Weight Watchers®

Greatest Hits

250 Classic Recipes from the Sixties to Today

WEIGHT WATCHERS PUBLISHING GROUP

Creative and Editorial Director
Nancy Gagliardi
Art Director
Ed Melnitsky
Production Manager
Alan Biederman
Office Manager/Publishing Assistant
Jenny Laboy-Brace

Food Editor
Joyce Hendley
Recipe Developers
Barbara Beltrami
David Bonom
Cynthia DePersio
Paul Picciuto
Patty Santelli

Photographer
Rita Maas
Food Stylist
Michael Pederson
Prop Stylist
Cathy Cook

Designer
Sue Llewellyn
Editorial Consultant
Barbara Turvett

A Word About Weight Watchers

Since 1963, Weight Watchers has grown from a handful of people to millions of enrollments annually. Today, Weight Watchers is recognized as the leading name in safe and sensible weight control. Weight Watchers members form a diverse group, from youths to senior citizens, attending meetings virtually around the globe. Weight-loss and weight-management results vary by individual, but we recommend that you attend Weight Watchers meetings, follow the Weight Watchers food plan, and participate in regular physical activity. For the Weight Watcher meeting nearest you, call 800-651-6000. Also, visit us at our Web site: WeightWatchers.com.

Icons

 hot/fiery

 no cooking

 one pot

 20 minutes or less

 vegetarian

WW THEN AND NOW
a classic Weight Watchers recipe, revisited and updated

table of contents

Introduction

My first experience at Weight Watchers was as a chunky 12-year-old attending meetings during a steamy summer, circa 1970. While my specifics may be sketchy, I do have some revealing recollections of those early days on the Program: liver, and lots of it (for iron); Weight Watchers Frozen Dessert, an icy confection that had lines embedded on the side of the box so you would know where to slice off a portion; diet chocolate soda; "marinara sauce" made from tomato juice (which my Italian-born mother found more difficult to make than I did to eat); having my sister help me with the mathematics of the infamous Food Selections; and the anxiety of weigh-ins. While my memories may be few, what is still clear in my mind is how I felt the summer I went back to school an amazing 30 pounds lighter.

When it comes to information about and experience with losing weight, I know I've come a long way—and Weight Watchers has, too. When Jean Nidetch, a Queens housewife armed with the New York City Board of Health diet, gathered a group of overweight friends and relatives in her basement and conducted what would soon be the blueprint for Weight Watchers meetings, she knew she was on to something—something big. Big, indeed, when you consider the cultural, economical, and personal implications of the fad-diet tsunami that's been barreling through the decades: from the grapefruit diet ("It burns fat!") to carbohydrates are king ("Carbo loading is the key to weight loss!") to learning to embrace your ample curves ("Love yourself no matter what your size!") to all protein, all the time ("Get zoned out!"). Through it all, Weight Watchers has remained steadfast—the gold standard of weight loss, if you will. We all may have dabbled with the other diets over the years, but when we're serious about losing weight, we always come back to Weight Watchers.

Forgive me if I sound a tad too salesperson-ish, but the fact remains that through decade after decade, Weight Watchers has helped millions of individuals lose weight. From those first Food Selections to today's ***POINTS*®,** Weight Watchers has always been based on science, as well as the needs of the society. No magic bullets—just the weight-loss facts, ma'am.

Weight Watchers Greatest Hits: 250 Classic Recipes from the Sixties to Today has been an exceedingly fun project to work on. From paging through past Weight Watchers cookbooks to hearing the stories from people who were there from the beginning, we've re-created some of those original Weight Watchers recipes with a modern twist (look for the WW Then and Now icon—it denotes a treasured Weight Watchers favorite that we've updated). We've also treaded lightly (and deliciously) into Mom's territory by tinkering with some tried-and-true American family classics.

Since this also is Weight Watchers fortieth anniversary, we've added a fun and nostalgic dieting timeline, as well as quotes and memories from early (and present) Leaders and members. By all means, try the recipes, but also take a moment to read this cookbook. It's a delightful, as well as telling, look into our past, and it just may provide clues to what the future holds for all of us.

Regards,
Nancy Gagliardi
Editorial Director

about our recipes

We make every effort to ensure that you will have success with our recipes. For best results and for nutritional accuracy, please keep the following guidelines in mind:

• All recipes feature approximate nutritional information; our recipes are analyzed for Calories (Cal), Total Fat (Fat), Saturated Fat (Sat Fat), Cholesterol (Chol), Sodium (Sod), Carbohydrates (Carb), Dietary Fiber (Fib), Protein (Prot), and Calcium (Calc).

• All recipes include ***POINTS*** values based on the Weight Watchers **Winning Points** Food System. ***POINTS*** are calculated from a proprietary formula that takes into account calories, total fat, and dietary fiber.

• Before serving, divide foods—including any vegetables, sauce, or accompaniments—into portions of equal size according to the designated number of servings per recipe.

• Any substitutions made to the ingredients will alter the "Per serving" nutritional information and may affect the ***POINTS*** value.

• Additionally, substituting fat-free foods for any low-fat ingredients specified in a recipe may affect the consistency, texture, or flavor of the finished dish.

• If you prefer to avoid using alcohol in any recipe, you may substitute an equal amount of water, broth, or juice.

• Nutritional information for recipes that include meat, fish, and poultry are based on cooked skinless boneless portions, with the fat trimmed as specified in the recipe.

The Start of Something Big

40 Years of Weight Watchers

LOSING WEIGHT THROUGH THE DECADES

1961

Weighing 214 pounds, Jean Nidetch visits the Obesity Clinic at the New York City Board of Health and follows Dr. Norman Joliffe's Prudent Diet. Finding a real need to talk to others, Jean invites six friends to her home. Within two months, the group expands to 40 members.

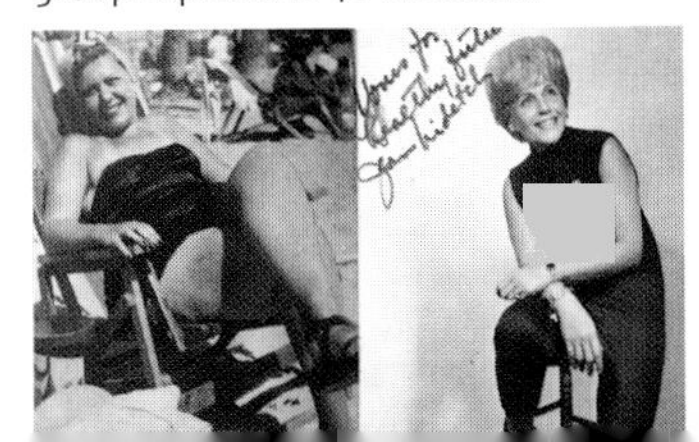

1962

Jean Nidetch begins to hold meetings in the cellar of her apartment building—and gives talks upon request at other sites.

1963

>>>

Jean Nidetch is invited by Al and Felice Lippert to host a meeting at their home. After losing several pounds, Al declares, "You have the beginnings of a real business here!" Felice, Al, and Jean (below, left to right) incorporate in May: Weight Watchers is born.

Deviled Eggs

MAKES 6 SERVINGS 

In the era known as B.C. (Before Cholesterol), deviled eggs were a mainstay of every picnic—until they fell out of favor with the Food Police. Luckily, our healthied-up version of this family classic works for either era; we've cut the yolks and mayonnaise and added chopped veggies. The result is more delicious and decidedly healthier than the fatty original.

- **8 large eggs**
- **1 small celery stalk, finely chopped (about ¼ cup)**
- **1 small carrot, shredded (about ¼ cup)**
- **2 tablespoons thinly sliced scallion**
- **2 tablespoons fat-free sour cream**
- **1 tablespoon low-fat mayonnaise**
- **2 teaspoons deli-style mustard**
- **1 teaspoon cider vinegar**
- **¼ teaspoon salt**
- **¼ teaspoon ground pepper**

1. Place the eggs in a saucepan large enough to hold them in a single layer; add enough cold water to cover. Bring to a boil over medium-high heat; reduce the heat and cook at a bare simmer, 12 minutes. Rinse under cold water and, when cool enough to handle, remove the shells.
2. Halve the eggs lengthwise. Place 4 whole yolks in a medium bowl and discard the remaining yolks. Chop 4 of the egg white halves and add to the bowl; mash well with a fork. Add the celery, carrot, scallion, sour cream, mayonnaise, mustard, vinegar, salt, and pepper; blend with a fork.
3. Spoon the filling into the hollows of the remaining 12 halves of whites, mounding to fill. Place on a platter, cover with plastic, and refrigerate at least 1 hour. Serve cold.

Per serving (2 stuffed egg halves): 73 Cal, 4 g Fat, 1 g Sat Fat, 142 mg Chol, 232 mg Sod, 3 g Carb, 0 g Fib, 7 g Prot, 36 mg Calc. ***POINTS: 2.***

> "I don't believe that [the Program] has changed all that much. People are always the same; they'll always care for each other. They'll always need to know that first of all, they're not alone; secondly, they're not bad people for being overweight; and third, if they really want something, it's within their power to go and get it."
>
> —*Jean Nidetch*

Cheese Ball

MAKES 16 SERVINGS 

You couldn't go to a party in the seventies without finding a cheese ball to dress up the appetizer table (and Paprika Cheese Balls were a beloved recipe in the first *Weight Watchers Cookbook* [1966]). We've cut the fat but added flavor and texture with subtle spices and dried vegetables. Whether you shape it into a ball or a log, the mixture is soft and spreadable. For a somewhat firmer texture, substitute an equal amount of farmer cheese for the cottage cheese (it's usually sold in brick form, like cream cheese, in the dairy case). Be sure to serve the cheese ball with plenty of crisp vegetables and a butter knife for spreading.

¾ cup shredded low-fat sharp cheddar cheese
¾ cup no-salt-added, reduced-fat (2%) cottage cheese
1 tablespoon Dijon mustard
⅛ teaspoon cayenne
1 (8-ounce) package fat-free cream cheese, cut into quarters, at room temperature
1 (.9-ounce) package dry vegetable soup/recipe mix
½ cup fresh parsley

1. Pulse the cheddar cheese, cottage cheese, mustard, and cayenne in a food processor until very smooth, about 2 minutes. Add the cream cheese and soup mix; process until smooth, scraping down the sides of the bowl as needed. Scrape with a spatula onto a large sheet of plastic wrap.
2. Wrap the plastic around the cheese mixture and shape it into a 4-inch ball or 7-inch-long log with your hands. Refrigerate until firm, at least 3 hours or overnight.
3. Just before serving, sprinkle about half of the chopped parsley in a circle onto a sheet of plastic wrap. Unwrap the cheese ball or log and place on the parsley. Sprinkle the remaining parsley on top and press to help the leaves adhere. Carefully roll any uncoated areas in the loose parsley, and smooth the shape, if needed. Place on a serving plate and surround with cut-up vegetables of your choice.

Per serving (2 tablespoons): 42 Cal, 1 g Fat, 1 g Sat Fat, 4 mg Chol, 219 mg Sod, 2 g Carb, 0 g Fib, 5 g Prot, 67 mg Calc. ***POINTS: 1.***

Cheese Blintzes

MAKES 8 SERVINGS

In Weight Watchers cookbooks past, "blintzes" were made from beaten eggs and should have properly been called omelettes. Today's version is thankfully faithful to the original—a filled paper-thin pancake. To make the creamy filling, we used whipped cottage cheese, a smooth cottage cheese found in some supermarkets. If you can't find it, simply puree the same amount of dry-curd cottage cheese in a food processor or blender until smooth. Serve the blintzes with unsweetened cinnamon applesauce or a sprinkling of cinnamon sugar.

- **⅓ cup fat-free cream cheese, room temperature**
- **¼ cup sugar**
- **1½ teaspoons grated lemon zest**
- **½ teaspoon vanilla extract**
- **1¾ cups whipped low-fat (1%) cottage cheese**
- **1 cup low-fat (1%) milk**
- **1 cup all-purpose flour**
- **2 large eggs**
- **2 egg whites**
- **1 tablespoon melted butter**
- **¼ teaspoon salt**

1. To prepare the filling, stir together the cream cheese, sugar, lemon zest, and vanilla in a medium bowl until smooth. Stir in the cottage cheese until combined; cover and refrigerate.
2. To prepare the pancakes, blend together the milk, flour, eggs, egg whites, butter, and salt in a blender or food processor until smooth. Pour into a bowl and let stand 20 minutes.
3. Place the oven rack in the center of the oven; preheat the oven to 350°F. Line a jelly-roll pan with foil and spray lightly with nonstick spray.
4. Spray a small nonstick skillet with nonstick spray; place over medium heat until hot. Pour about 3 tablespoons of the pancake batter into the pan, tilting the pan quickly to evenly coat the bottom. Cook until lightly browned underneath and dry on the top, about 30 seconds. Flip and cook 5 seconds. Remove to a plate and place a piece of wax paper on top. Repeat with the remaining batter (stirring occasionally) to make 16 pancakes, stacking the cooked pancakes between sheets of wax paper.
5. To assemble the blintzes, spoon 2 tablespoons of the cheese mixture on the lower third of the pale side of each pancake. Fold the right and left sides over the filling, then roll up to seal. Place, seam-side down, in the prepared pan and tent loosely with foil. Bake until the filling is hot, 10 minutes.

Per serving (2 blintzes): 166 Cal, 3 g Fat, 2 g Sat Fat, 61 mg Chol, 181 mg Sod, 21 g Carb, 0 g Fib, 12 g Prot, 68 mg Calc. ***POINTS: 4.***

top tip

You can easily freeze the assembled blintzes for another time. Just place them on a baking sheet and freeze until firm, then transfer to an airtight freezer container. Bake them, still frozen, on a baking sheet in a preheated 350°F oven, until heated through, about 12 minutes.

WW THEN AND NOW

Cheese Crisps

MAKES 16 SERVINGS

In the nineties, *frico*—crisp little discs of grated cheese, fried to an irresistible chewy crispness—were all the rage at trendy Italian eateries. Who'd have thought that Weight Watchers anticipated the trend as far back as the sixties, when members made Cheese Crisps in their Teflon frying pans? Now, as then, these savory little treats make great cocktail nibbles.

- **1 cup shredded part-skim mozzarella cheese**
- **2 tablespoons freshly grated Parmesan cheese**
- **1 tablespoon all-purpose flour**

1. Preheat oven to 400°F. Spray 2 baking sheets with nonstick spray.
2. Combine the mozzarella cheese, Parmesan cheese, and flour in a small bowl. Drop the cheese mixture by tablespoons onto the baking sheets, at least 2 inches apart, making 16 crisps. Bake until the cheese is melted and golden, with darker brown edges, 5–7 minutes.
3. Remove from the oven and let the crisps cool for 1 minute. Carefully remove the crisps from the baking sheets with a thin metal spatula and place on paper towels to cool completely. Serve at once, or store in an airtight container for up to 2 days at room temperature.

Per serving (1 crisp): 25 Cal, 2 g Fat, 1 g Sat Fat, 4 mg Chol, 52 mg Sod, 1 g Carb, 0 g Fib, 2 g Prot, 63 mg Calc. ***POINTS: 1.***

The weight I gained from having 3 children in 18 months is what sent me to Weight Watchers. At the time, I was living in the UK, a new wife and mother, with three babies in diapers and a weight problem. I told my husband, 'If I haven't lost the weight by the twins' first birthday, I'll join Weight Watchers.' It was two weeks after their first birthday, in 1983, when I joined by local Meeting. It was the best decision I ever made.

—Linda Huett, President and CEO, Weight Watchers International

Cheese Puffs

MAKES 15 SERVINGS

Looking for an easy crowd pleaser? Look back to this sixties classic, tasty morsels that were nothing short of a cocktail-party staple. Crispy on the outside with creamy centers, they're irresistible. Even better, you can make them in advance, freeze them, and reheat them at the last minute.

- **1 (12-ounce) can evaporated fat-free milk**
- **2 tablespoons unsalted butter**
- **¾ teaspoon dry mustard**
- **¾ teaspoon salt**
- **¼ teaspoon ground pepper**
- **1 cup all-purpose flour**
- **⅓ cup freshly grated Parmesan cheese**
- **2 large eggs**
- **1 teaspoon baking powder**
- **3 egg whites**
- **½ cup shredded reduced-fat cheddar cheese**

1. Bring the milk, butter, mustard, salt, and pepper to a boil in a medium saucepan; reduce the heat to medium. Beat in the flour and Parmesan cheese with a wooden spoon, stirring vigorously, until the mixture leaves the side of the pan. Cool for 10 minutes.
2. Adjust the racks to divide the oven into thirds; preheat the oven to 400°F. Line two baking sheets with foil and lightly coat with nonstick spray.
3. With an electric mixer on medium speed, beat the eggs into the flour mixture until well blended. Sift in the baking powder, then add the egg whites and continue beating until the mixture is glossy and smooth. Beat in the cheddar cheese on low speed until just combined.
4. Spoon the mixture into a pastry bag or a plastic food-storage bag with a corner cut off. Pipe into 1-inch mounds, spacing 1 inch apart. (You can also pipe the mixture into 1½-inch-long "fingers," if you prefer.) You should have about 75 puffs or fingers. Bake until golden brown and firm to the touch, 22 minutes. Serve hot or warm.

Per serving (5 puffs): 96 Cal, 4 g Fat, 2 g Sat Fat, 37 mg Chol, 255 mg Sod, 9 g Carb, 0 g Fib, 6 g Prot, 147 mg Calc. ***POINTS: 2.***

top tip

To freeze the cooled puffs, place them on a baking sheet in a single layer in the freezer until firm. Transfer them to zip-close freezer bags or plastic containers and store airtight for up to two months. To reheat the puffs, arrange them on baking sheets. Bake in a preheated 375°F oven until heated through and crisped, about 5 minutes (or 10 to 15 minutes if they're still frozen).

Cheese Crisps, Cheese Ball, Cheese Puffs, and Deviled Eggs (clockwise from top left)

Nachos Grande

MAKES 8 SERVINGS

Walk into any popular eighties bar/restaurant, and you'd find this appetizer on the menu—usually being washed down with Mexican beers or festive frozen Margaritas. You can create all that fun in your own kitchen too, minus the booze: Serve up this leaner version at your next party, or as a special midweek treat for the kids.

- **1 teaspoon canola oil**
- **1 cup cooked or rinsed drained canned red kidney beans**
- **¼ pound lean ground turkey breast**
- **1 small onion, chopped**
- **1 (14-ounce) can diced green tomatoes with green chiles**
- **2 teaspoons Mexican seasoning mix**
- **¼ teaspoon salt**
- **6 ounces reduced-fat restaurant-style tortilla chips**
- **¾ cup shredded reduced-fat cheddar cheese**
- **12 pitted small black olives, sliced**
- **¼ cup sliced pickled jalapeño peppers, drained**
- **½ cup fat-free sour cream**

1. Preheat oven to 425°F. Spray a baking sheet with nonstick spray.
2. Heat a large nonstick skillet over medium-high heat. Swirl in the oil, then stir in the beans, turkey, and onion. Cook, stirring to break up the meat, 3 minutes. Add the tomatoes, Mexican seasoning, and salt; cook until thickened, about 5 minutes. Remove from the heat and keep warm.
3. Spread the tortilla chips on the baking sheet. Sprinkle with the cheese, olives, and jalapeño peppers. Bake until the cheese just melts, about 5 minutes. Transfer the nachos to a serving platter. Top with the turkey mixture and sour cream and serve at once.

Per serving (1¼ cups): 204 Cal, 4 g Fat, 2 g Sat Fat, 17 mg Chol, 483 mg Sod, 29 g Carb, 4 g Fib, 13 g Prot, 141 mg Calc. ***POINTS: 4.***

"I was at a luncheon and ran into [a friend who] had lost a lot of weight. She told us about Jean Nidetch. Jean was also at the luncheon, so I invited her to come talk with my husband and me. She said she'd come if we got a group together, and I did—and she came with her scale. At first, my husband pooh-poohed the whole idea. But after the first week, he lost nearly four pounds; the next week, he lost three pounds more, and by week three, he told Jean, 'You have the beginnings of a business.' By May of that year [1963] we were incorporated."

—Felice Lippert, Cofounder, Weight Watchers International

Swiss Fondue

MAKES 10 SERVINGS

Fondues, the quintessential sixties gourmet treat, are back in style. If you've avoided the trend fearing a diet disaster, here's salvation: We've found a way to make fondue a lot more ***POINTS***-friendly without sacrificing taste or gooey cheesiness. It starts with substituting pureed beans for some of the cheese, then adding some shredded aged Asiago cheese for a flavor boost. This recipe makes enough for you to throw a fondue party; serve it with bread cubes, steamed vegetables like broccoli and carrots, and/or slices of tart apple.

1 (19-ounce) can cannellini (white kidney) beans, rinsed and drained
½ cup reduced-fat (2%) milk
½ small garlic clove
¾ cup dry white wine
5 ounces imported Swiss Gruyère cheese (about 1¾ cups)
1 ounce coarsely grated aged Asiago cheese (about ⅓ cup)
2 teaspoons cornstarch, dissolved in 1 tablespoon water
1 tablespoon kirsch (optional)
⅛ teaspoon nutmeg

1. Place the beans and milk in a food processor; puree, scraping the sides of the work bowl frequently, until absolutely smooth, at least 3 minutes.
2. Rub a medium nonreactive saucepan with the garlic; discard the garlic. Pour the wine into the saucepan and bring to a simmer over medium heat. Add the Gruyère cheese and Asiago cheese, a handful at a time, stirring constantly with a wooden spoon in a zigzag motion, until the cheese is melted, 5–8 minutes (do not boil or the cheese will clump). Stir in the bean mixture, dissolved cornstarch, kirsch (if using), and nutmeg; continue cooking, stirring gently, until smooth and slightly thickened, 5–6 minutes longer. Transfer to a large fondue pot and set over moderate heat. Serve at once.

Per serving (about ⅔ cup): 111 Cal, 5 g Fat, 3 g Sat Fat, 16 mg Chol, 222 mg Sod, 8 g Carb, 2 g Fib, 8 g Prot, 199 mg Calc. ***POINTS: 2.***

top tips

- If you have leftover fondue, it will keep, covered, in the refrigerator for three days. To reheat, place it in a microwavable bowl, cover loosely, and cook on Medium power, stirring every 10 seconds or so, until just melted.
- Kirsch, a German brandy distilled from cherries and cherry pits, is a traditional ingredient in Swiss fondue—but it's strictly optional in ours. The tablespoon called for contributes less than 5 calories per serving.
- No Asiago cheese in your pantry? Substitute freshly grated Parmesan cheese.

Vietnamese Summer Rolls with Peanut-Mirin Sauce

MAKES 4 ROLLS

Love the crispy fried spring rolls in Vietnamese restaurants—but not the ***POINTS*** tally? Try these equally authentic and delicious summer rolls instead. Wrapped in rice paper—thin, translucent sheets of rice-flour dough—they're a snap to make and beautiful to look at. Look for rice paper in Asian groceries and better supermarkets (they're often in the produce section with the Asian vegetables).

- **2 tablespoons rice vinegar**
- **1 tablespoon mirin**
- **1 tablespoon finely chopped unsalted roasted peanuts**
- **½ teaspoon sugar**
- **⅛ teaspoon salt**
- **1 ounce cellophane noodles**
- **1 cup boiling water**
- **4 (8-inch) round rice-paper sheets**
- **2 large romaine lettuce leaves, halved, with ribs removed to make 8 pieces**
- **1 cucumber, peeled, seeded and cut into long, thin strips**
- **1 medium carrot, peeled and grated**
- **4 scallions, green part only**
- **¼ cup cilantro leaves**
- **¼ cup mint leaves**

1. To prepare the peanut-mirin sauce, combine the vinegar, mirin, peanuts, sugar, and salt in a small bowl.
2. Combine the noodles with the boiling water in a medium heatproof bowl; let soak 12 minutes, then drain and pat dry with paper towels.
3. Fill a large skillet with warm water. Soak 1 rice-paper round in the water until just pliable, 30–45 seconds. Pat away the excess water with a paper towel. Arrange 1 piece of the lettuce on the bottom third of the rice paper, tearing the lettuce to fit as needed and leaving a 1-inch border. Top the lettuce with one-fourth of the noodles, cucumber, carrot, scallions, and cilantro. Tightly roll the rice paper around the filling; after rolling halfway, arrange one-fourth of the mint along the roll, then continue rolling into a neat cylinder. Transfer to a plate and cover with a damp paper towel. Repeat with the remaining ingredients to make 4 rolls.
4. With a serrated knife, slice each roll on the diagonal into 4 pieces. Serve with the peanut-mirin sauce.

Per serving (one 4-piece roll with ½ tablespoon sauce): 78 Cal, 1 g Fat, 0 g Sat Fat, 4 mg Chol, 87 mg Sod, 15 g Carb, 2 g Fib, 3 g Prot, 37 mg Calc. ***POINTS: 1.***

top tips

- Mirin is a sweet cooking wine traditionally made from fermented rice and grain alcohol. If you can't find it in an Asian grocery or your liquor store, use 1 tablespoon sake (Japanese rice wine) plus 2 teaspoons sugar. Or, for a nonalcoholic version, just omit the mirin and add an extra teaspoon of sugar in Step 1.
- Translucent cellophane noodles, sometimes called bean threads, are made from mung bean starch. They have a slippery texture and are virtually tasteless, absorbing their flavors from the dishes in which they are cooked. They are sold in bundles in Asian groceries and some supermarkets.

Spanakopita Triangles

MAKES 8 SERVINGS

Serve these classic Greek spinach triangles as an appetizer for eight—or as an entrée for four, with a salad or soup on the side. They can be baked up to 3 hours in advance, then reheated in a preheated 375°F oven until crisp, about 8 minutes.

- **1 (10-ounce) box frozen chopped spinach, thawed and squeezed dry**
- **⅔ cup crumbled reduced-fat feta cheese**
- **3 scallions, chopped**
- **1 large egg white**
- **1½ tablespoons fresh dill, or ¾ teaspoon dried**
- **¼ teaspoon freshly ground pepper**
- **8 (12 x 17-inch) sheets phyllo dough, room temperature**
- **2 tablespoons olive oil**

1. Place the oven rack in the center of the oven; preheat the oven to 375°F. Spray a baking sheet with nonstick spray.
2. Press the spinach between layers of paper towels to remove any excess moisture. Place the cheese in a medium bowl and mash with a fork. Add the spinach, cheese, scallions, egg white, dill, and pepper; stir together until combined.
3. Set the stack of phyllo sheets to one side; keep covered with a sheet of wax paper and a damp towel on top as you work.
4. Lay 1 phyllo sheet lengthwise in front of you and brush the sheet lightly with oil. Top with another sheet and brush lightly with oil. Cut crosswise into 6 even strips. Place a scant tablespoon of the spinach mixture at the end of each strip. Fold one corner up over the filling, then continue folding in a flag fashion, to form a triangle. Place on the baking sheet and repeat with the remaining filling and phyllo sheets to make 24 triangles. Brush the tops of the triangles lightly with any remaining oil.
5. Bake until golden brown, about 25 minutes. Cool for 5 minutes and serve hot or warm.

Per serving (3 triangles): 112 Cal, 5 g Fat, 2 g Sat Fat, 11 mg Chol, 223 mg Sod, 12 g Carb, 1 g Fib, 4 g Prot, 103 mg Calc. ***POINTS: 2.***

Mushroom "Peanuts" Revisited

MAKES 8 SERVINGS

Once upon a time, Weight Watchers members who craved nuts were encouraged to make "Roast Peanuts" by spreading canned mushrooms on a baking sheet and baking them for an hour in a slow oven. When we tried to re-create the process, we ended up with shriveled, unappetizing mushrooms and a very smelly kitchen; the recipe was definitely in need of an update. We broiled our mushrooms instead, flavoring them with garlic and herbs—and the results were addictive! Eat them right out of the oven as a snack, or toss them with pasta or grain salads. They're also yummy layered in a sandwich or on top of a pizza.

2 (10-ounce) packages sliced mushrooms, (about 7 cups)
2 tablespoons olive oil
2 teaspoons reduced-sodium soy sauce
1 tablespoon chopped rosemary or thyme, or 1 teaspoon dried
1 large garlic clove, minced
Freshly ground pepper

1. Preheat the broiler.
2. Spread the mushrooms in a broiler pan or large roasting pan. Whisk together the oil, soy sauce, rosemary or thyme, and garlic in a small bowl, then drizzle over the mushrooms. Toss well, then let stand for 15 minutes to allow the flavors to blend.
3. Broil 5 inches from the heat until the tops of the mushrooms are crisp, about 2 minutes; turn the pieces with a spatula and broil briefly to crisp the other sides. Sprinkle with the pepper and serve at once.

Per serving (¾ cup): 50 Cal, 4 g Fat, 1 g Sat Fat, 0 mg Chol, 53 mg Sod, 0 g Carb, 1 g Fib, 2 g Prot, 7 mg Calc. ***POINTS: 1.***

top tip

Although they're best piping hot, you can store the mushrooms in the refrigerator for up to four days. Let them come to room temperature before serving, or reheat them briefly in the microwave until just heated through.

Black Bean "Caviar"

MAKES 8 SERVINGS

This elegant appetizer would probably have been labeled "mock caviar" in an earlier Weight Watchers era, but back then the tasty black beans—its secret ingredient—would have been considered off-limits. Deep in color and wonderfully rich, this impostor tops a cracker quite nicely. Further the illusion by serving it with a dollop of fat-free sour cream and sprinkle of finely chopped fresh parsley, and serve the crackers wrapped in a cloth napkin on a small tray alongside.

- **1 (15-ounce) can black beans, drained and rinsed**
- **1 large garlic clove, minced**
- **1 tablespoon prepared tapenade**
- **1 tablespoon extra-virgin olive oil**
- **⅛ teaspoon freshly ground pepper**
- **24 water crackers**

Gently toss the beans, garlic, tapenade, oil, and pepper in a medium bowl using a rubber spatula, until just evenly mixed. Transfer to a small serving bowl and serve with the crackers on the side.

Per serving (3 crackers, each topped with 1 tablespoon "caviar"): 108 Cal, 3 g Fat, 0 g Sat Fat, 0 mg Chol, 134 mg Sod, 17 g Carb, 3 g Fib, 4 g Prot, 38 mg Calc. ***POINTS: 2.***

top tip

Tapenade, a savory paste that hails from France's Provençal region, is made with black olives, capers, anchovies, lemon, thyme, and other seasonings. A small spoonful packs a big flavor punch. Look for it in the olive section of better supermarkets and gourmet stores.

Buffalo Wings

MAKES 6 SERVINGS

Invented at the Anchor Bar in Buffalo, New York, in the late sixties, this still-popular bar fare requires more fat than you want to know about in its original version. Our version manages to trim quite a bit by skinning and broiling the wings and marinating them in a wonderfully tangy sauce. The wings can be made ahead and refrigerated for up to two days or frozen for up to three months. They're great to have on hand for an impromptu get-together.

- **3 pounds (12–14) chicken wings, skinned**
- **3 tablespoons cider vinegar**
- **2 tablespoons reduced-sodium chicken broth**
- **2 teaspoons vegetable oil**
- **2 teaspoons hot pepper sauce**
- **¼ cup crumbled blue cheese**
- **¼ cup plain fat-free yogurt**
- **1 tablespoon reduced-fat mayonnaise**
- **6 celery stalks, trimmed**

1. Wash and pat the wings dry with paper towels; cut off the tips and reserve for another use. Halve the wings at the joint.
2. Combine the vinegar, broth, oil, and pepper sauce in a large zip-close plastic bag; add the chicken. Squeeze out the air and seal the bag; turn the bag to coat the chicken. Refrigerate, turning the bag occasionally, 30 minutes. Drain and discard any remaining marinade.
3. Spray the broiler rack with nonstick spray; preheat the broiler.
4. Broil the chicken 5 inches from the heat, turning once, until golden and cooked through, about 10 minutes per side.
5. Meanwhile, combine the blue cheese, yogurt, and mayonnaise in a small bowl. Serve with the chicken wings and celery.

Per serving (4 wing halves with 1½ tablespoons dip and 1 celery stick): 156 Cal, 8 g Fat, 3 g Sat Fat, 47 mg Chol, 182 mg Sod, 3 g Carb, 1 g Fib, 18 g Prot, 76 mg Calc. ***POINTS: 4.***

top tip

Save the trimmed-off wing tips for making stock and soups. Freeze them in a zip-close freezer bag (along with other poultry scraps) until you've accumulated enough. It won't take long!

Nachos Grande
and Buffalo Wings

Chicken Liver Crostini

MAKES 8 SERVINGS

For a good decade or so the Weight Watchers Program required members to eat liver once a week, to make sure no one missed out on getting plenty of iron in their diets. How challenging that must have been for vegetarians—not to mention droves of confirmed liver haters! Cookbooks included plenty of liver recipes, and sometimes entire chapters were devoted to liver alone. Today, we include just one liver recipe in this cookbook, and we've taken a twenty-first-century approach of combining just a little liver with a lot of wonderful flavorings to make a simply divine pâté.

2 tablespoons unsalted butter or margarine
1 small onion, chopped
1 shallot, chopped
¼ pear, peeled and chopped
½ pound chicken livers, trimmed, preferably organic
1 tablespoon brandy or calvados (optional)
½ teaspoon salt
Freshly ground black pepper
16 (½-ounce) slices Italian or French bread, toasted
1 cup cornichons (small French pickles, optional)

1. Melt the butter or margarine in a large nonstick skillet. Add the onion, shallot, and pear; cook, stirring frequently, until the onion and shallot are translucent and the pear is soft, about 5 minutes. Add the livers and brown them, breaking them apart with a spoon, until they are no longer pink and cooked through, 8–10 minutes. Remove from the heat, and let cool slightly.
2. Combine the liver mixture with its liquid, the brandy or calvados, if using, the salt, and pepper in a food processor. Pulse until very smooth; transfer the mixture to a small bowl or crock. Cover tightly and refrigerate for at least 1 day or up to 5 days. Serve with the toasted bread and the cornichons, if using, on the side.

Per serving (2 crostini): 138 Cal, 5 g Fat, 2 g Sat Fat, 119 mg Chol, 321 mg Sod, 16 g Carb, 1 g Fib, 7 g Prot, 31 mg Calc. ***POINTS: 3.***

top tip

You can also freeze the pâté to have on hand for entertaining; it will last in the freezer for up to three months. Calvados, a dry apple brandy made in the Normandy region of France, lends a subtle apple flavor to meat and poultry dishes. It's well worth investing in a bottle for the kitchen.

I lost all that weight on the Obesity Clinics diet, but I added something else. I added talk. I found I couldn't do it on diet alone. I had to be able to talk about my eating problems and to tell other people what I was going through. So I called up a few fat friends and asked them to come to my home to talk. They came. And then they came every week after that, bringing other fat people with them. It was our little group, where we met to tell each other about being fat. Soon the group grew: My little private club has become an industry. I never intended it to. It was really just a group for me and my fat friends.

—Jean Nidetch

"I remember the first class, when Jean explained the Program to me: You have to have two milks, two breads [each day]...and liver once a week. I said, 'Gee, Mrs. Nidetch, I hate liver.' And she looked at me, with really piercing eyes, and said, 'Nobody said you have to like it; you just have to eat it!'"

—Florine Mark, Franchise Owner, Detroit

Ask anybody who's following a strict diet: Sometimes they just blow it. Then they go overboard the next day, because they think it's all over. But there's no such thing as blowing it on the ***POINTS*** Food System.

—Felice Lippert, Cofounder, Weight Watchers International

"Jean taught us to like ourselves, and that was the most important thing. And you learn to like yourself when you lose that kind of weight. You just can't help it."

—Florence Rogoff, former personal assistant to Jean Nidetch

Yummy, Yummy, Yummy

1964

Jean Nidetch realizes she can't do it all alone; Weight Watchers (original logo, below) begins licensing franchises.

1965

The cult of the impossibly thin fashion model begins as Twiggy appears in the pages of *Vogue*. Miniskirts and micromini skirts soon follow, to the despair of most normal-legged women. (The short-lived, floor-length maxi skirt is a brief respite.)

1966

>>>

The first *Weight Watchers Cookbook* sells well. Weight Watchers now has more than 200 branches worldwide.

To prepare for the film *Georgy Girl*, actress Lynn Redgrave puts on and loses several pounds, winning her critical acclaim—and a future role as spokesperson for Weight Watchers.

French Onion Soup Gratinée

MAKES 4 SERVINGS

A soup whose main ingredient was a "limited" vegetable like onions no doubt challenged early Weight Watchers cooks. The versions they created tended to be more broth than onion and bereft of the cheese crouton traditionally served on top. This modern, savory version makes peace with the past, reinventing the French-bistro staple with all the pleasure—and only a few of the ***POINTS***.

- **1 tablespoon + 1 teaspoon olive oil**
- **2 pounds onions, thinly sliced**
- **1 (32-ounce) can reduced-sodium chicken broth**
- **1½ teaspoons Worcestershire sauce**
- **Freshly ground pepper**
- **4 (1-ounce) slices French bread, toasted**
- **1 cup shredded reduced-fat Swiss or Jarlsberg cheese**

1. Heat a large nonstick skillet. Swirl in the oil, then add the onions. Cook, stirring frequently, until golden, about 15 minutes.
2. Preheat the oven to 450°F.
3. Bring the broth to a simmer in a large saucepan; add the cooked onions, Worcestershire sauce, and pepper. Reduce the heat to low and simmer, stirring occasionally, until the onions are tender, about 15 minutes.
4. Place 4 ovenproof soup bowls on a baking sheet. Ladle the soup into the bowls; top each with a slice of bread and ¼ cup of cheese. Bake until the cheese melts, about 5 minutes.

Per serving (1 cup): 299 Cal, 11 g Fat, 4 g Sat Fat, 9 mg Chol, 689 mg Sod, 34 g Carb, 5 g Fib, 18 g Prot, 410 mg Calc. ***POINTS: 6.***

top tip

Double this recipe and freeze half for another time. When ready to serve, just thaw at room temperature or in the refrigerator overnight, and reheat it on the stovetop or in the microwave. Then all you have to do at the last minute is toast the bread and shred the cheese. Voilà!

Asian Noodle Soup with Tofu and Shrimp

MAKES 8 SERVINGS

This delicately flavored soup is a meal in a bowl and a great way to enjoy heart-healthy tofu. Back in the early days of Weight Watchers, some of the ingredients would have required a trip to an Asian grocery. Today, they're easy to find in almost any supermarket.

- **2 (32-ounce) cans reduced-sodium chicken broth**
- **1 (8-ounce) head bok choy, trimmed and sliced (4 cups)**
- **¾ pound snow peas, trimmed and cut into 1-inch pieces**
- **¼ pound small fresh or frozen shrimp, peeled and deveined**
- **2 teaspoons reduced-sodium soy sauce**
- **2 teaspoons sesame oil**
- **1 bunch scallions, trimmed and sliced**
- **8 ounces firm tofu, sliced ¼-inch thick, then into 1-inch squares**
- **1 (8-ounce) can sliced water chestnuts, drained**
- **4 ounces capellini**
- **1 teaspoon rice or white-wine vinegar**
- **Freshly ground white pepper**

1. Bring the broth to a boil in a large saucepan or Dutch oven. Add the bok choy, snow peas, shrimp, soy sauce, and oil. Return to a boil, reduce the heat, and simmer until the bok choy and snow peas are tender but still crunchy and the shrimp are pink but still opaque, about 5 minutes.
2. Add the scallions, tofu, water chestnuts, capellini, vinegar, and pepper. Cook until the capellini are barely tender and the soup is heated through, about 5 minutes.

Per serving (1¾ cups): 196 Cal, 6 g Fat, 1 g Sat Fat, 28 mg Chol, 576 mg Sod, 21 g Carb, 4 g Fib, 16 g Prot, 139 mg Calc. ***POINTS: 4.***

> "A Weight Watchers meeting is like a time-out for people with busy lives—an hour when they can focus just on themselves, learn new things, and exchange information. I call it fun school."
>
> *—Kristen Prentiss Trapasso, Leader, Syracuse, New York*

Mediterranean Clam Chowder

MAKES 4 SERVINGS

Here are all the flavors of the briny Manhattan clam chowder with which we're familiar, but with the added Mediterranean flavors of fennel, olives, capers, and lemon. You'll love this version's chunky texture and tangy taste.

- **4 teaspoons olive oil**
- **1½ cups chopped fennel**
- **1 onion, chopped**
- **1 carrot, chopped**
- **1 celery stalk, chopped**
- **2½–3½ cups hot water**
- **1 (8-ounce) can stewed tomatoes, coarsely chopped, with their juice**
- **1 cup bottled clam juice or fish broth**
- **1 medium potato, peeled and chopped**
- **1½ teaspoons chopped thyme, or ½ teaspoon dried**
- **1½ teaspoons chopped oregano, or ½ teaspoon dried**
- **Freshly ground pepper**
- **1 (6 ½-ounce) can minced clams**
- **6 large or 10 small black olives, pitted and chopped**
- **2 tablespoons capers, drained**
- **½ teaspoon grated lemon zest (the colorful part of rind)**
- **1 teaspoon fresh lemon juice**

1. Heat a large nonstick saucepan. Swirl in the oil, then add the fennel, onion, carrot, and celery. Sauté until slightly wilted, about 5 minutes.
2. Add 2½ cups of the hot water, the tomatoes, clam juice or fish broth, potato, thyme, oregano, and pepper; simmer, adding more hot water ½ cup at a time, until the potatoes and vegetables are tender but not mushy, about 15 minutes. Stir in the clams with their juice, the olives, capers, lemon zest, and lemon juice. Cook until heated through (do not boil); serve at once.

Per serving (1½ cups): 156 Cal, 6 g Fat, 1 g Sat Fat, 16 mg Chol, 520 mg Sod, 19 g Carb, 4 g Fib, 8 g Prot, 86 mg Calc. ***POINTS: 3.***

Creamy Fish Chowder

MAKES 4 SERVINGS

Thank goodness, times have changed, and there's no need to call upon cottage cheese purees or dehydrated onion flakes to create a creamy soup like this one. Chunky with fish and potatoes and full of briny flavors, our chowder is a showcase for the freshest fish available at the market.

- **1 cup water**
- **2 medium potatoes, peeled and chopped**
- **1 onion, chopped**
- **1 cup chopped mushrooms**
- **1 celery stalk, chopped**
- **1 tablespoon + 1 teaspoon unsalted butter**
- **1 tablespoon all-purpose flour**
- **1 cup fat-free milk**
- **1 cup evaporated fat-free milk**
- **8 ounces firm-fleshed white fish fillets (blackfish, sea bass, monkfish, orange roughy, red snapper, or tile fish), cut into 1-inch pieces**
- **½ cup fish broth or bottled clam juice**
- **½ tablespoon chopped thyme, or ½ teaspoon dried**
- **Freshly ground white pepper**
- **2 teaspoons chopped thyme (optional)**

1. Combine the water, potatoes, onion, mushrooms, celery, and butter in a large saucepan or Dutch oven. Bring to a boil; reduce the heat and simmer, covered, until the potatoes are tender, about 20 minutes.
2. Place the flour in a medium bowl; whisk in the milk and evaporated milk. Stir into the potato mixture in the saucepan. Add the fish, broth or clam juice, thyme, and pepper. Cook, stirring frequently, over medium heat, until the fish is no longer opaque and the chowder has thickened slightly, about 15 minutes (do not boil). Sprinkle with the additional thyme, if using.

Per serving (1¼ cups): 215 Cal, 8 g Fat, 3 g Sat Fat, 45 mg Chol, 136 mg Sod, 21 g Carb, 2 g Fib, 16 g Prot, 106 mg Calc. ***POINTS: 5.***

"There was something magical about those meetings in the early days of Weight Watchers. Together, we felt we could do anything. I'd snack on slices of cucumber dipped in mustard, but in my mind, they were French fries dipped in ketchup."

—Patty Barnett, Editorial Consultant, Weight Watchers International

Split Pea Soup with
Ham and Cheese

Split Pea Soup with Ham and Cheese

MAKES 8 SERVINGS

Back in the old days, when legumes were considered fattening, Weight Watchers created Mock Split Pea Soup. Made from pureed green beans, asparagus, celery, and a few other ingredients, it only resembled the real thing in color. This split pea soup is not only made with the real stuff, it's also laced with delicious little morsels of ham and cheese. Change is good!

- **1 pound split peas, picked over, rinsed, and drained**
- **4 teaspoons vegetable oil**
- **2 carrots, chopped**
- **1 large onion, chopped**
- **1 celery stalk, chopped**
- **1 (32-ounce) can reduced-sodium chicken broth**
- **2 cups water**
- **¼ pound lean ham, cut into matchstick-size pieces**
- **Freshly ground pepper**
- **2 ounces reduced-fat cheddar cheese, cut into ½-inch cubes**

1. Place the peas in a large saucepan; add enough water to cover them by 2 inches and bring to a boil. Remove from the heat, then cover and let soak 1 hour. Drain.
2. Heat a large nonstick saucepan or Dutch oven. Swirl in the oil, then add the carrots, onion, and celery. Sauté until wilted, about 5 minutes. Add the peas, broth, water, ham, and pepper. Bring to a boil; reduce the heat and simmer, covered, stirring occasionally, until the peas are tender, about 1 hour. Top with the cheese and serve immediately, or set aside to cool to room temperature, then refrigerate up to 3 days.
3. To reheat, thin the soup with a little water, as needed (it will thicken as it stands); place over medium heat and cook, stirring until warmed through. Top with the cheese and serve.

Per serving (1 cup): 288 Cal, 6 g Fat, 2 g Sat Fat, 11 mg Chol, 455 mg Sod, 39 g Carb, 15 g Fib, 21 g Prot, 93 mg Calc. ***POINTS: 5.***

"After I lost 55 pounds, I thought, I can't stop talking about Weight Watchers anyway, so I might as well make money at it. I've been a Leader ever since."

—Susie Huebner, Leader, Des Moines

Gumbo

MAKES 4 SERVINGS

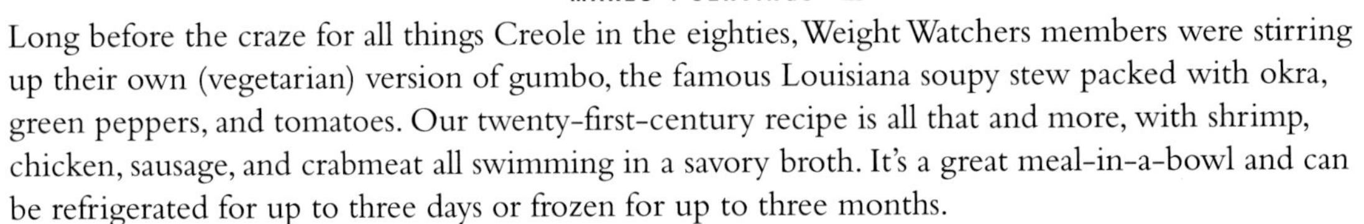

Long before the craze for all things Creole in the eighties, Weight Watchers members were stirring up their own (vegetarian) version of gumbo, the famous Louisiana soupy stew packed with okra, green peppers, and tomatoes. Our twenty-first-century recipe is all that and more, with shrimp, chicken, sausage, and crabmeat all swimming in a savory broth. It's a great meal-in-a-bowl and can be refrigerated for up to three days or frozen for up to three months.

- **4 teaspoons vegetable oil**
- **1 green bell pepper, chopped**
- **8 scallions, sliced**
- **1 celery stalk, chopped**
- **1 garlic clove, minced**
- **1 (14-ounce) can diced tomatoes, with their juice**
- **1 (14-ounce) can reduced-sodium chicken broth**
- **1 (10-ounce) box frozen okra, thawed**
- **1½ teaspoons chopped thyme, or 1 teaspoon dried**
- **1 bay leaf**
- **¼ teaspoon crushed red pepper**
- **½ cup long-grain rice**
- **12 medium shrimp, peeled and deveined**
- **2 ounces skinless boneless chicken breast, cut into ½-inch chunks**
- **2 ounces kielbasa, sliced**
- **1 cup cooked crabmeat, picked over**

1. Heat a large nonstick saucepan. Swirl in the oil, then add the bell pepper, scallions, celery, and garlic. Sauté until slightly wilted, 5 minutes. Add the tomatoes, broth, okra, thyme, bay leaf, and red pepper. Bring to a boil; reduce the heat and simmer, covered, until the vegetables are soft, about 15 minutes.
2. Stir in the rice and continue cooking until the rice is soft on the outside but still hard in the center, 15–20 minutes. Add the shrimp, chicken, and kielbasa; simmer, covered, until the shrimp is pink and opaque, the chicken is cooked through, and the rice is completely tender, 5–10 minutes more. Add the crabmeat; cook until just heated through. Remove the bay leaf before serving.

Per serving (2¼ cups): 311 Cal, 11 g Fat, 3 g Sat Fat, 79 mg Chol, 660 mg Sod, 32 g Carb, 4 g Fib, 22 g Prot, 166 mg Calc. ***POINTS: 6.***

top tip

Keeping resealable plastic bags of chopped onions, bell pepper, celery, and other frequently used vegetables in the freezer makes preparing soups like this a cinch; they'll last about a month in the freezer. A half cup of chopped veggies generally equals 1 medium unit (example: ½ cup chopped onion equals 1 medium onion).

Lentil Soup

MAKES 8 SERVINGS

Not so long ago lentils were only allowed once a week on the Weight Watchers program, but today we know how healthful (and deliciously filling) they are. In this classic soup, we've used no oil, making a virtually fat-free but hearty meal. More good news: It's a cinch to prepare, and like so many hearty soups, it's better after a day or two.

10 cups reduced-sodium beef broth
1 pound dried lentils, picked over, rinsed, and drained
4 carrots, chopped
2 large onions, peeled and chopped
1 celery stalk, chopped
1 bay leaf
3 canned whole plum tomatoes, drained and chopped
1 cup tomato juice
1 tablespoon red-wine or cider vinegar
Freshly ground pepper
1–2 cups hot water
Chopped scallion (optional)

Combine the broth, lentils, carrots, onions, celery, and bay leaf in a large saucepan or Dutch oven. Bring to a boil, reduce the heat, and simmer, covered, stirring occasionally, until the lentils and vegetables are tender, about 30 minutes. Add the tomatoes, tomato juice, vinegar, and pepper; add the water 1 cup at a time until desired thickness is reached. Cover and cook, stirring occasionally, until the flavors have blended, 10 minutes. Sprinkle with the chopped scallion, if using.

Per serving (1¾ cups): 261 Cal, 2 g Fat, 0 g Sat Fat, 0 mg Chol, 364 mg Sod, 44 g Carb, 15 g Fib, 19 g Prot, 72 mg Calc. ***POINTS: 5.***

top tip

You can store the soup in the refrigerator for up to five days or freeze it for up to three months. It will thicken slightly with time; just thin it with a little water when you reheat it on the stove or in the microwave.

Mushroom-Barley Soup

MAKES 8 SERVINGS

"Mushrooms, an unlimited vegetable, are a mainstay of the W.W. Program," notes the ample mushroom recipe section in the first *Weight Watchers Cookbook.* And we're still in love with these meaty, flavorful, and fat-free gems. This old-fashioned, hearty soup is a worthy homage—a perfect choice on a blustery winter day. The soup freezes well, so you might as well make up a double batch while you're at it. Serve it with some crusty bread and a crunchy green salad.

2 tablespoons olive oil
2 onions, chopped
3 carrots, chopped
3 celery stalks, chopped
½ cup dry white wine
9 cups reduced-sodium beef broth
⅓ cup pearl barley
2 (10-ounce) packages mushrooms
½ cup minced flat-leaf parsley
Freshly ground pepper
2–3 tablespoons minced flat-leaf parsley (optional)

1. Heat a large nonstick saucepan or Dutch oven. Swirl in the oil, then add the onions, carrots, and celery. Sauté until wilted, about 5 minutes. Add the wine; simmer until the liquid is reduced by one-fourth. Add the broth; bring to a steady simmer. Stir in the barley; cover and cook, stirring occasionally, until the barley is tender, about 45 minutes.
2. Meanwhile, clean and trim the mushrooms; separate the stems from the caps. Chop the stems and one-third of the caps; slice the remaining caps.
3. Transfer 1½ cups of the vegetables and barley and ½ cup of the liquid to a food processor; puree. Return the mixture to the saucepan.
4. Add the mushrooms, parsley, and pepper; stir and bring to a gentle boil. Simmer, covered, until the mushrooms are cooked, 15 minutes. Garnish with the additional parsley, if using.

Per serving (1½ cups): 133 Cal, 5 g Fat, 1 g Sat Fat, 0 mg Chol, 210 mg Sod, 17 g Carb, 4 g Fib, 6 g Prot, 43 mg Calc. ***POINTS: 2.***

top tip

The small amount of wine in this soup adds a great deal of flavor. However, if you'd like to leave it out, substitute ½ cup water and a tablespoon of white-wine vinegar instead.

Ribollita

MAKES 8 SERVINGS

The name of this chunky, satisfying soup means "twice boiled" in Italian, because it's based on reheating leftover soup with chunks of bread to thicken it (and making it a complete meal in a bowl). Traditional recipes call for *cavalo nero*, a dark, plumelike kale commonly found in Tuscany. The closest thing to it here is lacinato kale (sometimes called Tuscan kale); look for it in specialty-food stores or supermarkets. If you can't find that, regular kale makes a good substitute. As with any soup worthy of such a name, this one is much better the second day.

- **4 teaspoons olive oil**
- **2 onions, chopped**
- **1 slice Canadian-style bacon, cut into matchstick-size pieces**
- **2 garlic cloves, minced**
- **1 (28-ounce) can whole plum tomatoes, coarsely chopped, with their juice**
- **3 carrots, chopped**
- **3 celery stalks, chopped**
- **1 bunch lacinato or regular kale, trimmed and chopped**
- **2 (14-ounce) cans reduced-sodium beef broth**
- **2 (14-ounce) cans reduced-sodium chicken broth**
- **2 (14-ounce) cans cannellini (white kidney) beans, rinsed and drained**
- **2 tablespoons chopped sage, or 2 teaspoons dried**
- **Freshly ground pepper**
- **8 (1-ounce) slices stale Italian or French bread**
- **2–3 tablespoons slivered sage leaves (optional)**

1. Heat a large nonstick saucepan or Dutch oven. Swirl in the oil, then add the onions, bacon, and garlic. Sauté until the onions are translucent, about 5 minutes. Stir in the tomatoes, carrots, and celery. Reduce the heat and simmer until the celery and carrot are partially softened, about 10 minutes. Stir in the kale, beef broth, chicken broth, beans, sage, and pepper; bring to a boil. Reduce the heat and simmer, stirring frequently, until the kale is very tender and the soup has thickened, about 1 hour. (The ribollita can be prepared ahead at this point and stored, covered, in the refrigerator for up to 3 days or frozen for up to 3 months.)
2. Place a layer of 4 bread slices in the bottom of a large saucepan or Dutch oven. Add a few ladles of the soup, then cover the soup with another layer of bread slices. Pour in the remaining soup and bring to a boil. Reduce the heat and simmer until the bread is soft, about 10 minutes. Sprinkle with the sage leaves, if using.

Per serving (generous 2 cups): 245 Cal, 5 g Fat, 1 g Sat Fat, 2 mg Chol, 898 mg Sod, 38 g Carb, 8 g Fib, 13 g Prot, 145 mg Calc. ***POINTS: 5.***

Minestrone and
Bubble Bread with Herbs
and Sun-Dried Tomatoes

Minestrone

MAKES 8 SERVINGS

Vegetable soups have played an important role in the Weight Watchers Program right from the start: The first cookbook featured more than a dozen, and Garden Vegetable Soup continues to be one of the most requested and beloved Program recipes. Indeed, there's no better way to get your veggies than in a tasty, filling bowlful. To honor that tradition, we've created the ultimate vegetable soup in this Italian improvisation—whose name means, in one translation, "vegetable soup," and in another, "large bowl of soup." Loaded with veggies, beans, and pasta, and topped with grated Parmesan cheese, it is a meal in itself.

- **6 ounces cannellini (white kidney) beans, picked over, rinsed, and drained**
- **8 cups reduced-sodium beef broth**
- **¼ teaspoon salt**
- **Freshly ground pepper**
- **4 teaspoons olive oil**
- **2 onions, chopped**
- **2 carrots, chopped**
- **2 celery stalks, chopped**
- **1 garlic clove, minced**
- **1 (28-ounce) can whole plum tomatoes, drained and chopped (reserve 1 cup juice)**
- **1 small (1-pound) cabbage, cleaned and shredded**
- **3 medium (8-ounce) zucchini, chopped**
- **½ cup chopped flat-leaf parsley**
- **2 tablespoons chopped sage, or 2 teaspoons dried**
- **3 ounces tubetti or other small pasta**
- **¼ cup freshly grated Parmesan cheese**

1. Place the beans in a large saucepan or Dutch oven; add enough cold water to cover them by 2 inches and bring to a boil. Remove from the heat; cover and let soak until the beans have swelled to at least twice their size, about 1½ hours. Drain.
2. Place the saucepan over medium heat; add the broth, salt, and pepper. Bring to a simmer; reduce the heat and simmer, covered, until the beans are barely tender, about 1 hour.
3. Meanwhile, heat a large nonstick skillet. Swirl in the oil, then add the onions, carrots, celery, and garlic. Cook, stirring frequently, until wilted.
4. Stir the vegetable mixture into the bean mixture; add the tomatoes and their reserved juice, the cabbage, zucchini, parsley, and sage. Simmer, stirring occasionally, until the vegetables are tender, about 20 minutes. Stir in the tubetti; continue cooking until they are barely tender, about 10 minutes. Remove from the heat; cover and let stand 10 minutes. Sprinkle with the cheese.

Per serving (1½ cups): 221 Cal, 5 g Fat, 1 g Sat Fat, 2 mg Chol, 481 mg Sod, 34 g Carb, 8 g Fib, 12 g Prot, 143 mg Calc. ***POINTS: 4.***

Gazpacho with Cilantro Croutons

MAKES 4 SERVINGS

In the swinging seventies, no sophisticated summer dinner party was complete without gazpacho on the menu. The refreshing cold soup—an import from sunny Spain—is basically liquefied salad. It makes a great light lunch or late-afternoon pick-me-up. Why not pack some in a thermos and sip it throughout the day?

- **4 large plum tomatoes, peeled and chopped**
- **1 medium cucumber, peeled and chopped**
- **1 green bell pepper, chopped**
- **4 scallions, sliced**
- **2 cups tomato juice**
- **3 tablespoons chopped cilantro**
- **1 tablespoon white-wine or cider vinegar**
- **1 tablespoon fresh lemon juice**
- **¼ teaspoon hot pepper sauce**
- **4 teaspoons olive oil**
- **1 garlic clove, bruised**
- **2 slices white or whole-wheat bread, cut in 1-inch cubes**

1. Puree the tomatoes, cucumber, pepper, and scallions in a food processor. Pour into a large bowl. Stir in the tomato juice, 1 tablespoon of the cilantro, the vinegar, lemon juice, and pepper sauce. Cover tightly and refrigerate until well chilled, at least 2 hours and up to 2 days.
2. Just before serving, heat a medium nonstick skillet. Swirl in the oil, then add the garlic. Cook, stirring, until fragrant, about 30 seconds. Discard the garlic; add the bread cubes and cook, stirring frequently, until the bread just starts to brown. Transfer to a medium bowl. Toss to coat with the remaining 2 tablespoons cilantro. Serve the soup with the warm croutons.

Per serving (1¼ cups): 125 Cal, 5 g Fat, 1 g Sat Fat, 0 mg Chol, 517 mg Sod, 18 g Carb, 3 g Fib, 3 g Prot, 49 mg Calc. ***POINTS: 2.***

top tips

- To peel the tomatoes, immerse them in boiling water for 1 minute; quickly transfer them with a slotted spoon to a bowl of ice water. As soon as they're cool enough to handle, just slip off the skins with your fingers.
- Bruising garlic helps release its flavor. Here's how: Place a peeled clove on a cutting board and flatten it slightly with the side of a large knife.
- The croutons can be made ahead of time and stored in an airtight container for up to three days or frozen in a zip-close freezer bag for up to two months. Just crisp them in a toaster oven for a few minutes before using.

Butternut Squash Soup with Sage

MAKES 4 SERVINGS

Two of autumn's best flavors, sweet winter squash and earthy sage, make this colorful soup a wonderful way to welcome the season. It makes a great first course that's filling but also very easy on the *POINTS*.

- **2 teaspoons olive oil**
- **1 onion, chopped**
- **1 medium (2-pound) butternut squash, peeled, seeded, and coarsely chopped**
- **1 (32-ounce) can reduced-sodium chicken broth**
- **2 tablespoons chopped sage**
- **1–1½ cups water**
- **¼ cup fat-free sour cream**
- **2 tablespoons chopped sage (optional)**

1. Heat a large nonstick saucepan. Swirl in the oil, then add the onion. Sauté until translucent, about 5 minutes. Add the squash, broth, and sage; bring to a boil. Reduce the heat and simmer, adding the water ½ cup at a time, until the squash is very soft, about 20 minutes. Remove from the heat and let cool 30 minutes.
2. Pour the mixture through a strainer; reserve the liquid. Transfer the squash mixture remaining in the strainer to a food processor; pulse to a very smooth puree. Add 1–1½ cups of the strained liquid, ½ cup at a time, until the soup has a fluid but creamy consistency. (Refrigerate or freeze any leftover strained liquid for another use.)
3. Transfer the soup back to the saucepan and cook, stirring frequently, until just heated through. Garnish each serving with a tablespoon of the sour cream and a sprinkle of the additional sage, if using.

Per serving (1 cup): 184 Cal, 4 g Fat, 1 g Sat Fat, 0 mg Chol, 489 mg Sod, 33 g Carb, 7 g Fib, 8 g Prot, 136 mg Calc. ***POINTS: 3.***

top tip

If you have any strained liquid leftover in Step 2, save it for flavoring soups and stews. It will last up to three days in the refrigerator or two months in the freezer.

Potato-Leek Soup

MAKES 8 SERVINGS

Made with just potatoes, leeks, and chicken broth, this hearty potage has all the robust taste of the traditional one made with cream—but none of the fat. It can be completely or partially pureed and served hot or cold. (If you serve it cold, be sure to label it "vichyssoise," as sophisticated chefs did in the sixties.) It can be refrigerated for up to three days but not frozen.

2 (32-ounce cans) reduced-sodium chicken broth
8 medium (5-ounce) potatoes, peeled and chopped
3 leeks, cleaned and thinly sliced
Freshly ground pepper
2 tablespoons minced chives (optional)

1. Combine the broth, potatoes, leeks, and pepper in a large saucepan or Dutch oven; cover and simmer until the vegetables are very soft, about 30 minutes. Uncover and let cool slightly.
2. Puree at least 2 cups or up to all of the potatoes and leeks (depending on the texture you want), with 1–2 cups of the broth in a food processor; pour the mixture back into the remaining soup, stir, and reheat. Serve hot, or cover and refrigerate and serve cold; hot or cold, garnish with the minced chives, if using.

Per serving (1½ cups): 153 Cal, 1 g Fat, 0 g Sat Fat, 0 mg Chol, 477 mg Sod, 28 g Carb, 3 g Fib, 7 g Prot, 44 mg Calc. ***POINTS: 3.***

top tip

To clean the leeks, trim the roots, leaving the root ends intact to hold the layers together. Slice them lengthwise, fan open the layers, and swish them in a large bowl of cool water. Let them stand a few minutes to allow the grit to fall to the bottom, then lift them out.

Borscht with Sour Cream

MAKES 4 SERVINGS

Once upon a Weight Watchers time, borscht was an occasional treat only to be eaten at dinner, because it was made with beets—a "limited" vegetable. But today we can enjoy it anytime and enrich it with a dollop of sour cream, to boot.

- **¾ pound beets, shredded (2 cups)**
- **1 (14-ounce) can reduced-sodium beef broth**
- **1½ cups water**
- **½ red onion, finely chopped**
- **½ cup finely shredded red cabbage**
- **½ teaspoon packed dark brown sugar**
- **2 tablespoons chopped dill**
- **2 tablespoons fresh lemon juice**
- **¼ teaspoon salt**
- **Freshly ground pepper**
- **¼ cup fat-free sour cream**
- **2 tablespoons chopped dill (optional)**

1. In a large nonreactive saucepan, combine the beets, broth, water, onion, cabbage, and sugar. Bring to a boil; reduce the heat and simmer, covered, until the cabbage is tender, about 20 minutes. Add the dill; simmer 5 minutes. Remove from the heat.
2. Stir in the lemon juice, salt, and pepper. Pour into a 1-quart storage container and refrigerate until chilled, at least 2 hours and up to 3 days. Garnish each serving with a tablespoon of the sour cream and a sprinkle of the additional dill, if using.

Per serving (1 cup): 68 Cal, 1 g Fat, 0 g Sat Fat, 0 mg Chol, 294 mg Sod, 13 g Carb, 2 g Fib, 4 g Prot, 62 mg Calc. ***POINTS: 1.***

"I must have joined Weight Watchers 15 times over the years, and dropped out of it just as many times. But the last time, I made two commitments to myself: First, I was going to come to a meeting every week, no matter what—not just on the weeks I knew I'd lost weight; second, I was going to do it for as long as it took, and not put a time limit on it. It took me 14 months to lose 32 pounds, but they never came back."

—Stephanie Del Valle, Leader and Area Trainer, New York City

Chilled Broccoli Soup with Lemon and Herbs

MAKES 4 SERVINGS

This tasty, healthy soup requires no extra fat. It's just broccoli, broth, and flavorings, all cooked together and then pureed in a food processor. What could be easier or more Weight Watchers Program–friendly? If you don't have fresh herbs, it's better to omit them altogether than to substitute dried ones.

- **2 (32-ounce) cans reduced-sodium chicken broth**
- **1 bunch broccoli, trimmed and broken into florets; stalks peeled and chopped**
- **1 onion, chopped**
- **2 garlic cloves, finely chopped**
- **2 tablespoons fresh lemon juice**
- **2 tablespoons chopped flat-leaf parsley**
- **1 tablespoon chopped mint**
- **¼ cup fat-free sour cream or yogurt cheese (optional)**

1. Combine the broth, broccoli, onion, and garlic in a large saucepan. Bring to a boil; reduce the heat and simmer, covered, until the broccoli is very tender, about 20 minutes.
2. Pour the mixture through a strainer; reserve the broth. Transfer the broccoli mixture remaining in the strainer to a food processor. Add the lemon juice, parsley, and mint; puree, adding the reserved broth ¼ cup at a time, until the mixture is liquid but creamy. Let cool to room temperature, then cover tightly and refrigerate until chilled, at least 2 hours and up to 1 day. (Refrigerate or freeze any remaining broth for another use.) Garnish each serving with 1 tablespoon of the sour cream or yogurt cheese, if using.

Per serving (1 cup): 119 Cal, 3 g Fat, 1 g Sat Fat, 0 mg Chol, 965 mg Sod, 11 g Carb, 4 g Fib, 13 g Prot, 85 mg Calc. ***POINTS: 2.***

top tip

To make ¼ cup yogurt cheese, spoon ½ cup plain fat-free yogurt into a coffee filter or cheesecloth-lined strainer; place over a bowl. Refrigerate, covered, at least 8 hours or overnight.

MORE WEIGHT WATCHERS MEMORIES...

"The Weight Watchers Program has evolved to be much more flexible over the years. That has made it harder to take the weight off in the beginning, but easier to keep it off in the long term—and that's where it really matters."

—Carol Kramer, Manager, New Service Development and Training (and former Leader), Weight Watchers International

"The best thing Weight Watchers ever did was to introduce the ***POINTS*** Food System. It gave us so much flexibility. With ***POINTS***, you don't have to change your life, you just make choices. Instead of saying, "I can't order lasagna at this restaurant," you ask yourself, "Do I want to spend ***8 POINTS*** on this meal?" It's living in the real world."

—Sharon Claye, Leader, Detroit

"We don't sell a diet. We sell self-respect."

—Florine Mark, Franchise Owner, Detroit

"During the [1965] New York City blackout, I got a call from one of my Leaders, saying, 'I'm on a street corner, pulling a meeting together.' That didn't surprise me. That devotion is what never changes. The Program may change, but the people won't."

—Jean Nidetch

Tossin' and Turnin'

1968

Good health is a good buy, too: Weight Watchers goes public; the stock opens at $11.25 but by end of day is valued at $30.

The first spark in the fitness boom is struck: Dr. Kenneth Cooper, founder of the Cooper Aerobics Center in Dallas, publishes *Aerobics,* which touts the benefits of exercise to health and longevity.

1969

Man walks on the moon, and Weight Watchers earthly holdings are bigger than ever—with a line of frozen foods, *Weight Watchers Magazine* (which features a monthly column by Jean Nidetch), and summer camps for overweight teens.

1970

Jean Nidetch's *The Story of Weight Watchers* becomes an instant best-seller.

The Food and Drug Administration bans cyclamates, a popular noncaloric sweetener. Saccharin becomes the calorie-free sweetener of choice.

>>>

Artichoke-Green Bean-Asparagus Salad with Dijon Vinaigrette

MAKES 4 SERVINGS

What a pity that glamorously delicious, fiber-rich, and nearly fat-free artichoke hearts were once considered "limited" vegetables on the Weight Watchers eating plan. This elegant and savory salad makes amends, celebrating them with style. Since the vegetables are prepared, dressed, and marinated for hours, it's a good do-ahead dish for company.

- **1 (10-ounce) box frozen artichoke hearts**
- **1 (10-ounce) box frozen green beans**
- **1 (10-ounce) box frozen asparagus spears**
- **2 tablespoons reduced-sodium chicken broth**
- **4 teaspoons olive oil**
- **1 tablespoon chopped thyme**
- **1 tablespoon white-wine or cider vinegar**
- **2 garlic cloves, minced**
- **1 tablespoon Dijon mustard**
- **1 teaspoon dry mustard**
- **¼ teaspoon salt**
- **Freshly ground pepper**
- **1 hard-cooked egg, finely chopped**
- **1 tablespoon minced flat-leaf parsley**

1. Cook the artichoke hearts, green beans, and asparagus according to package directions. Drain, then arrange the vegetables on a platter in an attractive pattern.
2. Puree the broth, oil, thyme, vinegar, garlic, Dijon mustard, dry mustard, salt, and pepper in a blender or food processor. Drizzle the dressing evenly over the vegetables; sprinkle with the egg and parsley. Cover tightly with plastic wrap; refrigerate up to 8 hours or overnight. Let stand at room temperature 30 minutes before serving.

Per serving (1 cup): 138 Cal, 7 g Fat, 1 g Sat Fat, 53 mg Chol, 242 mg Sod, 16 g Carb, 7 g Fib, 7 g Prot, 94 mg Calc. ***POINTS: 3.***

top tip

If you have the time, substitute fresh, trimmed green beans and asparagus spears for the frozen ones; you'll need about 2 cups of each. Steam them until tender-crisp before using. You can also use canned quartered artichoke hearts instead of frozen; a 14-ounce can will work nicely.

Arugula-Pear Salad with Gorgonzola Dressing

MAKES 4 SERVINGS

Pears and Gorgonzola cheese are a favorite combination in Italian cuisine, especially after a meal. Why not serve this elegant salad as a last course at a dinner party? The salad and the dressing can be made ahead of time, refrigerated for up to eight hours, then combined just before serving.

- **1 pear, thinly sliced**
- **1 tablespoon fresh lemon juice**
- **1 bunch arugula, cleaned**
- **⅓ cup crumbled Gorgonzola cheese**
- **¼ cup reduced-sodium vegetable broth**
- **4 teaspoons olive oil**
- **1 tablespoon white-wine or cider vinegar**
- **1 garlic clove, bruised**
- **Freshly ground pepper**

1. Combine the pear with the lemon juice in a small bowl; toss to coat. Arrange the arugula and pear slices on a platter.
2. To prepare the dressing, combine the cheese, broth, oil, vinegar, garlic, and pepper in a small bowl; let stand at least 5 minutes to allow the flavors to blend, then remove the garlic.
3. Drizzle the dressing over the salad just before serving.

Per serving (1½ cups): 115 Cal, 8 g Fat, 3 g Sat Fat, 11 mg Chol, 182 mg Sod, 8 g Carb, 1 g Fib, 3 g Prot, 97 mg Calc. ***POINTS: 3.***

top tip

Bruising garlic helps release its flavor. Here's how: Place a peeled clove on a cutting board and flatten it slightly with the side of a large knife.

Arugula, Radicchio, and Belgian Endive Salad with Creamy Garlic Dressing

MAKES 4 SERVINGS

Inspired by the Salad Bouquet of lettuce, endive, and asparagus featured in the first *Weight Watchers Cookbook*, this colorful trio of salad greens features a creamy garlic dressing you'll want to drizzle on everything. Make it ahead, if you like; the dressing will keep in a tightly sealed container in the refrigerator for up to three days.

- **½ cup plain fat-free yogurt**
- **4 teaspoons vegetable oil**
- **1 tablespoon white-wine or cider vinegar**
- **½ tablespoon light corn syrup**
- **1 garlic clove, minced**
- **½ teaspoon salt**
- **Freshly ground pepper**
- **1 bunch arugula, cleaned**
- **1 head radicchio, cleaned**
- **1 head Belgian endive, cleaned**
- **1 tablespoon minced chives (optional)**

1. To prepare the dressing, pulse the yogurt, oil, vinegar, corn syrup, garlic, salt, and pepper in a food processor or blender until smooth. Cover and refrigerate until ready to serve.
2. Arrange the arugula, radicchio, and endive leaves on a platter. Just before serving, drizzle the dressing over the salad. Sprinkle with the chives, if using.

Per serving (2 cups): 100 Cal, 5 g Fat, 1 g Sat Fat, 1 mg Chol, 356 mg Sod, 11 g Carb, 4 g Fib, 4 g Prot, 158 mg Calc. ***POINTS: 2.***

"My son and his wife wanted to lose a little weight for their wedding, so they decided to sign up for my meetings—and they both ended up becoming Lifetime Members."
—*Wendy Brintnall, Leader, Omaha*

Fennel, Orange, and Red Cabbage Salad with Citrus Vinaigrette

MAKES 4 SERVINGS 

Designer vinegars such as raspberry and balsamic were a hallmark of the excessive eighties, but they're used to wonderful effect in this beautiful salad. The sweet-and-sour combination of vinegars, lemon juice, orange, and honey is a perfect complement to the licorice-y taste of the fennel—and the cabbage pulls it all together.

- **2 tablespoons reduced-sodium vegetable broth or dry white wine**
- **1 teaspoon grated orange zest**
- **2 tablespoons fresh orange juice**
- **4 teaspoons olive oil**
- **1 tablespoon honey**
- **1 teaspoon lemon juice**
- **1 teaspoon red-wine or cider vinegar**
- **1 teaspoon raspberry vinegar**
- **1 teaspoon balsamic vinegar**
- **¼ teaspoon salt**
- **Freshly ground pepper**
- **1 small (1-pound) red cabbage, shredded (4 cups)**
- **1 fennel bulb, trimmed and thinly sliced**
- **2 oranges, peeled, sliced, and cut into bite-size pieces**

Whisk together the broth or wine, orange zest, orange juice, oil, honey, lemon juice, red-wine or cider vinegar, raspberry vinegar, balsamic vinegar, salt, and pepper in a large salad bowl. Add the cabbage, fennel, and oranges to the bowl; toss to coat evenly. Serve at once.

Per serving (2 cups): 133 Cal, 5 g Fat, 1 g Sat Fat, 0 mg Chol, 201 mg Sod, 23 g Carb, 5 g Fib, 3 g Prot, 100 mg Calc. ***POINTS: 2.***

Field Greens with Roasted Beets, Goat Cheese Croutons, and Dijon Vinaigrette

Field Greens with Roasted Beets, Goat Cheese Croutons, and Dijon Vinaigrette

MAKES 4 SERVINGS

Field greens, microgreens, mesclun, baby greens—all these terms became salad buzzwords in upscale nineties restaurants, but the idea is an old one. French cooks have been creating salads from mixed bunches of tender baby greens for years. Today, it's common to find a colorful mix of greens at farmers' markets, supermarkets, and even in prebagged salad kits (they're usually labeled "spring mix"). Paired with those other nineties staples, beets, goat cheese, and Dijon vinaigrette, they make a classy but easy salad.

2 beets, peeled, trimmed, and cubed
1 teaspoon chopped thyme, or ¼ teaspoon dried
4 (1-ounce) slices toasted French or Italian bread
2 ounces goat cheese
2 tablespoons chopped flat-leaf parsley
3 tablespoons dry white wine or reduced-sodium chicken broth
4 teaspoons olive oil
2 teaspoons white- or red-wine vinegar, or cider vinegar
1 teaspoon Dijon mustard
1 garlic clove, bruised
¼ teaspoon salt
Freshly ground pepper
8 ounces mixed baby greens

1. Preheat the oven to 400°F.
2. Spray a small baking pan with nonstick spray. Combine the beets and thyme in the pan; toss to coat and spray again with nonstick spray. Roast, stirring occasionally, until tender, about 25 minutes. Set aside to cool.
3. To prepare the croutons, spread the toasted bread slices with the goat cheese; sprinkle with the parsley and set aside.
4. To prepare the dressing, combine the wine or chicken broth, oil, vinegar, mustard, garlic, salt, and pepper in a large bowl; let stand 2 minutes, then discard the garlic. Whisk until smooth.
5. To assemble the salad, drizzle a teaspoon of the dressing over the beets in the pan and toss to coat evenly. Add the greens to the bowl with the remaining dressing; toss to coat evenly. Divide the greens among 4 salad plates. Top each with one-fourth of the beets, then with a crouton.

Per serving (2 cups with 1 crouton): 199 Cal, 9 g Fat, 3 g Sat Fat, 13 mg Chol, 437 mg Sod, 21 g Carb, 3 g Fib, 7 g Prot, 163 mg Calc. ***POINTS: 4.***

top tip

A bit of creamy goat cheese makes this elegant salad a hearty meal. In the eighties and nineties, health-conscious eaters flocked to the tangy cheese, touting it as a lower-fat alternative to cow's-milk cheese. In fact, the fat content is virtually the same, ounce per ounce. The good news is that the assertive, nutty flavor of a good goat cheese goes quite a long way so, as in this salad, you only need a little to make a big impact.

Caesar Salad

MAKES 4 SERVINGS  

Caesar salad had its heyday in the sixties, was rediscovered in the nineties, and is better than ever today. We've eliminated the raw egg, so you can serve it with confidence.

- **1 large garlic clove, bruised**
- **¼ cup reduced-sodium chicken broth**
- **4 teaspoons olive oil**
- **1 tablespoon fresh lemon juice**
- **¾ teaspoon anchovy paste**
- **½ teaspoon dry mustard**
- **Freshly ground pepper**
- **1 head romaine lettuce, torn into bite-size pieces (6 cups)**
- **1 cup fat-free croutons**
- **2 tablespoons freshly grated Parmesan cheese**

Rub a large salad bowl with the garlic clove, then combine the garlic with the broth, oil, lemon juice, anchovy paste, mustard, and pepper in the bowl. Let stand 5 minutes, then discard the garlic. Add the lettuce to the bowl; toss to coat evenly. Sprinkle with the croutons and cheese.

Per serving (2 cups): 94 Cal, 6 g Fat, 1 g Sat Fat, 4 mg Chol, 184 mg Sod, 6 g Carb, 2 g Fib, 4 g Prot, 83 mg Calc. ***POINTS*: 2.**

"I once had a member come in in tears. She had been staying within her ***POINTS*** range, exercising regularly, really following the Program—but she had gained weight. I asked to look at her journal and found that she wasn't adding any fat to her diet. I said, 'How about adding a little peanut butter here? Or some dressing on that salad?' She gave it a try, and the next week she had lost four pounds. It's hard to convince people that their bodies need fat, even when they're trying to lose weight."

—Susie Huebner, Leader, Des Moines

Chef's Salad with Russian Dressing

MAKES 4 SERVINGS 

Weight Watchers members were among the first to be clued in that a typical American chef's salad—loaded with cold cuts and cheese and doused in dressing—was anything but diet food. Here's our latest take on the classic, with more veggies and a leaner but still creamy-rich dressing.

- **2 tablespoons reduced-calorie mayonnaise**
- **¼ cup plain fat-free yogurt**
- **2 tablespoons ketchup**
- **Freshly ground pepper**
- **1 head romaine lettuce, torn into bite-size pieces (6 cups)**
- **1 cucumber, peeled and sliced**
- **1 green bell pepper, sliced into thin rings**
- **1 tomato, cut into 8 wedges**
- **2 ounces reduced-sodium turkey breast, cut into matchstick-size strips**
- **2 ounces reduced-fat Swiss cheese, cut into matchstick-size strips**
- **1 hard-cooked egg, quartered**

Whisk together the mayonnaise, yogurt, ketchup, and ground pepper in a salad bowl. Add the lettuce and cucumber to the bowl; toss to coat evenly. Arrange the bell pepper, tomato, turkey, cheese, and egg on top of the salad in an attractive pattern and serve at once.

Per serving (2½ cups): 139 Cal, 7 g Fat, 2 g Sat Fat, 66 mg Chol, 289 mg Sod, 10 g Carb, 2 g Fib, 12 g Prot, 244 mg Calc. ***POINTS: 3.***

top tip

For a chunkier, tangier Russian dressing, substitute salsa for the ketchup.

Cobb Salad with
Green Goddess Dressing

Cobb Salad with Green Goddess Dressing

MAKES 4 SERVINGS

Like so many of our classic salads, this one comes from 1920s California. Bob Cobb, of the famed Brown Derby restaurant in Hollywood, is said to have created the salad out of leftovers in the refrigerator. The dressing, named to honor the actor George Arliss and a play he starred in, *The Green Goddess*, hails from San Francisco's Palace Hotel.

- **4 slices turkey bacon**
- **½ small iceberg lettuce head, chopped (about 3 cups)**
- **1 bunch arugula, chopped (about 1 cup)**
- **8 ounces skinless cooked chicken breast, sliced**
- **3 large hard-cooked egg whites, chopped**
- **½ medium (8-ounce) Hass avocado, peeled and chopped**
- **4 plum tomatoes, seeded and chopped**
- **½ cup plain fat-free yogurt**
- **¼ cup fat-free mayonnaise**
- **½ cup chopped parsley**
- **¼ cup chopped chives**
- **1 scallion, chopped**
- **1 teaspoon white-wine vinegar**
- **¼ teaspoon salt**
- **⅛ teaspoon freshly ground pepper**

1. Heat a medium nonstick skillet over medium heat. Add the bacon and cook until crisp. Drain on paper towels until cool enough to handle; coarsely chop.
2. Scatter the lettuce and arugula over a platter. Top with neat rows of the chicken, egg whites, avocado, tomatoes, and bacon.
3. To prepare dressing, place the yogurt, mayonnaise, parsley, chives, scallion, vinegar, salt, and pepper in blender; pulse until smooth.
4. Lightly drizzle half of the dressing over the salad and serve at once, passing the remaining dressing separately.

Per serving: (1½ cups with ¼ cup dressing): 224 Cal, 8 g Fat, 2 g Sat Fat, 56 mg Chol, 580 mg Sod, 12 g Carb, 3 g Fib, 26 g Prot, 110 mg Calc. ***POINTS: 5.***

top tips

- To seed the tomatoes, just cut them in half horizontally, then squeeze out and discard the seeds.
- We prefer Hass avocados for this recipe, and not just because of their Californian origins. With their distinctive black pebbly skin, Hass avocados contain slightly more fat than the smaller, green-skinned Mexican types grown in Florida—but their buttery taste and velvety texture justify every ***POINT.***

Greek Salad with Oregano Dressing

MAKES 4 SERVINGS

Forty years ago, you'd find this salad featured at any corner diner. Now that it's become a classic, you're just as likely to find it today. This savory version includes all the traditional ingredients but only a fraction of the fat. Try it with toasted pita bread.

- **¼ cup reduced-sodium vegetable broth**
- **4 teaspoons olive oil**
- **1 tablespoon white- or red-wine vinegar, or cider vinegar**
- **1½ tablespoons chopped oregano, or 1½ teaspoons dried**
- **1 garlic clove, bruised**
- **¼ teaspoon salt**
- **Freshly ground pepper**
- **1 head romaine, Bibb, iceberg, or green-leaf lettuce, torn into bite-size pieces (6 cups)**
- **1 cucumber, peeled, seeded and chopped**
- **1 green bell pepper, seeded, and cut into ½-inch strips**
- **1 tomato, cut into 8 wedges**
- **¼ cup chopped dill**
- **10 small black olives, pitted and sliced**
- **4 anchovies, rinsed and chopped (optional)**
- **½ cup crumbled feta cheese**

1. Combine the broth, oil, vinegar, oregano, garlic, salt, and black pepper in a small bowl. Let stand 5 minutes to allow the flavors to blend, then discard the garlic.
2. Meanwhile, combine the lettuce, cucumber, bell pepper, tomato, dill, and olives in a large salad bowl. Pour the dressing over the salad; toss to coat evenly. Top with the anchovies, if using, and sprinkle with the cheese.

Per serving (2½ cups): 128 Cal, 10 g Fat, 4 g Sat Fat, 17 mg Chol, 449 mg Sod, 7 g Carb, 3g Fib, 4 g Prot, 134 mg Calc. ***POINTS: 3.***

Spinach-Mushroom-Bacon Salad with Warm Onion Dressing

MAKES 6 SERVINGS

The nineties bistro craze made this favorite salad even more popular; who knows how many diners thought their bacon-and-dripping-soaked salads were light eating? Our version cuts the fat dramatically, with a savory, warm dressing that wilts the spinach just enough to make it tender.

- **1 (10-ounce) bag triple-washed fresh spinach, torn into bite-size pieces, or 8 cups spinach leaves**
- **1 (10-ounce) package sliced mushrooms**
- **2 tablespoons vegetable oil**
- **2 cups reduced-sodium vegetable broth**
- **1 red onion, thinly sliced and separated into rings**
- **1 teaspoon grated orange zest**
- **¼ cup fresh orange juice**
- **2 tablespoons red-wine or cider vinegar**
- **¼ teaspoon salt**
- **1 crisp-cooked bacon slice, crumbled**
- **Freshly ground pepper**

1. Place the spinach and mushrooms in a salad bowl; set aside.
2. Heat a large nonstick skillet. Swirl in the oil, then add the broth, onion, orange zest, orange juice, vinegar, and salt. Cook over medium heat, stirring occasionally, until the onions are very tender and the liquid has thickened and reduced to ½ cup, about 15 minutes. Let stand 10 minutes.
3. Pour the warm dressing over the spinach and mushrooms; sprinkle with the bacon pieces and pepper. Serve at once.

Per serving (2 cups): 86 Cal, 5 g Fat, 1 g Sat Fat, 1 mg Chol, 238 mg Sod, 8 g Carb, 2 g Fib, 3 g Prot, 58 mg Calc. ***POINTS: 2.***

top tip

If you're using bunch spinach, you'll need to wash it carefully. Immerse the leaves in cold standing water and swish gently to free the grit. Let soak for a minute or two while the grit settles to the bottom. Lift the spinach out of the water and repeat the rinsing with clean water until the spinach is free of grit, usually three changes of water. Drain and dry in a salad spinner. Store the cleaned spinach in a loosely closed plastic bag in the refrigerator for up to three days.

Pickled Beet and Onion Salad

MAKES 4 SERVINGS

Back in the old days when beets and onions were "limited" vegetables, a recipe for Beet Relish combined canned cooked beets, dehydrated onion flakes, artificial sweetener, and vinegar. Compare that with this twenty-first-century version that uses lots of beets, fresh onion, a little oil, balsamic vinegar, and, yes, real sugar!

3 tablespoons red-wine or cider vinegar
2 tablespoons dry red wine or reduced-sodium vegetable broth
1 tablespoon balsamic vinegar
2 teaspoons sugar
2 teaspoons olive oil
¼ teaspoon salt
Freshly ground pepper
4 cups cooked sliced beets or 2 (15-ounce) cans sliced beets, drained
1 red onion, chopped

Combine the wine or cider vinegar, wine, balsamic vinegar, sugar, oil, salt, and pepper in a large bowl. Add the beets and onion; toss to coat. Cover tightly and refrigerate to blend the flavors, at least 30 minutes and up to 1 day before serving.

Per serving (¾ cup): 117 Cal, 3 g Fat, 0 g Sat Fat, 0 mg Chol, 278 mg Sod, 23 g Carb, 3 g Fib, 3 g Prot, 35 mg Calc. ***POINTS: 2.***

top tip

To cook fresh beets, scrub them, then boil or roast them in their skins until tender (30 minutes to an hour, depending on the size of the beets). When they are cool enough to handle, peel off their skins under a stream of cold running water; they should slip off easily. Wear rubber gloves if you don't want to stain your hands.

California Salad Sandwiches

MAKES 4 SERVINGS 

There was a time when this sandwich's alfalfa sprouts, avocado, and whole-grain bread would have pegged it as pure Californian, if not pure hippie. But today, these ingredients are commonplace. Instead of slathering the sandwiches with mayonnaise, we use flavorful pureed beans. We also streamline the assembly by pan-grilling the sandwiches instead of toasting the bread. Far out!

- **1 cup cooked small white beans (such as Great Northern or flageolets), or rinsed drained canned white beans**
- **2 tablespoons water**
- **1 tablespoon fresh lemon juice**
- **2 tablespoons Dijon mustard**
- **8 slices multigrain bread**
- **8 slices low fat Swiss or cheddar cheese, about 4 ounces**
- **1 small avocado, peeled, pitted, and thinly sliced**
- **2 cups alfalfa sprouts**
- **1 medium tomato, cut into 8 slices**

1. Combine the beans, water, and lemon juice in a blender; puree until smooth.
2. Spread 1½ teaspoons of the mustard onto each of 4 bread slices, then spread all 8 slices with a layer of the bean puree. Layer each mustard-spread bread slice in the following order: 1 slice of cheese, ¼ of the avocado slices, ½ cup alfalfa sprouts, 2 tomato slices, and another cheese slice. Top each sandwich with the remaining (bean-puree-spread) bread slices.
3. Heat a large nonstick skillet over medium heat. Lightly spray both sides of each sandwich with nonstick spray, then place in the skillet. Cover and cook, turning once, until the cheese melts and the bread toasts slightly, 4 minutes. Serve at once.

Per serving (1 sandwich): 339 Cal, 13 g Fat, 4 g Sat Fat, 9 mg Chol, 418 mg Sod, 42 g Carb, 10 g Fib, 20 g Prot, 445 mg Calc. ***POINTS: 7.***

top tip

Alfalfa sprouts add lots of crunch and potassium, but they have been identified as a source of bacterial contamination in rare cases. The sprouts may become infected with bacteria from runoff from pasture land and, since the sprouts are eaten raw, any harmful bacteria present are not killed by cooking. Therefore, be sure to wash the sprouts well before you use them: Soak them in a large quantity of water and shake dry. Pregnant women, young children, the elderly, and people whose immune systems are compromised should avoid alfalfa sprouts altogether; for them, lettuce is a better choice for this sandwich.

Not Your Mama's
Three-Bean Salad

Not Your Mama's Three-Bean Salad

MAKES 6 SERVINGS

Remember the boring vinegar-soaked salad of the past? This dish takes on a new profile with fresh slivers of basil, tangy lemon juice, and green soybeans (edamame) for their sweet flavor and bright color. And unlike the original three-bean salad, the beans won't turn drab olive green during storage; the salad will keep up to two days in the refrigerator.

- **1 teaspoon grated lemon zest**
- **1½ tablespoons fresh lemon juice**
- **1 tablespoon extra-virgin olive oil**
- **½ teaspoon salt**
- **Freshly ground pepper**
- **1 (15-ounce) can black beans, rinsed and drained**
- **1 (15-ounce) can small white beans, rinsed and drained**
- **⅔ cup cooked green soybeans (edamame)**
- **⅓ sweet onion, finely diced**
- **⅓ red bell pepper, finely diced**
- **5 large basil leaves, thinly sliced**

Combine the lemon zest, lemon juice, oil, salt, and ground pepper in a medium bowl. Add the black beans, white beans, soybeans, onion, bell pepper, and basil; toss to coat evenly. Serve at once, or cover and refrigerate for up to 2 days.

Per serving (¾ cup): 160 Cal, 3 g Fat, 0 g Sat Fat, 0 mg Chol, 427 mg Sod, 26 g Carb, 8 g Fib, 9 g Prot, 94 mg Calc. ***POINTS: 3.***

Fruit Salad with Yogurt-Mint Dressing

MAKES 4 SERVINGS

In the old days of Weight Watchers, fruit salads were served in limited quantities—and usually bulked up with vegetables like green peppers and pimientos. The dressings tended to be made with pureed cottage cheese, diet ginger ale, artificial sweetener, and other alchemy. And, of course, kiwi fruits were unknown and bananas were forbidden. What a pleasure it is to improve on the past and enjoy this refreshing fruit salad, as perfect for lunch as it is for dessert.

- **1 cup sliced strawberries**
- **2 medium kiwi fruit, pared and sliced**
- **1 banana, sliced**
- **1 (8-ounce) can unsweetened pineapple chunks, drained**
- **3 tablespoons orange juice**
- **¼ cup aspartame-sweetened fat-free vanilla yogurt**
- **2 tablespoons chopped mint**
- **4 small fresh mint sprigs (optional)**

1. Combine the strawberries, kiwi, banana, and pineapple with 1 tablespoon of the orange juice in a large bowl.
2. Puree the yogurt, chopped mint, and the remaining 2 tablespoons orange juice in a food processor. Pour over the fruit mixture; toss to coat evenly. Refrigerate, covered, until thoroughly chilled, at least 1 hour and up to 8 hours. Garnish with the mint sprigs, if using, and serve.

Per serving (¾ cup): 92 Cal, 1 g Fat, 0 g Sat Fat, 0 mg Chol, 10 mg Sod, 22 g Carb, 3 g Fib, 2 g Prot, 43 mg Calc. ***POINTS: 1.***

top tip

If time—and your budget—allows, seek out fresh pineapple to use in place of canned. The taste difference is incomparable and well worth the effort.

When we opened the Program in a foreign country, I'd bring an interpreter wherever I went. But I'd find that the audiences understood me anyway. They reacted to the emotion; they knew what I was saying. They laughed at the same things people laughed at in Brooklyn, New York.

—Jean Nidetch

It's hard getting people off the quick-weight-loss mentality. I always ask them, 'Do you want quick weight loss—or permanent weight loss?' That's the choice. If a member compares herself to someone who goes on a quick-weight-loss diet, she'll see that it's like the tortoise and the hare. The other person will lose the weight—but also gain it back—in the same time period that it takes the Weight Watchers member to reach her goal. So she's still losing the weight faster, in the long run.

—Sharon Claye, Leader, Detroit

The **Tools for Living** have been there from the beginning—I taught them in my very first class, in 1968. It's just easier to teach them now, because we've given them a name and made them more professional.

—Florine Mark, Franchise Owner, Detroit

Our knowledge of nutrition has changed, and that has a lot to do with our culture. Back in the early days of Weight Watchers, Americans were concerned about nutrient deficiencies; we were worried about people getting enough protein and iron. We used to require members to eat a serving of liver once a week, to help prevent anemia in women of child-bearing age. Today, dietary excesses are our most important concerns—too much fat, too many calories. And, with the availability of fortified foods and nutritional supplements, nutrient deficiencies are not such an issue.

—Karen Miller-Kovach, R.D., Chief Scientist, Weight Watchers International

Beat It!

eggs

1971

William Henry Sebrell, Jr., M.D., (left, with Jean Nidetch) former director of the National Institutes of Health, becomes Weight Watchers first Medical Director.

1973

Weight Watchers holds its tenth anniversary party at Madison Square Garden. Bob Hope, Pearl Bailey, and others entertain a sold-out crowd of more than 17,000. Times Square is renamed "Weight Watchers Square."

1975

The French nouvelle cuisine movement hits these shores. Gourmets are thrilled by the artful, elegant foods; others are turned off by overpriced meals that leave them hungry. Weight Watchers members rejoice: Now the rest of the world knows the concept of portion size.

>>>

eggs

Fried Egg

MAKES 1 SERVING

Founding Weight Watchers members probably remember "frying" their eggs in Teflon pans with nary a dot of butter. They'd probably rather forget all the eggs that stuck to the pan or burned! Today's more enduring nonstick finishes, plus the removal of butter from the banned list, makes our updated recipe much simpler, tastier, and foolproof.

1 teaspoon unsalted butter
1 large egg

Melt the butter in a small nonstick skillet over high heat until bubbling. Break the egg into a small cup or saucer, then slide it gently into the skillet. Cover, reduce the heat to low, and cook until the white is set and opaque. Serve at once.

Per serving (1 egg): 108 Cal, 8 g Fat, 4 g Sat Fat, 223 mg Chol, 64 mg Sod, 1 g Carb, 0 g Fib, 6 g Prot, 26 mg Calc. ***POINTS: 3.***

"Weight Watchers understood that it was necessary to have a scientific background to address weight loss—and we became recognized as leaders. Each time we updated the Program, it reflected the best science...and with each update, we simplified the Program to make it easier for members to use."

—Reva Frankle, M.S., Ed.D., former Director of Nutrition, Weight Watchers International

Omelettes for Two

MAKES 2 SERVINGS

Fat-free omelettes were a staple in the old days of Weight Watchers. The one caveat was that eggs could only be eaten at breakfast or lunch. Break the rules deliciously with this foolproof omelette technique; it makes a great impromptu supper. We've given a mushroom and Swiss variation, but you can also fill the omelette with any variety of cooked vegetables, meats, or poultry. If cholesterol is a concern, substitute 1 cup of fat-free egg substitute for the eggs and egg whites.

- **2 large eggs**
- **3 egg whites**
- **1 tablespoon water**
- **¼ teaspoon salt**
- **¼ teaspoon ground pepper**
- **½ teaspoon olive oil**

1. Beat together the eggs, egg whites, water, salt, and pepper in medium bowl until slightly frothy.
2. Heat ¼ teaspoon of the oil in a large nonstick skillet over medium-high heat. Add half of the egg mixture and cook, occasionally lifting the edges of the egg and tilting the pan to allow the uncooked mixture to flow underneath, 2 minutes. When almost set, loosen edges of the omelette with a spatula and fold into a half-moon shape. Reduce heat to low and cook 1 minute more, or until set. Repeat with the remaining egg mixture.

Per serving (1 omelette): 110 Cal, 6 g Fat, 2 g Sat Fat, 213 mg Chol, 436 mg Sod, 1 g Carb, 0 g Fib, 12 g Prot, 29 mg Calc. ***POINTS: 3.***

Mushroom-Swiss Omelettes

MAKES 2 SERVINGS 

- **1½ cups sliced mushrooms**
- **2 large eggs**
- **3 egg whites**
- **1 tablespoon water**
- **¼ teaspoon salt**
- **¼ teaspoon ground pepper**
- **½ teaspoon olive oil**
- **4 tablespoons shredded reduced-fat Swiss cheese**

1. Spray a large nonstick skillet with nonstick spray and place over medium heat. Add the mushrooms, spreading them in a single layer. Cover and cook until golden, 3 minutes, stirring halfway through cooking. Set aside the mushrooms and wipe out the skillet with paper towels.
2. Prepare the omelette as directed in Omelettes for Two, up to Step 2. Before folding the omelette, sprinkle on 2 tablespoons of the cheese and half of the mushrooms. Continue with Step 2 as directed, adding the remaining cheese and mushrooms.

Per serving (1 omelette): 157 Cal, 8 g Fat, 3 g Sat Fat, 217 mg Chol, 455 mg Sod, 4 g Carb, 1 g Fib, 17 g Prot, 198 mg Calc. ***POINTS: 4.***

Hash Browns, Egg, and Cheese Casserole

MAKES 6 SERVINGS

This homey, hearty casserole is a great addition to a brunch buffet. The turkey bacon gives it a rich, smoky flavor without adding a lot of fat. If you find yourself with any leftovers, you can refrigerate the casserole for up to two days and reheat individual portions in the microwave.

- **6 strips turkey bacon, sliced crosswise into ¼-inch strips**
- **3 cups (12 ounces) frozen hash brown potatoes**
- **4 scallions, sliced**
- **3 large eggs**
- **3 egg whites**
- **¾ cup low-fat (1%) small-curd cottage cheese**
- **⅔ cup shredded reduced-fat cheddar cheese**
- **3 tablespoons freshly grated Parmesan cheese**
- **3 tablespoons all-purpose flour**
- **¾ teaspoon poultry seasoning or ground sage**
- **½ teaspoon baking powder**
- **¼ teaspoon salt**
- **¼ teaspoon ground pepper**

1. Place the oven rack in the center of the oven; preheat oven to 375°F. Spray a 1½-quart shallow baking dish with nonstick spray.
2. Spray a nonstick skillet with nonstick spray and set over medium heat. Add the bacon and cook until nearly crisp, stirring occasionally, 4 minutes. Add the potatoes and scallions; continue cooking and stirring until tender, about 7 minutes. Remove from the heat and let cool slightly.
3. Beat together the eggs and egg whites in a large bowl until blended. Beat in the cottage cheese, ⅓ cup of the cheddar cheese, the Parmesan cheese, flour, poultry seasoning or sage, baking powder, salt, and pepper until combined. Stir in the cooled potato mixture and spread evenly into the baking dish. Bake until golden and set in the center, about 30 minutes. Sprinkle evenly with the remaining ⅓ cup cheddar cheese. Let stand until the cheese is melted, about 10 minutes, and serve hot or warm.

Per serving (⅙ of casserole): 235 Cal, 8 g Fat, 4 g Sat Fat, 129 mg Chol, 665 mg Sod, 22 g Carb, 2 g Fib, 18 g Prot, 205 mg Calc. ***POINTS: 5.***

Swiss Cheese Strata

MAKES 6 SERVINGS

Back in the seventies, strata—a layered casserole of bread, flavorings, and egg custard—may have lost some ground to quiche as the brunch staple of choice. But for some of us, this easy, make-ahead dish will always be first in our hearts. Try it for a Sunday buffet or an easy weekend breakfast.

- **5 slices whole-wheat bread, quartered**
- **¾ cup diced bottled roasted red peppers**
- **½ cup shredded reduced-fat Swiss cheese**
- **3 scallions, thinly sliced**
- **2 cups low-fat (1%) milk**
- **2 large eggs**
- **3 egg whites**
- **2 tablespoons freshly grated Parmesan cheese**
- **1 tablespoon Dijon mustard**
- **¼ teaspoon salt**
- **¼ teaspoon ground pepper**

1. Spray a 2-quart baking dish with nonstick spray. Arrange the bread pieces in the bottom of the baking dish, overlapping them slightly. Scatter the red peppers, Swiss cheese, and scallions on top.
2. Whisk together the milk, eggs, egg whites, Parmesan cheese, mustard, salt, and pepper in a medium bowl. Pour over the bread and let stand for at least 20 minutes, or cover and refrigerate for up to 12 hours.
3. Place the oven rack in the center of the oven; preheat the oven to 350°F. Bake the strata until golden and a knife inserted in the center comes out clean, 40–45 minutes. Let stand 10 minutes, then serve hot.

Per serving (⅙ of casserole): 166 Cal, 6 g Fat, 3 g Sat Fat, 79 mg Chol, 395 mg Sod, 17 g Carb, 2 g Fib, 13 g Prot, 276 mg Calc. ***POINTS: 3.***

"I loved being a Leader for Weight Watchers. Seeing my members lose weight and reach their goals was almost as exciting as reaching my own Weight Goal. In fact, I've loved every job I've had with the company, including this one."

—Linda Huett, President and CEO, Weight Watchers International

Spinach, Caramelized Onion, and Tomato Quiche

MAKES 6 SERVINGS

Quiche, a staple of the Alsace-Lorraine region of France, was so popular in the United States in the early eighties that it spawned a 1982 satirical book on male masculinity called *Real Men Don't Eat Quiche.* Yet few men—or women, for that matter—can resist this savory tart, as colorful as it is flavorful. Enjoy it hot, cold, or at room temperature.

- **2 teaspoons extra-virgin olive oil**
- **3 medium onions, chopped**
- **2 garlic cloves, minced**
- **1 teaspoon sugar**
- **1 (10-ounce) package frozen chopped spinach, thawed and squeezed dry**
- **1 (10-ounce) package refrigerated pizza dough**
- **¾ cup evaporated fat-free milk**
- **2 large eggs, lightly beaten**
- **¼ cup light sour cream**
- **1 egg white, lightly beaten**
- **½ teaspoon salt**
- **⅛ teaspoon nutmeg**
- **⅛ teaspoon freshly ground pepper**
- **½ cup shredded reduced-fat Monterey Jack cheese**
- **12 cherry tomatoes, halved**

1. Heat a large nonstick skillet over medium-high heat. Swirl in the oil, then add the onions, garlic, and sugar. Cook, stirring occasionally, until the onions are lightly golden, about 8 minutes. Add the spinach and cook 2 minutes longer; remove from the heat and let cool 10 minutes.
2. Preheat the oven to 350°F. Spray a 9-inch pie plate with nonstick spray.
3. Place the dough on a lightly floured work surface and shape it into a 4-inch circle. Cover lightly with plastic wrap and let rest 10 minutes. Roll the dough into an 11-inch circle; fit the dough into the pie plate, and flute the edges.
4. Combine the milk, eggs, sour cream, egg white, salt, nutmeg, and pepper in a medium bowl. Sprinkle the cheese over the bottom of the pie crust. Top evenly with the spinach mixture, then pour in the egg mixture. Arrange the tomato halves, cut-side up, on top of the quiche, in a circular pattern. Place on a baking sheet and bake until quiche is just set, about 45 minutes. Remove from the oven and let stand 10 minutes before cutting. Serve immediately or at room temperature.

Per serving (⅙ of quiche): 279 Cal, 9 g Fat, 3 g Sat Fat, 80 mg Chol, 571 mg Sod, 38 g Carb, 3 g Fib, 14 g Prot, 250 mg Calc. ***POINTS: 6.***

top tip

The quiche makes a great party appetizer, too. Simply cut it into very thin wedges and arrange on a serving platter.

Spinach,
Caramelized Onion,
and Tomato Quiche

Broccoli-and-Bacon Egg Cups

MAKES 4 SERVINGS

These savory bites look like muffins but taste like little omelettes, so we consider them mini frittatas. They're perfect to serve for a Sunday brunch, and if you have leftovers, they reheat beautifully in the microwave. You can make the vegetable mixture and the egg mixture (minus the buttermilk) up to a day in advance; store them in separate containers in the refrigerator. Simply whisk in the buttermilk right before cooking.

- **6 slices turkey bacon, sliced crosswise into ¼-inch strips**
- **2 cups frozen chopped broccoli**
- **1 small red onion, chopped**
- **1½ teaspoons bottled roasted or minced garlic**
- **2 teaspoons Italian seasoning**
- **2 tablespoons all-purpose flour**
- **1 cup low-fat buttermilk**
- **3 large eggs**
- **3 egg whites**
- **¼ cup freshly grated Parmesan cheese**
- **½ teaspoon salt**
- **½ teaspoon ground pepper**

1. Place the oven rack in the center of the oven; preheat the oven to 350°F. Heavily spray a 12-cup muffin pan with nonstick spray.
2. Spray a nonstick skillet with nonstick spray; place over medium heat. Add the bacon and sauté until crispy, 6 minutes. Transfer to a plate.
3. Return the skillet to the heat. Add the broccoli, onion, garlic, and Italian seasoning; cook until the vegetables are just tender, 7 minutes. Remove from the heat; stir in the flour and the cooked bacon. Set aside to cool.
4. Whisk together the buttermilk, eggs, egg whites, cheese, salt, and pepper in a large bowl until blended. Stir in the cooled vegetable mixture, then spoon evenly into the muffin cups. Bake until set in the center, about 20 minutes. To remove, run a narrow rubber spatula or knife around the edge of each muffin cup.

Per serving (3 mini egg cups): 206 Cal, 10 g Fat, 4 g Sat Fat, 185 mg Chol, 882 mg Sod, 12 g Carb, 2 g Fib, 18 g Prot, 216 mg Calc. ***POINTS: 5.***

top tip

Choose bagged frozen broccoli over the solid-brick type. Its flavor and texture are usually better, and it's easy to measure out the allotted amount.

Ham-and-Mushroom Crêpes

MAKES 6 SERVINGS

Any devoted watcher of Julia Child's cooking show in the seventies would have attempted making these thin French-style pancakes. The technique takes a little practice to master but is well worth knowing.

CRÊPES

- **½ cup all-purpose flour**
- **¼ teaspoon salt**
- **¾ cup low-fat (1%) milk**
- **2 large eggs**

FILLING

- **¾ cup low-fat (1%) milk**
- **¾ cup reduced-sodium chicken broth**
- **3 tablespoons all-purpose flour**
- **5 tablespoons dry sherry**
- **⅛ teaspoon nutmeg**
- **⅛ teaspoon cayenne**
- **Freshly ground pepper**
- **½ cup freshly grated Parmesan cheese (preferably Parmigiano-Reggiano)**
- **2 tablespoons chopped parsley**
- **8 ounces sliced cremini mushrooms (about 2 cups)**
- **3 cloves garlic, minced**
- **¼ teaspoon salt**
- **6 slices deli-sliced cooked lean ham (about 6 ounces)**

1. To prepare crêpes, combine the flour and salt in a medium bowl. Whisk the milk and eggs in a separate bowl. Slowly whisk the milk mixture into flour mixture until smooth. Let stand 15 minutes.
2. Spray a small nonstick skillet or crêpe pan with nonstick spray and set over medium heat. Stir the batter, then pour a scant ¼ cup into the skillet, tilting in all directions to form a thin, even layer. Cook until top is set and bottom is golden, 1–1½ minutes. Flip and cook until the second side is lightly browned, 15–20 seconds. Transfer to a plate and repeat with remaining batter to make 6 crêpes. Cover loosely with plastic wrap and reserve.
3. To prepare the filling, whisk together the milk, broth, flour, 3 tablespoons of the sherry, the nutmeg, cayenne, and pepper in a medium saucepan until smooth. Cook over medium heat, whisking constantly, until thickened, 6–7 minutes. Remove from heat and stir in the cheese and 1 tablespoon of parsley; cover and keep warm.
4. Spray a large nonstick skillet with nonstick spray and set over medium-high heat. Add the mushrooms, garlic, and salt; cook, stirring occasionally, until mushrooms soften, about 6 minutes. Stir in the remaining 2 tablespoons sherry and cook until the liquid evaporates, 1–2 minutes. Remove from the heat and stir in the remaining 1 tablespoon parsley. Let cool slightly.
5. Preheat the oven to 450°F. Spray a 7 x 11-inch baking dish with nonstick spray. Arrange the crêpes side-by-side on a work surface. Lay one slice of the ham across the center of each crêpe. Spread each with 1 tablespoon of the sauce, then top with one-sixth (about 2 tablespoons) of the mushrooms. Roll up the crêpes jelly-roll style and transfer to the baking dish. Spoon the remaining sauce over the crêpes to cover. Bake until the sauce is bubbly and lightly browned, about 15 minutes.

Per serving (1 filled crêpe): 207 Cal, 7 g Fat, 3 g Sat Fat, 95 mg Chol, 806 mg Sod, 19 g Carb, 1 g Fib, 17 g Prot, 212 mg Calc. ***POINTS: 5.***

Huevos Rancheros
in Tortilla Cups

Huevos Rancheros in Tortilla Cups

MAKES 4 SERVINGS

For many Americans, these ranch-style eggs were the first wave of the Mexican food craze of the seventies and early eighties. Today, they taste better than ever, especially in this pretty presentation, where the eggs are spooned into free-form crisp tortillas. If you prefer a soft tortilla, simply stack the tortillas, wrap them in foil, and warm in a 350°F oven until heated through. To serve, place the tortillas flat on luncheon plates and spoon the Huevos Rancheros on top.

- **4 (6-inch) corn tortillas**
- **1 (14-ounce) can diced tomatoes with green pepper, celery, and onion**
- **1 (15-ounce) can black beans, rinsed and drained**
- **½ cup canned diced mild green chiles, drained**
- **2–3 tablespoons mild pepper sauce, such as Frank's Red Hot**
- **¾ teaspoon ground cumin**
- **3 tablespoons chopped cilantro**
- **4 large eggs**
- **¼ cup shredded reduced-fat cheddar cheese**

1. Place the oven rack in the center of the oven; preheat the oven to 425°F. Lightly spray both sides of the tortillas with nonstick spray. Place 4 inverted custard cups on a baking sheet, and drape a tortilla over each to give it a bowl shape. (You may also use an inverted 12-cup muffin pan, placing the tortillas over alternate cups.) Bake until the tortillas are crisped and lightly golden around the edges, 10 minutes. Remove the tortillas and set them on a rack to cool.
2. Combine the diced tomatoes, beans, chiles, pepper sauce, cumin, and 2 tablespoons of the cilantro in an ovenproof skillet. Bring to a boil over medium heat, reduce the heat to low, and simmer until the flavors are blended, 4 minutes. Break the eggs one at a time, on top of the sauce, spacing them evenly apart.
3. Immediately place the pan in the oven and bake until the eggs are almost set, 6–8 minutes. Sprinkle the cheese on top of the eggs and bake until melted, 1 minute. To serve, place the tortilla cups on serving plates and spoon the eggs and sauce into the tortilla cups. Garnish with the remaining tablespoon of chopped cilantro and serve immediately.

Per serving (1 filled tortilla cup): 289 Cal, 8 g Fat, 3 g Sat Fat, 216 mg Chol, 840 mg Sod, 40 g Carb, 8 g Fib, 17 g Prot, 200 mg Calc. ***POINTS: 6.***

top tip

Make the tortilla cups up to two days ahead; just store them in a zip-close freezer bag at room temperature. Recrisp them in a 425°F oven for 2 minutes before using.

pasta and pizza

That's Amore!

1976

Recognizing that losing weight isn't just about dieting, Weight Watchers introduces a pioneering behavior-modification plan, developed by leading psychologist Richard Stuart, Ph.D. The plan is an integral part of the Weight Watchers Program.

1977

Fitness guru Jim Fixx writes *The Complete Book of Running*—and the nation puts on jogging shoes. Seven years later, Fixx dies of a heart attack while running, giving us a sobering dose of perspective.

1978

Weight Watchers is purchased by the Heinz Corporation for more than $70 million. An exercise component is added to the Program, designed by Lenore Zonman, M.D., and later revised by William McArdle, Ph.D. The first U.S. Dietary Goals are introduced, and Weight Watchers revises its Program accordingly: less protein, more carbs.

>>>

Marinara Sauce

MAKES 8 SERVINGS 

Weight Watchers veterans from the sixties will be glad to know they no longer need to boil down tomato juice to make marinara sauce (or serve it over canned bean sprouts and call it spaghetti). This fresher, tastier version is quick and versatile—and the recipe can be easily doubled if you'd like to keep some extra in the freezer.

- **1 (28-ounce) can whole Italian plum tomatoes**
- **1 teaspoon olive oil**
- **¼ medium onion, finely chopped**
- **2 garlic cloves, minced**
- **1 teaspoon sugar**
- **½ teaspoon salt**
- **¼ teaspoon ground pepper**
- **2 tablespoons chopped basil**

1. Pulse the tomatoes in a food processor or blender until coarsely chopped; set aside.
2. Heat a medium soup pot or Dutch oven. Swirl in the oil, then add the onion. Sauté until translucent, about 3 minutes. Add the garlic, and sauté until just fragrant, 30 seconds more.
3. Stir in the tomatoes, sugar, salt, and pepper; bring to a boil. Reduce the heat to low and simmer until thickened, at least 20 minutes and up to 1 hour. Stir in the basil during the last 5 minutes of cooking time.

Per serving (½ cup): 30 Cal, 1 g Fat, 0 g Sat Fat, 0 mg Chol, 307 mg Sod, 5 g Carb, 1 g Fib, 1 g Prot, 29 mg Calc. ***POINTS: 0.***

> "If you talk to healthy thin people, they're living by Weight Watchers principles. Whether they know it or not, they're following the Weight Watchers Program."
>
> *—Carol Kramer, Manager, New Service Development and Training (and former Leader), Weight Watchers International*

Fusilli with Pesto and Roasted Tomatoes

MAKES 4 SERVINGS

Americans discovered the delights of pesto sauce in the eighties and have never looked back. Despite all the cilantro, parsley-mint, and goat-cheese variations that followed, the classic basil version remains the most beloved. In our recipe, we've added garden-ripe tomatoes. Make this dish in the summer; you need really fresh tomatoes and basil to make it sing.

8 small plum tomatoes, halved lengthwise
2 tablespoons olive oil
2 cups packed basil leaves
2 tablespoons freshly grated Parmesan cheese
1 tablespoon pine nuts
Freshly ground pepper
2 cups fusilli

1. Preheat the oven to 400°F.
2. Place the tomato halves, cut-side up, in a medium shallow baking dish; drizzle 1 tablespoon of the oil over them. Roast the tomatoes until slightly browned on top but still firm, about 20 minutes. Set aside to cool.
3. Pulse the basil, cheese, nuts, the remaining 1 tablespoon oil, and the pepper in a food processor; scrape the sides with a rubber spatula, then pulse a few more times until the ingredients are well blended and have formed a coarse, bright green paste.
4. Meanwhile, cook the fusilli according to package directions. Drain, reserving 1½ tablespoons of the cooking water, and place in a warmed serving bowl. Stir the cooking water into the pesto; then add to pasta and toss to coat. Arrange the roasted tomatoes on top. Serve hot or at room temperature.

Per serving (1 cup pasta with 2 tomato halves): 280 Cal, 10 g Fat, 2 g Sat Fat, 2 mg Chol, 70 mg Sod, 40 g Carb, 3 g Fib, 9 g Prot, 90 mg Calc. ***POINTS: 6.***

top tip

Why not make extra pesto to have on hand for future meals? Just freeze it in ice cube trays until solid, transfer the cubes to a zip-close freezer bag, and freeze for up to a month. You can also make the pesto up to a week ahead, substituting hot tap water for the cooking water. Place it in a small airtight container just large enough to hold the pesto, lay a sheet of plastic wrap directly onto the surface of the pesto, seal the container, and refrigerate.

Rotelle with
Walnut-Gorgonzola Sauce

Rotelle with Walnut-Gorgonzola Sauce

MAKES 4 SERVINGS

Walnuts and Gorgonzola cheese were a winning combination in the popular bistro salads of the nineties, and they work brilliantly in this hearty pasta dish. We've chosen rotelle, a stubby, spiral-shaped pasta, because its twists capture and hold bits of cheese and nuts. But any ridged, chunky pasta, such as cavatappi or rigatoni, will also do nicely.

- **2 cups rotelle**
- **½ cup part-skim ricotta cheese**
- **¼ cup reduced-sodium chicken broth**
- **1 teaspoon grated lemon zest**
- **½ cup coarsely chopped walnuts**
- **¼ cup crumbled Gorgonzola cheese**
- **2 tablespoons chopped flat-leaf parsley**

1. Cook the rotelle according to package directions. Drain and place in a warmed serving bowl.
2. Meanwhile, combine the ricotta, broth, and lemon zest in a medium bowl; mix until smooth. Spoon over the rotelle, then add the walnuts, Gorgonzola cheese, and parsley; toss to coat. Serve hot or at room temperature.

Per serving (1 cup): 339 Cal, 15 g Fat, 4 g Sat Fat, 17 mg Chol, 193 mg Sod, 38 g Carb, 2 g Fib, 13 g Prot, 152 mg Calc. ***POINTS: 8.***

top tip

To make this dish ahead of time, just cover and refrigerate for up to a day. However, it doesn't reheat well; instead, take it out of the refrigerator about 30 minutes before serving time and enjoy it at room temperature. Do not freeze.

Farfalle with Tomatoes, Goat Cheese, and Basil

MAKES 4 SERVINGS

In the eighties and nineties, goat cheese and fresh basil were standard ingredients in every yuppie's pantry. Here, they're combined to bring out the best of summer's bounty. Farfalle, sometimes called bow-ties or butterflies, are particularly attractive shapes. But any pasta will show off these super garden flavors. Only fresh basil and tomatoes will do for this recipe (as any yuppie knows).

2 cups farfalle
4 teaspoons olive oil
1 garlic clove, bruised
6 medium plum tomatoes, peeled and chopped
¼ teaspoon salt
Freshly ground pepper
2 ounces herbed or plain goat cheese, crumbled
½ cup chopped basil

1. Cook the farfalle according to package directions. Drain and place in a warmed serving bowl.
2. Meanwhile, heat a large nonstick skillet. Swirl in the oil, then add the garlic. Sauté until fragrant, about 30 seconds; discard the garlic. Add the tomatoes, salt, and pepper. Cook, stirring occasionally, until the tomatoes have begun to release some of their juice, about 3 minutes.
3. Pour the tomatoes over the farfalle, then top with the cheese and basil. Toss to coat. Serve hot or at room temperature.

Per serving (1½ cups): 235 Cal, 8 g Fat, 3 g Sat Fat, 13 mg Chol, 202 mg Sod, 33 g Carb, 2 g Fib, 8 g Prot, 91 mg Calc. ***POINTS: 5.***

top tips

- The goat cheese (or any soft cheese) will be easier to crumble if you freeze it until firm, then let it stand 10 minutes at room temperature to thaw slightly.
- To peel the tomatoes, immerse them in boiling water for 1 minute; quickly transfer them to a bowl of ice water with a slotted spoon. As soon as they're cool enough to handle, just slip off the skins with your fingers.

Penne alla Vodka

MAKES 4 SERVINGS

For many, this is the classic eighties pasta dish, and it still makes people swoon. With its creamy tomato sauce spiked with just a splash of vodka, it looks and tastes sinfully rich but isn't. Even if it's loaded with restaurant-style sophistication, it's incredibly easy to make. And, yes, that's real cream on the ingredients list. Weight Watchers has come a long way, baby!

- **2 cups penne**
- **2 tablespoons reduced-calorie tub margarine**
- **1 shallot, finely chopped**
- **1 plum tomato, peeled and chopped**
- **¼ cup reduced-sodium chicken broth**
- **1 tablespoon tomato paste**
- **¼ teaspoon crushed red pepper**
- **¼ cup heavy cream**
- **2 tablespoons vodka**
- **¼ cup diced tomato**
- **2 tablespoons freshly grated Parmesan cheese**
- **2 tablespoons minced flat-leaf parsley**

1. Cook the penne according to package directions; drain and keep warm.
2. Meanwhile, melt the margarine in a medium nonstick skillet, then add the shallot and tomato. Sauté until softened, about 5 minutes. Add the broth, tomato paste, and pepper. Reduce the heat to low, then add the cream and vodka. Cook, stirring constantly, until just heated through (do not boil). Pour the sauce over the penne and toss to coat. Sprinkle with the diced tomato, cheese, and parsley and serve at once.

Per serving (¾ cup): 278 Cal, 9 g Fat, 4 g Sat Fat, 19 mg Chol, 201 mg Sod, 36 g Carb, 2 g Fib, 8 g Prot, 73 mg Calc. ***POINTS: 6.***

Linguine with Red Clam Sauce

MAKES 4 SERVINGS

Forty years ago, this classic combination was a staple on Italian restaurant menus. Today, it remains a favorite, despite all the competition from exotic pasta shapes, risottos, and polentas. Thank goodness, it's easy to make at home too!

- **12 medium clams**
- **¼ cup dry white wine or reduced-sodium vegetable broth**
- **1 tablespoon fresh thyme leaves, or 1 teaspoon dried**
- **1 tablespoon chopped fresh oregano, or 1 teaspoon dried**
- **3 large garlic cloves, minced**
- **¼ teaspoon crushed red pepper**
- **6 ounces linguine**
- **4 teaspoons olive oil**
- **8 plum tomatoes, chopped**
- **2 tablespoons chopped basil**
- **3 tablespoons finely chopped flat-leaf parsley**
- **½ teaspoon anchovy paste**

1. Scrub the clams well with a vegetable brush under cold running water. Place them in a large pot of cold water; let them soak a few minutes to release any residual grit, then drain. Repeat for several changes of water until no sand falls to the bottom of the pot.
2. Combine the clams, wine or broth, thyme, oregano, garlic, and pepper in a large saucepan. Cover and cook over medium heat until the clams open, about 5 minutes. Discard any clams that don't open. As soon as they are cool enough to handle, remove the clams from their shells, coarsely chop them, cover, and set aside. Reserve a few of the shells for garnish; reserve the cooking liquid (including the garlic and herbs) separately.
3. Cook the linguine according to package directions. Drain and place in a warmed serving bowl; keep warm.
4. Meanwhile, heat a medium nonstick skillet. Swirl in the oil, then add the tomatoes, basil, 2 tablespoons of the parsley, and the anchovy paste. Sauté over medium heat 5 minutes, then add the reserved clam cooking liquid; reduce the heat and simmer until thickened. Stir the clams into the sauce and heat just to serving temperature. Pour over the linguine, toss to coat, and garnish with the reserved clam shells. Sprinkle with the remaining 1 tablespoon parsley and serve at once.

Per serving (1 cup): 270 Cal, 6 g Fat, 1 g Sat Fat, 14 mg Chol, 71 mg Sod, 41 g Carb, 3 g Fib, 12 g Prot, 50 mg Calc. ***POINTS: 5.***

Capellini with Seafood

MAKES 4 SERVINGS

Capellini are thin, delicate strands of pasta that are sometimes (aptly) called angel hair. Best served in soups rather than topped with a sauce, they shine in this simple combination of clams, mussels, scallops, shrimp, and fresh herbs in a briny, light broth.

12 medium clams
12 medium mussels
¼ cup dry white wine or reduced-sodium vegetable broth
2 garlic cloves, minced
2 teaspoons olive oil
½ pound bay scallops, rinsed and patted dry
¼ pound medium shrimp, peeled and deveined
2 tablespoons chopped parsley
1 tablespoon thyme leaves
1 tablespoon minced oregano
6 ounces capellini
Freshly ground pepper
Parsley, thyme, and/or oregano sprigs (optional)

1. Scrub the clams and mussels well with a vegetable brush under cold running water. Pull off the hairy beards that may be attached to some of the mussels; if difficult, use a small knife. Place the clams and mussels in a large pot of cold water; let them soak a few minutes to release any residual grit, then drain. Repeat for several changes of water, until no sand falls to the bottom of the pot.
2. Combine the clams, mussels, wine or broth, and garlic in a large saucepan; cover and cook over medium heat until the shells open, about 8 minutes; discard any that don't open. Set the clams and mussels aside with their cooking liquid.
3. Heat a large nonstick skillet. Swirl in the oil, then add the scallops, shrimp, parsley, thyme, and oregano. Sauté until the shrimp are pink and the scallops are just opaque, 5–10 minutes. Remove from the heat, and add the clams and mussels with their cooking liquid.
4. Meanwhile, cook the capellini according to package directions; drain and place in a warmed serving bowl. Top with the seafood, sprinkle with the pepper, and toss to combine. Garnish with the herb sprigs, if using, and serve at once.

Per serving (1 cup): 321 Cal, 5 g Fat, 1 g Sat Fat, 81 mg Chol, 303 mg Sod, 39 g Carb, 2 g Fib, 29 g Prot, 110 mg Calc. ***POINTS: 6.***

Tagliatelle with Vegetable Ragu

MAKES 8 SERVINGS

Once you've prepared this savory, vegetable-packed sauce, you'll find it as versatile as the famous Weight Watchers Vegetable Soup recipe. It's great on any type of pasta (we like thin, ribbonlike tagliatelle), spread onto a pizza shell, or atop omelettes, chicken, or fish. Although this recipe calls for specific quantities of vegetables, don't be afraid to noodle around with amounts, especially if they're ***POINTS***-free. While you're at it, make a double batch of the sauce and freeze it. It can be thawed overnight in the refrigerator or reheated without thawing.

- **2 tablespoons olive oil**
- **1 onion, finely chopped**
- **1 small (5-ounce) zucchini, finely chopped**
- **1 celery stalk, finely chopped**
- **1 frying pepper, seeded and finely chopped**
- **1 carrot, peeled and finely chopped**
- **5 mushrooms, finely chopped**
- **1 (28-ounce) can whole plum tomatoes, pureed, with juice**
- **½ cup chopped flat-leaf parsley**
- **¼ cup chopped basil**
- **1 tablespoon chopped oregano**
- **1 garlic clove, minced**
- **1 bay leaf**
- **½ teaspoon salt**
- **Freshly ground pepper**
- **6 ounces tagliatelle**
- **¼ cup freshly grated Parmesan cheese**

1. Heat a large nonstick saucepan. Swirl in the oil, then add the onion. Sauté over medium heat until translucent, about 8 minutes. Add the zucchini and celery and sauté until softened. Add the frying pepper, carrot, and mushrooms; cook stirring frequently, until the mushrooms have released and reabsorbed their juices and the carrots are softened, about 10 minutes.
2. Add the tomatoes, parsley, basil, oregano, garlic, bay leaf, salt, and ground pepper. Cover and simmer, stirring occasionally, until the vegetables are tender and the sauce has thickened, about 30 minutes.
3. Cook the tagliatelle according to package directions. Drain and place in a warmed serving bowl. Pour the sauce over the tagliatelle and toss to coat. Sprinkle with the cheese and serve.

Per serving (1½ cups): 159 Cal, 6 g Fat, 1 g Sat Fat, 21 mg Chol, 381 mg Sod, 23 g Carb, 3 g Fib, 6 g Prot, 97 mg Calc. ***POINTS: 3.***

top tip

Frying peppers, sometimes labeled "Italian" or "Cubanelle" peppers, are similar to bell peppers, with the same color spectrum and a more slender, tapered shape. Their flesh is thinner than that of bells, with slightly sweeter flavor. Look for them in better supermarkets and farmers' markets in the summer months. If unavailable, substitute ½ to 1 large green bell pepper.

Tagliatelle with
Vegetable Ragu

Spaghetti Carbonara

MAKES 4 SERVINGS

Some say this Roman specialty was originally created by carbonari, or coal miners; others claim it's called carbonara, or "charcoal-style," because it was originally made with squid-ink pasta. Or maybe it's those bits of freshly ground black pepper, so essential to the flavor. Whatever its origins, this is a great-tasting dish, even with egg substitute and Canadian-style bacon replacing the usual whole eggs and pancetta (Italian-style unsmoked bacon). Timing is everything in this impromptu dish: The sauce ingredients should be ready just as the spaghetti finishes cooking; then, the hot pasta cooks the sauce as you toss it.

6 ounces spaghetti
1 tablespoon + 1 teaspoon unsalted butter
4 (1-ounce) slices Canadian bacon, trimmed of all visible fat and cut into matchstick-size pieces
1 shallot, finely chopped
2 garlic cloves, bruised
⅔ cup fat-free egg substitute
¼ cup freshly grated Romano cheese
1 tablespoon finely chopped flat-leaf parsley
Freshly ground pepper

1. Cook the spaghetti according to package directions.
2. Meanwhile, melt the butter in a large nonstick skillet, then add the bacon, shallot, and garlic. Sauté until the bacon and shallot are browned and the garlic is golden, about 5 minutes, then discard the garlic. (If the spaghetti is not quite done at this point, remove the skillet from the heat.)
3. Drain the spaghetti and immediately add it to the skillet; set the skillet over low heat. Add the egg substitute and cheese; toss to coat. Cook, stirring constantly, until the egg is just cooked through, about 2 minutes. Sprinkle with the parsley and pepper and serve at once.

Per serving (¾ cup): 288 Cal, 8 g Fat, 4 g Sat Fat, 29 mg Chol, 475 mg Sod, 36 g Carb, 2 g Fib, 16 g Prot, 78 mg Calc. ***POINTS: 6.***

top tip

Bruising garlic helps release its flavor. Here's how to do it: Place a peeled clove on a cutting board and flatten it slightly with the side of a large knife.

Shells with Spinach, Ricotta, and Raisins

MAKES 4 SERVINGS

In southern Italy, spinach, ricotta, and raisins are a popular trio. It's one of those perfect combinations of taste and texture (and one that would have been forbidden in the early days of Weight Watchers, when raisins and pasta were not allowed!). The sauce just gets better when it's tossed with a pasta that traps those savory little chunks of flavor, such as shells; rigatoni will also work well. This is also a perfect pasta for company; you can assemble it ahead of time, refrigerate it, and bring it to room temperature for 30 minutes before serving.

¼ cup golden raisins
1 tablespoon olive oil
1 onion, chopped
1 (10-ounce) box frozen chopped spinach, thawed and squeezed dry
¼ teaspoon salt
2 cups medium pasta shells
¼ cup part-skim ricotta
¼ cup freshly grated Parmesan cheese
Freshly ground white pepper

1. Put the raisins in a small bowl of hot water until plump and soft, about 10 minutes; drain and set aside.
2. Heat a medium nonstick skillet. Swirl in the oil, then add the onion. Sauté until translucent, about 8 minutes; reduce the heat to low. Stir in the spinach and salt; cook, stirring, until heated through. Set aside and keep warm.
3. In a large pot of boiling water, cook the shells according to package directions. Drain and place in warmed serving bowl. Add the spinach mixture, the raisins, ricotta, and Parmesan cheese; toss to coat. Sprinkle with the pepper and serve at once.

Per serving (1¼ cups): 298 Cal, 7 g Fat, 3 g Sat Fat, 10 mg Chol, 325 mg Sod, 47 g Carb, 4 g Fib, 12 g Prot, 217 mg Calc. ***POINTS: 6.***

top tip

Instead of the spinach, other greens like broccolini, broccoli, broccoli rabe, or Swiss chard would also work beautifully in this recipe. Steam them until tender but still bright green, about 10 minutes; drain in a colander under cold running water to stop the cooking, then proceed with the recipe.

Baked Ziti
with Meatballs

Baked Ziti with Meatballs

MAKES 8 SERVINGS

Here's an Italian-American all-time favorite, straight from many a Sunday dinner (minus much of the usual fat and calories). It's a little time-consuming to prepare, but the results are definitely worth it—and much can be done ahead of time. If you prefer, you can substitute lean ground turkey for all or part of the meat.

- **1 tablespoon olive oil**
- **1 onion, finely chopped**
- **1 (28-ounce) can diced plum tomatoes in juice, drained (reserve the juice)**
- **1 garlic clove, minced**
- **¼ pound lean ground beef (10% or less fat)**
- **¼ pound lean ground veal**
- **¼ pound lean ground pork**
- **¼ cup freshly grated Parmesan cheese**
- **1 cup chopped flat-leaf parsley**
- **½ cup plain dried bread crumbs**
- **3 egg whites, or ¼ cup fat-free egg substitute**
- **1 tablespoon chopped basil, or 1 teaspoon dried**
- **1 teaspoon chopped oregano or marjoram, or ½ teaspoon dried**
- **1 teaspoon chopped thyme, or ¼ teaspoon dried**
- **¼ teaspoon salt**
- **Freshly ground pepper**
- **4 cups ziti**
- **¼ cup shredded part-skim mozzarella cheese**

1. Heat a large nonstick saucepan. Swirl in the oil, then add the onion. Sauté until translucent, about 5–8 minutes. Stir in the tomatoes and garlic. Reduce the heat to medium-low; cook, stirring occasionally, until bubbling.
2. Meanwhile, combine the beef, veal, pork, Parmesan cheese, ½ cup of the parsley, the bread crumbs, egg whites, basil, oregano, thyme, salt, and pepper in a large bowl. Form the mixture into 40 walnut-size meatballs, then drop them gently and carefully into the bubbling sauce (watch for splashing).
3. Reduce the heat to low; simmer, without stirring, until the meatballs are resistant to gentle pressure from a wooden spoon, about 15 minutes. Stir in the remaining ½ cup parsley. Continue cooking, stirring occasionally and adding the reserved tomato juice ¼ cup at a time, until the meatballs are tender and the sauce has thickened, about 20 minutes.
4. Cook the ziti according to package directions. Drain well, then toss with the sauce and meatballs in a large bowl. (The dish may be made up to a day ahead at this point; just cover and refrigerate until ready to bake.)
5. Preheat the oven to 400°F. Spray a 9 x 13-inch baking dish with nonstick spray. Place the ziti mixture in the baking dish, and sprinkle evenly with the mozzarella. Cover with foil and bake until heated through, 15–20 minutes (if the mixture has been refrigerated, it will take 5–10 minutes longer). Uncover; bake until bubbling and golden on top, 5–10 minutes more.

Per serving (1 cup ziti with 5 meatballs): 332 Cal, 8 g Fat, 3 g Sat Fat, 32 mg Chol, 417 mg Sod, 45 g Carb, 3 g Fib, 19 g Prot, 140 mg Calc. ***POINTS: 7.***

Rigatoni with Meat Sauce

MAKES 4 SERVINGS

Pasta with meat sauce is a staple in any Italian kitchen—yesterday, today, and forever. This recipe calls for rigatoni, which have a thick tubular shape, but any thick pasta, such as shells, penne, or ziti, works just as well. Make a double, triple, or quadruple batch of sauce and freeze it for up to three months. In a pinch, the sauce can be heated up even in its frozen state, but it's best to thaw it overnight in the refrigerator if you have time.

2 teaspoons olive oil
1 onion, finely chopped
1 celery stalk, finely chopped
1 carrot, peeled and finely chopped
1 garlic clove, peeled and minced
8 ounces lean ground beef (10% or less fat), turkey, or veal
1 (28-ounce) can diced tomatoes in juice
¼ cup finely chopped flat-leaf parsley
¼ cup dry red wine or reduced-sodium beef broth
1 rosemary sprig
1 bay leaf
¼ teaspoon salt
Freshly ground pepper
2 cups rigatoni
¼ cup freshly grated Parmesan cheese

1. Heat a large nonstick saucepan. Swirl in the oil, then add the onion. Sauté until translucent, about 8 minutes. Add the celery, carrot, and garlic; sauté until wilted, 5 minutes more.
2. Add the ground meat and brown, breaking it apart with a spoon, until it is no longer pink. Add the tomatoes, parsley, wine or broth, rosemary, bay leaf, salt, and pepper, and cook, stirring occasionally, until the sauce is bubbling. Immediately lower the heat and simmer, uncovered, stirring occasionally, until thickened, about 45 minutes. Discard the rosemary and bay leaf.
3. Cook the rigatoni according to package directions. Drain and place in a warmed serving bowl. Pour the tomato sauce over the rigatoni and toss. Sprinkle with the cheese and serve at once.

Per serving (1½ cups): 312 Cal, 9 g Fat, 3 g Sat Fat, 37 mg Chol, 634 mg Sod, 36 g Carb, 4 g Fib, 21 g Prot, 170 mg Calc. ***POINTS: 6.***

Cheese Ravioli with Butternut Squash Sauce

MAKES 4 SERVINGS

Thanks to ready-made wonton wrappers, available in most supermarkets, homemade cheese ravioli is a fairly simple task—and even more fun if you have your family (or dinner guests) help assemble them. The rich butternut squash sauce topping is especially sweet for Weight Watchers members who can remember when winter squash was a "limited" vegetable, only to be eaten at dinnertime!

- **4 teaspoons olive oil**
- **3 shallots, peeled and chopped**
- **1 garlic clove, chopped**
- **1 (1¼–1½ pound) butternut squash, peeled, seeded, and coarsely chopped**
- **3 cups reduced-sodium chicken broth**
- **1 tablespoon minced thyme, or 1 teaspoon dried**
- **1 tablespoon minced sage, or 1 teaspoon dried**
- **½ teaspoon ground pepper**
- **⅛ teaspoon nutmeg**
- **½ cup part-skim ricotta**
- **5 tablespoons freshly grated Parmesan cheese**
- **2 tablespoons minced flat-leaf parsley**
- **1 large egg white**
- **24 wonton wrappers (one 12-ounce package)**
- **5–10 sage leaves (optional)**

1. Heat a large nonstick skillet. Swirl in the oil, then add the shallots and garlic. Sauté until fragrant, about 1 minute. Add the squash, broth, thyme, sage, ¼ teaspoon of the pepper, and the nutmeg; cook, stirring frequently, until the squash is very tender and the liquid has evaporated, about 15 minutes. Remove from the heat and let cool 15 minutes.
2. Meanwhile, combine the ricotta, 3 tablespoons of the Parmesan cheese, the parsley, egg white, and the remaining ¼ teaspoon pepper in a medium bowl.
3. To assemble the ravioli, lightly dust a work surface with flour. Lay out 12 wonton wrappers and put 1½ teaspoons of the cheese mixture in the center of each. Wet the area around the filling with a pastry brush dipped lightly in water, then place another wrapper on top of each, pressing the air out as you seal the edges. Cover lightly with a damp towel and set aside.
4. Meanwhile, puree the squash mixture in a food processor. If it is too thick for a sauce, add 1 tablespoon of water at a time until it reaches a smooth, thick consistency. Place it in a saucepan and bring to a gentle simmer, stirring frequently; keep warm.
5. Cook the ravioli, half a batch at a time, in gently boiling water until they are tender and float to the surface, about 4 minutes. Transfer them with a slotted spoon to a colander, drain well, and place in a warmed serving bowl. Cover the ravioli generously with the sauce, sprinkle with the remaining 2 tablespoons Parmesan cheese, and garnish with the sage leaves, if using.

Per serving (6 ravioli with ½ cup sauce): 358 Cal, 11 g Fat, 4 g Sat Fat, 40 mg Chol, 598 mg Sod, 48 g Carb, 6 g Fib, 17 g Prot, 281 mg Calc. ***POINTS: 7.***

Vegetable Lasagna

MAKES 4 SERVINGS

No-boil lasagna noodles came to supermarkets in the nineties, raising lasagna's status from a laborious special-occasion dish to almost a convenience food. Here, we've created a chock-full-of-veggies version that's easy to prepare—especially if you roast the vegetables and prepare the sauce ahead of time.

- **1 medium (1 pound) eggplant, peeled and sliced ¼-inch thick**
- **1 medium (8-ounce) zucchini, sliced ¼-inch thick**
- **¼ teaspoon salt**
- **Freshly ground pepper**
- **1 tablespoon olive oil**
- **1 garlic clove, minced**
- **1 (28-ounce) can whole tomatoes, chopped, with their juice**
- **1 (10-ounce) package mushrooms, sliced**
- **2 frying peppers (or 1 large green bell pepper), finely chopped**
- **½ cup chopped flat-leaf parsley**
- **5 (6½ x 7-inch) sheets or 10 (3½ x 6½-inch) sheets no-boil lasagna noodles**
- **¼ cup freshly grated Parmesan cheese**

1. Preheat the oven to 400°F. Spray 2 baking sheets and an 8-inch-square baking dish with nonstick spray. Arrange the eggplant and zucchini slices on the baking sheets, overlapping a few slices, if necessary. Spray the tops with nonstick spray, sprinkle with the salt and pepper, and bake until tender, 15 minutes. Set aside (leave the oven on).
2. Heat a large nonstick skillet. Swirl in the oil, then add the garlic. Sauté until fragrant, about 30 seconds. Add the tomatoes, mushrooms, frying peppers, parsley, and another grinding of the pepper; cook over medium-low heat until the sauce is bubbling but not yet thickened. Remove from the heat. (The sauce can be made up to 3 days ahead at this point; just transfer to an airtight container and refrigerate.)
3. Spread ½ cup of the sauce evenly over the bottom of the baking dish. Cover with 1 or 2 lasagna noodles (depending on the size you are using); top with one-fourth of the eggplant and zucchini slices, then top with another ½ cup of the sauce. Sprinkle with 1 tablespoon of the Parmesan cheese. Repeat the procedure to make 4 more layers, ending with a layer of noodles topped with sauce. If any sauce remains, pour it on the top and around the edges of the lasagna. Be sure to use all the sauce (it's needed to cook the noodles). Press down gently on the lasagna with a spatula to help the noodles absorb the sauce; the lasagna will compact as it cooks.
4. Cover with foil and bake until bubbling, about 35 minutes. Remove the foil and continue baking until all the sauce has been absorbed, about 10–15 minutes.

Per serving (2 cups): 365 Cal, 8 g Fat, 2 g Sat Fat, 5 mg Chol, 599 mg Sod, 62 g Carb, 9 g Fib, 15 g Prot, 182 mg Calc. ***POINTS: 7.***

Vegetable Lasagna

Basic Pizza Crust

MAKES 8 SERVINGS (TWO 12-INCH CRUSTS)

Not so long ago, Weight Watchers members made their own "pizzaiolas" by topping a slice of white bread with cooked-down tomato juice and a sprinkling of cheese. But today we can enjoy the real thing, with a crisp homemade crust and our choice of toppings. This recipe uses quick-rise yeast, so there's hardly any kneading—and it's a cinch to whirl in your food processor. What's more, the recipe makes enough dough for two pizzas; enjoy one now and refrigerate the rest of the dough for up to two days—or freeze it for up to two months, so you're pizza-ready anytime.

- **3 cups all-purpose flour**
- **2 teaspoons quick-rise yeast**
- **1 teaspoon salt**
- **1 cup warm (105°F–115°F) water**
- **4 teaspoons olive oil**
- **2 tablespoons cornmeal**

1. Pulse the flour, yeast, and salt in a food processor 2 or 3 times to blend. With the machine running, add the water and oil through the feed tube; process until the mixture forms a ball, about 10 seconds. Turn the dough out onto a lightly floured work surface; knead a few minutes until it forms a smooth ball and is lightly coated with flour.
2. Spray a large bowl with nonstick spray; place the dough in the bowl. Cover lightly with plastic wrap and let rise in a warm place until it doubles in size, 45–60 minutes. Or let the dough rise in the refrigerator for at least 8 hours or overnight. (At this point, the dough can be frozen. To reuse, thaw overnight in the refrigerator.)
3. Turn the dough out onto a lightly floured work surface, divide it in half, and knead each half until it just forms a smooth ball and is lightly coated with flour. Spray 2 large bowls with nonstick spray; put a dough ball in each bowl. Cover lightly with plastic wrap and let rise in a warm spot until they puff up a little, 10–15 minutes.
4. To assemble the pizza(s), preheat the oven to 500°F. For each crust, lightly spray a 12-inch nonstick pizza pan with nonstick spray; dust each pan with one tablespoon of the cornmeal.
5. Turn the dough out onto a lightly floured work surface, and shape it into a round, flat disk; let it rest for a few minutes, then place it in the pizza pan. Pat and gently stretch it to the desired thickness and shape. Sprinkle with toppings of your choice, and bake until the crust is crisp and golden brown, about 15 minutes.

Per serving (¼ pizza crust): 201 Cal, 3 g Fat, 0 g Sat Fat, 0 mg Chol, 292 mg Sod, 38 g Carb, 2 g Fib, 5 g Prot, 9 mg Calc. ***POINTS: 4.***

Pizza Margherita

MAKES 4 SERVINGS (ONE 12-INCH PIZZA)

This is the world's favorite pizza from time immemorial, perhaps for the sunny simplicity of its toppings: tomato sauce, mozzarella cheese, and herbs (representing, not unintentionally, the red, white, and green colors of the Italian flag).

- **Dough for 1 pizza [see Basic Pizza Crust, page 96], or 1 prebaked thin pizza crust**
- **¾ cup prepared fat-free tomato sauce**
- **¼ cup shredded part-skim mozzarella cheese**
- **2 teaspoons olive oil**
- **1 tablespoon chopped flat-leaf parsley**
- **½ tablespoon chopped oregano, or ½ teaspoon dried**
- **½ tablespoon chopped basil, or ½ teaspoon dried**
- **¼ teaspoon salt**
- **⅛ teaspoon crushed red pepper**

1. Preheat the oven according to the directions for the crust you are using.
2. Spread the tomato sauce evenly over the crust; sprinkle with the cheese. Drizzle with the oil, then sprinkle with the parsley, oregano, basil, salt, and pepper. Bake until the cheese is bubbling, 10–15 minutes. Serve at once.

Per serving (¼ pizza): 256 Cal, 6 g Fat, 1 g Sat Fat, 4 mg Chol, 681 mg Sod, 41 g Carb, 2 g Fib, 8 g Prot, 76 mg Calc. ***POINTS: 5.***

top tips

- To shape and stretch the dough like a pro, place one hand over the dough, and, with your other hand, gently pull on one side of the dough as far as it will stretch without breaking. Turn the dough a quarter turn and repeat until it has reached the desired size and thickness. If the dough starts to tear, let it rest for 5 to 10 minutes. This relaxes the proteins in the dough and makes it easier to stretch.
- One of the secrets to a great pizza crust is a very hot oven. Be sure your oven has reached the recommended temperature before you slide that pizza in.
- To make the dough by hand, combine 1½ cups of the flour with the yeast and salt in a large bowl. Add the water and oil; stir until the dough starts to gather around the spoon. Add the remaining flour, a little at a time, until the dough can no longer be stirred. Turn it out onto a lightly floured work surface; knead until smooth and elastic, about 10 minutes.

Broccoli-Cheddar-Mushroom Pizza

MAKES 4 SERVINGS (ONE 12-INCH PIZZA)

Sometimes a little break with tradition can be fun and delicious. This veggie pizza was inspired by the tasty toppings at a salad bar.

- **Dough for 1 pizza [see Basic Pizza Crust, page 96], or 1 prebaked thin pizza crust**
- **1 cup shredded reduced-fat cheddar cheese**
- **1 (10-ounce) box frozen chopped broccoli, thawed and squeezed dry**
- **1 (10-ounce) package mushrooms, sliced**
- **¼ teaspoon salt**
- **Freshly ground pepper**

1. Preheat the oven according to the directions for the crust you are using.
2. Sprinkle the cheese evenly over crust; top with the broccoli, mushrooms, salt, and pepper. Bake until the crust is golden, the cheese is bubbling, and the mushrooms are cooked through, 10–15 minutes. Serve at once.

Per serving (¼ pizza): 318 Cal, 8 g Fat, 4 g Sat Fat, 15 mg Chol, 606 mg Sod, 46 g Carb, 5 g Fib, 17 g Prot, 254 mg Calc. ***POINTS: 6.***

top tip

For an even quicker pizza, use broccoli florets and sliced mushrooms from the salad bar of your supermarket. Give the broccoli a quick steam in the microwave before using.

Seafood Pizza

MAKES 4 SERVINGS (ONE 12-INCH PIZZA)

This pizza calls for the crust to bake separately while the shellfish are steaming. Don't skimp on the seafood; only the freshest will do. For an especially dramatic presentation, serve a few of the clams and mussels in their shells.

- **12 littleneck clams**
- **1 pound medium mussels**
- **Dough for 1 pizza [see Basic Pizza Crust, page 96], or 1 prebaked thin pizza crust**
- **½ pound medium shrimp, peeled and deveined**
- **½ cup dry white wine or vegetable broth**
- **¼ cup chopped flat-leaf parsley**
- **2 tablespoons chopped basil**
- **1 tablespoon chopped thyme**
- **3 garlic cloves, minced**
- **¼ teaspoon crushed red pepper**
- **1 (14-ounce) can diced tomatoes in juice, drained**

1. Scrub the clams and mussels well with a vegetable brush under cold running water. Pull off the hairy beards that may be attached to some of the mussel shells; if it's difficult, use a small knife. Place the clams and mussels in a large pot of cold water; let them soak a few minutes to release any residual grit, then drain. Repeat for several changes of water until no sand falls to the bottom of the pot.
2. Preheat the oven to 500°F. Bake the pizza crust until crispy but still pale, about 8 minutes. Remove from the oven, but leave it on.
3. Meanwhile, combine the clams, mussels, shrimp, wine or broth, parsley, basil, thyme, garlic, and pepper in a large saucepan; cover and cook over medium heat until the clams and mussels open and the shrimp turn pink, 7–8 minutes (do not overcook). Discard any clams or mussels that don't open. Transfer the clams and mussels to a large bowl with a slotted spoon; set them aside until they are cool enough to handle, then remove them from their shells. Reserve ¼ cup of their cooking liquid, and a few shells, if desired, for garnish.
4. Combine the tomatoes and the reserved cooking liquid in a medium nonstick skillet; cook over medium heat until thickened, about 5 minutes.
5. Spread the tomato sauce over the crust. Place a few mussels and clams in the reserved shells, if using, then distribute all the shellfish evenly over the tomato sauce. Return the pizza to the oven and bake until heated through and the crust is golden, 4–5 minutes. Serve at once.

Per serving (¼ pizza): 301 Cal, 4 g Fat, 1 g Sat Fat, 77 mg Chol, 592 mg Sod, 77 g Carb, 3 g Fib, 21 g Prot, 79 mg Calc. ***POINTS: 6.***

Pizza all'Insalata

MAKES 4 SERVINGS (ONE 12-INCH PIZZA)

This unusual pizza started appearing on restaurant tables in the Italian-obsessed eighties. Insalata, Italian for salad, makes for a deliciously healthy, fresh pizza topping—no gooey cheese needed!

Dough for 1 pizza [see Basic Pizza Crust, page 96], or 1 prebaked thin pizza crust
6 medium plum tomatoes, sliced
3 tablespoons dry white or red wine, or vegetable broth
4 teaspoons olive oil
1 tablespoon red-wine vinegar, white-wine vinegar, or cider vinegar
1 teaspoon balsamic vinegar
1 garlic clove, bruised
¼ teaspoon dried oregano, marjoram, or basil
¼ teaspoon salt
Freshly ground pepper
1 medium bunch arugula, trimmed
2 cups trimmed and torn romaine or Bibb lettuce leaves
1 Belgian endive, sliced
2 medium carrots, peeled and shredded
1 cup chopped seeded peeled cucumber
2 tablespoons freshly grated Parmesan cheese

1. Preheat the oven according to the directions for the crust you are using.
2. Arrange the sliced tomatoes on the crust; spray with nonstick spray. Bake until the crust is golden and the tomatoes are cooked through, 10–15 minutes.
3. Meanwhile, combine the wine or broth, oil, wine vinegar, balsamic vinegar, garlic, oregano, salt, and pepper in a large bowl; let stand 10 minutes. Whisk vigorously to blend; discard the garlic. Add the arugula, lettuce, endive, carrots, and cucumber to the bowl and toss with the dressing.
4. When the pizza crust is done, remove it from the oven and top with the salad. Sprinkle with the cheese and serve at once.

Per serving (¼ pizza): 333 Cal, 10 g Fat, 2 g Sat Fat, 2 mg Chol, 549 mg Sod, 52 g Carb, 8 g Fib, 10 g Prot, 174 mg Calc. ***POINTS: 7.***

Pizza all'Insalata

Tex-Mex Pizza

MAKES 4 SERVINGS (ONE 12-INCH PIZZA)

The Tex-Mex craze of the eighties led to some wild, and sometimes forgettable, experimentation. But here's one combination that worked nicely: Pizza meets quesadilla.

Dough for 1 pizza [see Basic Pizza Crust, page 96], or 1 prebaked thin pizza crust
½ cup salsa
1 (15-ounce) can black beans, rinsed and drained
½ cup shredded reduced-fat cheddar cheese
½ onion, chopped
½ teaspoon chili powder
½ cup fat-free sour cream (optional)

1. Preheat the oven according to the directions for the crust you are using.
2. Spread the salsa over the crust. Top with the beans, cheese, and onion; sprinkle with the chili powder. Bake until the crust is golden, the cheese is bubbling, and the onion has started to brown, 10–15 minutes.
3. Top with dollops of the sour cream, if using, and serve at once.

Per serving (¼ pizza): 360 Cal, 6 g Fat, 2 g Sat Fat, 8 mg Chol, 631 mg Sod, 61 g Carb, 8 g Fib, 16 g Prot, 183 mg Calc. ***POINTS: 7.***

top tip

This pizza is particularly freezer-friendly, so why not make a double batch and keep the extra one on hand for quick meals? Just allow 5 to 10 minutes extra baking time when you put a frozen pizza in the oven, and add the sour cream, if using, just before serving.

White Pizza

MAKES 4 SERVINGS (ONE 12-INCH PIZZA)

In the United States, so-called white pizza (or pizza bianca) may have any number of toppings, from feta cheese to clams; the only essential is a pale color. In our version, gooey mozzarella cheese and sweet, crunchy Vidalia onion rings play the starring roles.

Dough for 1 pizza [see Basic Pizza Crust, page 96], or 1 prebaked thin pizza crust
1 cup shredded part-skim mozzarella cheese
1 large Vidalia onion, sliced and separated into rings
¼ teaspoon salt
Freshly ground white pepper

1. Preheat the oven according to the directions for the crust you are using.
2. Sprinkle the cheese and onion rings evenly over the crust. Spray lightly with nonstick spray; sprinkle with the salt and pepper. Bake until the crust is golden, the cheese is melted, and the onions are tender and starting to brown, about 15 minutes. Serve at once.

Per serving (¼ pizza): 295 Cal, 8 g Fat, 3 g Sat Fat, 15 mg Chol, 588 mg Sod, 42 g Carb, 2 g Fib, 14 g Prot, 224 mg Calc. ***POINTS: 6.***

"I still follow the Weight Watchers rules; I've never lost that thinking. It's part of my nature, just like I always remember to put a napkin in my lap when I eat."
—Jean Nidetch

Ham, Pepper, and Onion Calzone

Ham, Pepper, and Onion Calzones

MAKES 4 SERVINGS

A calzone, which means "pant leg" in Italian, is a pizza that is folded in half to form a closed, filled pocket—sort of the Neapolitan version of an empanada. When making calzones, use fresh or frozen pizza dough from your supermarket, or a full (8-serving) recipe of Basic Pizza Crust [page 96]. Just don't use the ready-made dough that comes in a pop-open tube; it doesn't yield enough dough for this recipe.

- **1 tablespoon olive oil**
- **1 medium onion, sliced**
- **1 green bell pepper, seeded and cut into thin strips**
- **1 red bell pepper, seeded and cut into thin strips**
- **2 garlic cloves, minced**
- **1 teaspoon dried oregano**
- **4 ounces deli-thin-sliced lean ham, cut crosswise into thin strips**
- **1 pound refrigerated or thawed frozen pizza dough**
- **1 cup shredded part-skim mozzarella**

1. Preheat the oven to 400°F. Spray a baking sheet with nonstick spray.
2. Heat a large nonstick skillet over medium-high heat. Swirl in the oil, then add the onion, bell peppers, garlic, and oregano; cook, stirring occasionally, until softened, 5–7 minutes. Stir in the ham and cook 3 minutes; remove from the heat and let cool slightly.
3. Turn out the dough onto a lightly floured work surface and divide it in half. Stretch or roll each dough half into a 10-inch circle. Spread half of the ham mixture over one-half of each circle, leaving a 1-inch border, then top each with half of the cheese. Fold the dough over, making a half circle, and firmly pinch the edges together to seal. Using a spatula, transfer the calzones to the baking sheet. Bake until tops are golden brown, about 20 minutes. Cool 5 minutes, then cut each calzone in half, crosswise, to make 4 portions.

Per serving (½ calzone): 494 Cal, 15 g Fat, 5 g Sat Fat, 30 mg Chol, 979 mg Sod, 67 g Carb, 4 g Fib, 23 g Prot, 237 mg Calc. ***POINTS: 10.***

Lullaby of Birdland

1979

Weight Watchers introduces the revolutionary Garden of Eating program, a public-service nutrition education program for children in public schools designed by Reva Frankle R.D., Ed.D., Director of Nutrition. Congress commends it.

1980

The first Dietary Guidelines for Americans are released by the Departments of Agriculture and Health and Human Services, and are revised every five years thereafter. Weight Watchers Food Plan conforms to the guidelines each time.

1981

The FDA approves the artificial sweetener Aspartame for use in confections, desserts, chewing gum, and drinks. The downside: It loses its sweetness when heated.

Jane Fonda's Workout Book hits bookstores and is an instant hit.

>>>

Roast Chicken with Lemon and Herbs

MAKES 8 SERVINGS

There are few comfort foods quite as satisfying as a simple roasted chicken. Herbs, lemon, and garlic make this version extra special. When you serve it for a relaxed Sunday dinner, you can brown-bag any leftovers for the next week's lunches.

1 (4½-pound) roasting chicken
½ teaspoon salt
½ teaspoon ground pepper
1 lemon, halved
6 garlic cloves, peeled
3 thyme sprigs, or 1 teaspoon dried thyme
3 sage sprigs, or 1 teaspoon dried sage
Thyme sprigs (optional)
Sage sprigs (optional)

1. Preheat the oven to 350°F. Rub the chicken inside and out with the salt and pepper. Squeeze the lemon halves over the outside of the chicken. Place the squeezed lemon halves, the garlic, thyme, and sage into the large cavity of the chicken; truss.
2. Place the chicken, breast-side up, on a rack in a roasting pan; roast until the juices run clear when pierced with a fork, or until an instant-read thermometer inserted in the thigh registers 180°F, 2–2¼ hours. Remove from the oven; let stand 10 minutes before carving.
3. Remove the lemons, garlic, and herbs from the cavity and discard. Carve the chicken. Garnish with the additional thyme and sage, if using. Remove the skin before eating.

Per serving (⅛ chicken, without skin): 161 Cal, 6 g Fat, 2 g Sat Fat, 74 mg Chol, 216 mg Sod, 0 g Carb, 0 g Fib, 26 g Prot, 19 mg Calc. ***POINTS: 4.***

top tips

- Defrost chicken in the refrigerator or in a microwave, not on the counter. Poultry standing at room temperature provides a perfect environment for salmonella bacteria to grow and multiply.
- Cook chicken thoroughly. For chicken with bones, a meat thermometer should register 180°F; boneless parts should be cooked to an internal temperature of 160°F. When done, the juices of the chicken will be clear, not pink.
- Never leave raw or cooked chicken at room temperature for more than an hour.

Chicken Satay with Peanut Sauce

MAKES 8 SERVINGS

A Southeast Asian treat that became ubiquitous in the Asian food–obsessed nineties, satays make great party fare. We've lightened the traditional peanut dipping sauce considerably by using unsweetened light or "lite" coconut milk, available in most supermarkets. It has most of the flavor of regular coconut milk but less than half the fat and calories.

- **2½ tablespoons Thai fish sauce**
- **1 tablespoon minced peeled fresh ginger**
- **2 garlic cloves, minced**
- **1 tablespoon + 2 teaspoons fresh lime juice**
- **1½ pounds skinless boneless chicken breast halves, cut into thin 2-inch strips**
- **6 tablespoons light coconut milk**
- **3 tablespoons reduced-fat chunky peanut butter**
- **2 tablespoons chopped cilantro**
- **4 teaspoons honey**
- **1 teaspoon grated lime zest**
- **⅛ teaspoon crushed red pepper**

1. Combine 1½ tablespoons of the fish sauce, the ginger, garlic, and 2 teaspoons of the lime juice in a zip-close plastic bag; add the chicken. Squeeze out the air and seal the bag; turn to coat the chicken. Refrigerate, turning the bag occasionally, 1 hour.
2. Meanwhile, soak 40 long wooden skewers in enough cold water to cover for at least 30 minutes (this prevents them from burning); drain and set aside.
3. To prepare the peanut sauce, combine the coconut milk, peanut butter, cilantro, honey, the remaining 1 tablespoon each fish sauce and lime juice, the lime zest, and red pepper in a medium bowl; whisk until smooth.
4. Preheat the broiler or prepare the grill for a hot fire; spray the broiler pan or grill rack with nonstick spray. Thread the chicken strips onto the skewers, then broil or grill the skewers 4 inches from the heat, turning once, until they are cooked through, 3–4 minutes per side. Serve at once with the peanut sauce.

Per serving (5 skewers with about 2 tablespoons peanut sauce): 162 Cal, 6 g Fat, 2 g Sat Fat, 47 mg Chol, 200 mg Sod, 7 g Carb, 0 g Fib, 21 g Prot, 18 mg Calc. ***POINTS: 4.***

top tips

- Thai fish sauce (*nam pla*) is a clear brown, subtly fishy flavoring made from fermented fish; it can be found in the international section of supermarkets or in Asian groceries. A bottle will last several years in the pantry.
- Freeze the leftover coconut milk in an airtight container for future recipes; it will stay fresh for up to two months.

Chicken Salad Véronique

MAKES 4 SERVINGS

In the French culinary canon, any dish labeled "Véronique" includes grapes—and it is indeed a pleasure to add these sweet, juicy (and formerly forbidden) morsels to a chicken salad. Serve it with multigrain bread or rolls and sweet pickles.

- **½ cup plain fat-free yogurt**
- **2 tablespoons reduced-fat mayonnaise**
- **1 tablespoon honey**
- **1 teaspoon cider vinegar**
- **½ teaspoon Dijon mustard**
- **¼ teaspoon celery seeds**
- **¼ teaspoon salt**
- **Freshly ground pepper**
- **¾ pound cooked skinless boneless chicken breast, coarsely chopped**
- **1 cup seedless green grapes**
- **1 celery stalk, finely chopped**
- **¼ cup chopped walnuts**
- **4 small grape bunches (optional)**

Combine the yogurt, mayonnaise, honey, vinegar, mustard, celery seeds, salt, and pepper in a large bowl. Add the chicken, grapes, celery, and walnuts; toss to coat evenly. Cover and refrigerate at least 1 hour or up to 8 hours. Garnish with the small grape bunches, if using, and serve.

Per serving (¾ cup): 277 Cal, 11 g Fat, 2 g Sat Fat, 66 mg Chol, 303 mg Sod, 16 g Carb, 1 g Fib, 29 g Prot, 95 mg Calc. ***POINTS: 6.***

top tip

Here's how to chop the walnuts quickly and neatly: Place them in a small zip-close plastic bag, squeeze out the air, and seal the bag. Place the bag on a heavy work surface and pound with a heavy frying pan or rolling pin.

Mexican Chicken Wraps

MAKES 4 SANDWICHES

The wrap—a sandwich made by rolling a soft flat bread around any number of fillings—was one of the hottest grab-and-go eating concepts in the nineties. Like much of the global-fusion cuisine of that era, wraps can be made with just about any flat bread, from lavash to crêpes, but the most popular is the flour tortilla. Here, we've stuffed tortillas with a mildly spicy warm chicken filling that's tamed with cool, crunchy salad vegetables.

- **4 (¼-pound) skinless boneless chicken breast halves**
- **1 teaspoon olive oil**
- **1 tablespoon Mexican seasoning mix**
- **¼ teaspoon salt**
- **⅓ cup reduced-fat mayonnaise**
- **2 tablespoons chopped cilantro**
- **1 tablespoon fresh lime juice**
- **2 teaspoons chopped canned chipotles in adobo**
- **4 (8-inch) fat-free flour tortillas**
- **1 bunch arugula, cleaned**
- **1 plum tomato, seeded and chopped**
- **½ red onion, chopped**

1 Preheat the broiler or grill; spray the broiler pan or grill rack with nonstick spray. (Or, if you have one, spray a ridged grill pan with nonstick spray and set over medium-high heat until hot.)

2. Combine the chicken and oil in a small bowl. Sprinkle with the Mexican seasoning and salt, tossing to coat. Grill or broil the chicken, turning once, until cooked through, 10–12 minutes. Let cool 5 minutes, then slice ¼ inch thick.

3. Combine the mayonnaise, cilantro, lime juice, and chipotles in a small bowl.

4. To assemble the wraps, place the tortillas on a work surface. Spread each with 1½ tablespoons of the mayonnaise mixture. Top each tortilla with one-fourth of the arugula, then with one-fourth of the chicken. Sprinkle each with one-fourth of the tomato and onion. Fold the bottom flap up over the filling, then fold over the sides to enclose; roll up to form a package. Wrap the bottom of each sandwich in foil, if desired, to prevent them from opening.

Per serving (1 wrap): 348 Cal, 12 g Fat, 2 g Sat Fat, 69 mg Chol, 700 mg Sod, 30 g Carb, 2 g Fib, 30 g Prot, 126 mg Calc. ***POINTS: 8.***

top tips

- Chipotle chiles are smoked jalapeño peppers, sold ground, dried whole, or packed in adobo (tomato-onion) sauce in Latino markets and many supermarkets. Their complex, smoky flavor goes a long way; stir a little into soups, stews, and chili, and you'll marvel at the difference. Refrigerate the leftover chipotles in adobo in an airtight container for up to a year.
- To seed the tomato, halve it lengthwise, then squeeze out and discard the seeds.

Chicken Cordon Bleu

MAKES 4 SERVINGS

Cordon bleu, or blue ribbon, once connoted the highest level of culinary achievement for female chefs in France. It's also the name of a glamorous dish that graced many a dinner-party table in the sixties. The method is simple: A layer of fine ham and cheese is sandwiched between thin medallions of chicken or veal, then sautéed. Here, we've simplified and lightened the recipe to use a single layer of chicken rolled around the filling to make an elegant presentation.

4 (¼-pound) skinless boneless chicken breast halves, pounded to ¼-inch thickness
4 thin slices lean ham (about 2 ounces)
4 thin slices reduced-fat Swiss cheese (about 2 ounces)
4 tablespoons all-purpose flour
½ teaspoon salt
Freshly ground pepper
1 large egg, lightly beaten
½ cup cornflake crumbs
½ cup reduced-fat (2%) milk
½ cup reduced-sodium chicken broth
1 tablespoon Madeira
⅛ teaspoon nutmeg
2 tablespoons freshly grated Parmesan cheese

1. Preheat the oven to 400°F. Spray a baking sheet with nonstick spray.
2. Working one at a time, place a chicken breast half on a work surface. Top with one slice of the ham, then one slice of the Swiss cheese. Roll up, jelly-roll style, and secure with a toothpick. Repeat with the remaining chicken, ham and cheese.
3. Combine 2 tablespoons of the flour, ¼ teaspoon of the salt, and a grinding of the pepper on a sheet of wax paper. Place the egg in a shallow bowl, and the cornflake crumbs in another shallow bowl.
4. Working one at a time, lightly coat the chicken rolls first with the flour mixture, shaking off the excess, then dip into the egg to coat. Lightly coat with the cornflake crumbs, and place on the baking sheet (discard any leftover flour mixture, egg, and crumbs). Lightly spray the chicken rolls with nonstick spray. Bake until a thermometer inserted into the thickest part of each roll reaches 160°F, 30–35 minutes.
5. Meanwhile, to prepare the sauce, combine the milk, broth, the remaining 2 tablespoons flour, the Madeira, nutmeg, the remaining ¼ teaspoon salt, and another grinding of the pepper in a medium saucepan. Whisk until smooth; cook over medium heat, whisking constantly, until thickened, about 6 minutes. Remove from the heat and stir in the Parmesan cheese; cover and keep warm.
6. When the chicken rolls are ready, drizzle with the sauce and serve them at once.

Per serving (1 breast with ¼ cup sauce): 294 Cal, 9 g Fat, 4 g Sat Fat, 0 mg Chol, 744 mg Sod, 14 g Carb, 0 g Fib, 38 g Prot, 280 mg Calc. ***POINTS: 7.***

Chicken Cordon Bleu

Chicken Parmigiana

MAKES 4 SERVINGS

This is one of those beloved dishes that will never go out of style. You can make it with turkey cutlets or, if you're feeling fancy, veal cutlets. Serve the cutlets with pasta and tomato sauce, or on crusty bread with plenty of grilled or roasted vegetables.

1 large egg
1 tablespoon water
⅓ cup plain dried bread crumbs
¼ cup chopped flat-leaf parsley
3 tablespoons freshly grated Parmesan cheese
Freshly ground pepper
4 (¼-pound) skinless boneless chicken breasts, pounded thin

1. Preheat the oven to 400°F. Spray a 1-quart shallow baking dish with nonstick spray.
2. Beat the egg with the water in a shallow bowl. Combine the bread crumbs, parsley, cheese, and pepper on a sheet of wax paper.
3. Dip the chicken breasts first in the egg mixture, then coat lightly on both sides with the bread crumb mixture, shaking off the excess, and place them in the baking dish. (Discard any leftover egg or bread crumb mixture.) Bake until cooked through, golden and crisp-edged, about 15 minutes.

Per serving (1 breast): 210 Cal, 6 g Fat, 2 g Sat Fat, 119 mg Chol, 239 mg Sod, 7 g Carb, 1 g Fib, 29 g Prot, 111 mg Calc. ***POINTS: 5.***

top tip

The chicken breasts need to be uniformly thin to cook evenly and quickly. You can buy thin-sliced chicken breast halves that are about ¼ inch thick to save time. Or pound your own: Just lay the breasts between two sheets of plastic wrap, or put them in a partially sealed zip-close plastic bag (don't seal the bag completely, or it will pop). Use a rubber mallet or heavy skillet to pound them to uniform thinness.

Poached Chicken Breasts with Green Sauce

MAKES 4 SERVINGS

Poaching is one of the all-time-great low-fat cooking techniques, and Weight Watchers members have relied upon it for years. The technique of gently cooking foods in not-quite-simmering liquid is well suited for delicate and mild-flavored foods. In this case, chicken breasts soak up the subtle flavors of vegetables, chicken broth, and white wine. The green sauce makes for a tangy contrast.

CHICKEN

- **2 teaspoons olive oil**
- **1 onion, chopped**
- **1 green bell pepper. seeded and chopped**
- **1 carrot, peeled and chopped**
- **1 celery stalk, chopped**
- **4 (¼-pound) skinless boneless chicken breasts**
- **3 cups reduced-sodium chicken broth**
- **½ cup dry white wine**
- **2 tablespoons chopped flat-leaf parsley**
- **1 tablespoon chopped thyme**
- **1 garlic clove**
- **1 bay leaf**
- **Freshly ground white pepper**

SAUCE

- **1 cup packed flat-leaf parsley leaves**
- **5 small green olives, pitted and chopped**
- **1 tablespoon fresh lemon juice**
- **½ tablespoon plain dried bread crumbs**
- **1 teaspoon capers, drained**
- **1 teaspoon olive oil**
- **1 garlic clove**
- **Freshly ground white pepper**

1. To prepare the chicken: Heat a large nonstick skillet; swirl in the oil, then add the onion, green pepper, carrot, and celery. Sauté until the vegetables are wilted, about 5 minutes.
2. Add the chicken, broth, wine, parsley, thyme, garlic, bay leaf, and white pepper. Bring to a boil; reduce the heat and simmer, covered, until the chicken is cooked through, 12–15 minutes.
3. Meanwhile, prepare the sauce: Pulse the parsley, olives, lemon juice, bread crumbs, capers, oil, garlic, and pepper in a food processor until the mixture forms a coarse pesto-like sauce.
4. Transfer the chicken and vegetables with a slotted spoon to a warmed platter. Discard the bay leaf; reserve the liquid remaining in the pan for another use. Arrange the chicken and vegetables on a platter, and top each chicken breast with a dollop of the sauce.

Per serving (1 breast with ¼ cup vegetables and 2 tablespoons sauce): 213 Cal, 8 g Fat, 2 g Sat Fat, 62 mg Chol, 302 mg Sod, 9 g Carb, 2 g Fib, 27 g Prot, 62 mg Calc. ***POINTS: 5.***

Chicken with 40 Cloves of Garlic

MAKES 8 SERVINGS

Why 40 garlic cloves and not 35? Who knows where the number came from, but it's nothing to fear: The long cooking time mellows the garlic to a nutty creaminess. Serve the unpeeled cloves with the chicken, and let everyone have fun squeezing them out of their jackets onto toasted French bread rounds. Add a salad, and voilà! Dinner is served.

- **1 tablespoon extra-virgin olive oil**
- **4 skin-on bone-in chicken breast halves (about 2 pounds)**
- **4 skin-on bone-in chicken thighs (about 2 pounds)**
- **½ cup dry white wine**
- **½ cup reduced-sodium chicken broth**
- **2 tablespoons tomato paste**
- **40 garlic cloves, unpeeled**
- **1 rosemary sprig, or ½ teaspoon dried**
- **1 thyme sprig, or ½ teaspoon dried**
- **1 bay leaf**
- **¾ teaspoon salt**
- **¼ teaspoon freshly ground pepper**

1. Preheat the oven to 375°F.
2. Heat a large heavy-bottomed casserole or roasting pan large enough to hold the chicken in a single layer over medium heat. Swirl in the oil, then add the chicken breast and thigh pieces, skin-side down. Cook until browned on all sides, about 5 minutes, and transfer the chicken pieces to a plate.
3. Pour off and discard any fat remaining in the skillet. Stir in the wine, broth, and tomato paste, scraping up any browned bits from the bottom of the pan. Remove from the heat and add the garlic, rosemary, thyme, bay leaf, salt and pepper. Return the chicken to the skillet and toss to coat with the sauce. Cover tightly with foil and bake until the chicken is cooked through and the garlic is softened, 1¼–1½ hours. Remove the skin before eating.

Per serving (1 chicken piece with 5 garlic cloves and 2–3 tablespoons sauce): 158 Cal, 5 g Fat, 1 g Sat Fat, 56 mg Chol, 337 mg Sod, 6 g Carb, 1 g Fib, 22 g Prot, 46 mg Calc. ***POINTS: 3.***

top tip

For an alcohol-free version of this dish [as well as the Poached Chicken Breasts on page 115] substitute ½ cup nonalcoholic dry white wine and a tablespoon of white vinegar for the white wine—or omit the wine, and increase the chicken broth by ½ cup.

Shake-in-the-Bag Chicken

MAKES 4 SERVINGS 

Remember those commercials for that oven-fried-chicken coating mix, so common in the seventies? Little did we know how easy it was to make our own version—with a lot less sodium and fresher flavorings. Best of all, our mix makes skinless chicken breasts seem positively decadent. Enjoy the chicken hot or cold.

- **⅔ cup cornflake crumbs**
- **1 tablespoon all-purpose flour**
- **2 teaspoons paprika**
- **1 teaspoon dark brown sugar**
- **¾ teaspoon garlic powder**
- **¾ teaspoon onion powder**
- **¾ teaspoon salt**
- **½ teaspoon ground cumin**
- **4 bone-in chicken breast halves, skinned (about 2 pounds)**

1. Preheat oven to 400°F. Spray a baking sheet with nonstick spray.
2. Combine the cornflake crumbs, flour, paprika, sugar, garlic powder, onion powder, salt, and cumin in a large zip-close plastic bag. Spray the chicken pieces lightly with nonstick spray, then place one piece in the bag. Shake the bag to evenly coat the chicken, then transfer chicken to the baking sheet. Repeat with the remaining chicken pieces; discard any remaining coating mix.
3. Bake until a thermometer inserted into the thickest part of each breast registers 160°F, 40–45 minutes.

Per serving (1 breast half): 244 Cal, 5 g Fat, 1 g Sat Fat, 89 mg Chol, 597 mg Sod, 11 g Carb, 1 g Fib, 36 g Prot, 28 mg Calc. ***POINTS: 5.***

I want eating to be a pleasure for my members. If someone is struggling, I'll sit with her and do a cupboard check: 'How many fat-free products do you have in your kitchen?' If she has a lot, that's a sign that she's not getting it. If something doesn't taste good, you shouldn't put up with it. Spit it out!

—Wendy Brintnall, Leader, Omaha

Orange Chicken

Orange Chicken

MAKES 6 SERVINGS

Anyone who joined Weight Watchers in the seventies will remember this beloved recipe, which we've updated with fresher flavors. Juicy chicken thighs are a nice switch from the usual breasts, and a lot more forgiving of overcooking. Just be sure to trim them well, as they tend to have lots of fatty pockets.

- **1 medium orange**
- **1 teaspoon olive oil**
- **1 teaspoon paprika**
- **1 teaspoon dried rosemary, crumbled**
- **½ teaspoon garlic salt**
- **¼ teaspoon ground pepper**
- **6 (¼-pound) skinless, boneless chicken thighs, trimmed of visible fat**

1. Preheat the oven to 350°F. Peel off the zest (the colorful outer layer of the orange rind) with a zester or vegetable peeler, making sure to avoid the bitter white pith underneath; mince the zest. Trim off the remaining orange rind with a knife, then cut the orange into 8 wedges.
2. Stir the orange zest, oil, paprika, rosemary, garlic salt, and pepper in a small bowl. Rub the orange mixture all over the chicken. Transfer to a roasting pan and scatter the orange wedges around the chicken pieces.
3. Roast until the juices run clear and an instant-read thermometer inserted into the chicken reads 175°F, about 45 minutes. Cover loosely with foil and let stand 5 minutes before serving (the temperature will continue to rise 5 degrees out of the oven).

Per serving (1 thigh): 189 Cal, 8 g Fat, 2 g Sat Fat, 77 mg Chol, 155 mg Sod, 3 g Carb, 1 g Fib, 25 g Prot, 33 mg Calc. ***POINTS: 4.***

top tip

If you have one, use a razor-sharp rasp grater to remove the zest from the orange—it will produce paper-thin shreds.

Marinated Mediterranean Chicken

MAKES 8 SERVINGS

Almost every eighties dinner party served up a version of this sunny chicken dish, and no wonder: It's easy to make, delicious left over or reheated, great hot or at room temperature, and perfect for toting in a covered dish. Be sure to serve it over steamed brown rice or couscous to soak up all those delicious juices.

- **8 skinless bone-in chicken thighs (about 2 pounds)**
- **1 (14-ounce) can quartered artichoke hearts, drained**
- **¾ cup chopped pitted dates**
- **⅓ cup packed light brown sugar**
- **¼ cup golden raisins**
- **12 pimiento-stuffed Manzanilla olives, halved**
- **2 tablespoons balsamic vinegar**
- **3 garlic cloves, minced**
- **1 tablespoon dried basil**
- **1 tablespoon drained capers**
- **1 tablespoon extra-virgin olive oil**
- **2 teaspoons dried oregano**
- **½ teaspoon salt**
- **¼ teaspoon freshly ground pepper**
- **½ cup reduced-sodium chicken broth**

1. Combine the chicken, artichoke hearts, dates, sugar, raisins, olives, vinegar, garlic, basil, capers, oil, oregano, salt, and pepper in a large zip-close plastic bag. Squeeze out the air and seal the bag; turn to coat the chicken. Refrigerate, turning the bag occasionally, at least 8 hours or overnight.
2. Preheat the oven to 350°F. Remove the chicken pieces from the marinade and arrange them in a single layer in a large roasting pan. Pour the marinade over the chicken, then pour in the broth. Bake until a thermometer inserted into the thickest part of the chicken registers 160°F, 35–45 minutes.

Per serving (1 thigh with about ½ cup sauce): 251 Cal, 7 g Fat, 2 g Sat Fat, 50 mg Chol, 510 mg Sod, 30 g Carb, 4 g Fib, 18 g Prot, 61 mg Calc. ***POINTS: 5.***

Tandoori-Marinated Turkey Breast

MAKES 8 SERVINGS

It's hard to believe that until the seventies, yogurt was hard to find in this country, outside of ethnic or health-food stores. Today, it's available in every fat content and flavor imaginable, and every color of the rainbow. In Indian cookery, yogurt is often used as a marinade; its acid is a great tenderizer, and its tangy flavors are a great match for spices and herbs. Here, it turns a plain turkey breast into something juicy and special. Serve the turkey on a bed of sautéed spinach, with fragrant basmati rice on the side.

- **¾ cup plain fat-free yogurt**
- **1 small onion, finely chopped**
- **2 tablespoons grated peeled fresh ginger**
- **2 tablespoons red-wine vinegar**
- **1 tablespoon Dijon mustard**
- **1 teaspoon ground cumin**
- **1 garlic clove, minced**
- **½ teaspoon cinnamon**
- **¼ teaspoon crushed red pepper**
- **8 (¼-pound) skinless turkey cutlets**

1. Combine the yogurt, onion, ginger, vinegar, mustard, cumin, garlic, cinnamon, and red pepper in a large zip-close plastic bag; add the turkey. Squeeze out the air and seal the bag; turn to coat the turkey. Refrigerate, turning the bag occasionally, at least 2 hours or overnight. Drain and discard the marinade.
2. Spray the broiler rack with nonstick spray; preheat the broiler. Broil the turkey 5 inches from the heat, turning once, until cooked through, about 4 minutes per side.

Per serving (1 cutlet): 156 Cal, 3 g Fat, 1 g Sat Fat, 67 mg Chol, 83 mg Sod, 2 g Carb, 0 g Fib, 27 g Prot, 43 mg Calc. ***POINTS: 3.***

If you gained or if you cheated, they never made you feel as if you did a terrible thing.
They just said, 'Well, next week, you'll lose it.'
You always had a lot of encouragement from everyone around you.

—Florence Rogoff, former personal assistant to Jean Nidetch

Turkey Tetrazzini Casserole

MAKES 8 SERVINGS

This comfort-food specialty—originally made with chicken—is said to have been created in honor of the Italian opera singer Luisa Tetrazzini. But for decades Americans have preferred to look at it as a creative way to recycle leftover Thanksgiving turkey. Either way, it's irresistible, especially with our creative seasonings.

- **8 ounces spaghetti**
- **3 cups cooked cubed skinless turkey breast (about 1 pound)**
- **2 (10-ounce) cans reduced-fat condensed cream of mushroom soup**
- **1 cup low-fat (1%) milk**
- **⅓ cup grated Romano cheese**
- **½ teaspoon garlic powder**
- **½ teaspoon ground cumin**
- **¼ teaspoon freshly ground pepper**
- **¼ cup plain dried bread crumbs**
- **2 tablespoons unsalted light butter, melted**

1. Preheat the oven to 375°F. Spray a 7 x 11-inch baking dish with nonstick spray. Cook the spaghetti according to package directions. Drain and keep warm.
2. Combine the turkey, soup, milk, cheese, garlic powder, cumin, and pepper in a large bowl; add the spaghetti and toss well. Transfer to the baking dish.
3. Combine the bread crumbs and butter in a small bowl. Sprinkle over the spaghetti mixture and bake until the top is golden, 20–25 minutes.

Per serving: (1 cup): 296 Cal, 9 g Fat, 4 g Sat Fat, 58 mg Chol, 403 mg Sod, 30 g Carb, 1 g Fib, 23 g Prot, 105 mg Calc. ***POINTS: 6.***

Turkey Meatballs

MAKES 4 SERVINGS

These are not your traditional serve-with-pasta meatballs. Our herb-laced little orbs in a chock-full-of-veggies tomato sauce are great with rice, mashed potatoes, noodles—and, come to think of it, spaghetti! What a great idea for a covered-dish supper or buffet.

¾ pound ground skinless turkey breast
3 tablespoons plain dried bread crumbs
1 large egg white, lightly beaten
2 tablespoons chopped flat-leaf parsley
2 tablespoons chopped dill
1 tablespoon Dijon mustard
1 teaspoon grated lemon zest
4 teaspoons olive oil
1 medium (8-ounce) zucchini, chopped
1 onion, finely chopped
1 green bell pepper, finely chopped
1 (28-ounce) can whole plum tomatoes, chopped, with their juice
1 (10-ounce) package frozen cut green beans, thawed
¼ teaspoon salt
Freshly ground pepper

1. Combine the turkey, bread crumbs, egg white, parsley, dill, mustard, and lemon zest in a large bowl. Shape into 20 meatballs.
2. Heat a large nonstick skillet over medium heat. Swirl in the oil, then add the meatballs. Cook, turning frequently, until browned on all sides, about 6 minutes. Transfer to a heatproof plate with a slotted spoon; keep warm.
3. Return the skillet to the heat and add the zucchini, onion, and green bell pepper; sauté until wilted, about 5 minutes. Stir in the tomatoes, beans, salt, and black pepper; bring to a simmer. Add the meatballs to the sauce; simmer, partially covered, frequently spooning the sauce over the meatballs, until the meatballs are cooked through and tender, 10 minutes.

Per serving (5 meatballs with ½ cup sauce): 257 Cal, 8 g Fat, 2 g Sat Fat, 50 mg Chol, 631 mg Sod, 22 g Carb, 6 g Fib, 26 g Prot, 129 mg Calc. ***POINTS: 5.***

top tips

- Mince the fresh herbs by hand if you can; a food processor does the job quickly but also crushes and bruises them.
- At many fresh-produce markets and farm stands, you can find herbs with their roots still attached. In that form, they will keep fresh for weeks. Just place them in a glass with enough water to cover their roots, cover their leaves loosely with an upturned plastic bag, and refrigerate.

Turkey Sloppy Joes

MAKES 4 SERVINGS

Nobody knows who Joe was, but these belovedly messy sandwiches certainly deserve the other half of their name. Why buy the salty packaged flavoring mix, when you can so easily make them yourself?

- **1 tablespoon canola oil**
- **1 medium onion, finely chopped**
- **1 green bell pepper, finely chopped**
- **2 garlic cloves, minced**
- **1 teaspoon chili powder**
- **½ teaspoon dried oregano**
- **½ teaspoon dry mustard**
- **1 pound ground skinless turkey breast**
- **1 cup prepared barbecue sauce**
- **4 multigrain hamburger rolls**

1. Heat a large nonstick skillet over medium heat. Swirl in the oil, then add the onion, pepper, and garlic. Cook, stirring occasionally, until softened, about 5 minutes. Stir in the chili powder, oregano, and mustard; let cool 1 minute.
2. Add the turkey and cook, stirring to break up the meat, until no longer pink, 3–4 minutes. Stir in the barbecue sauce and cook until slightly thickened, about 2 minutes. Remove from the heat and serve on the hamburger rolls.

Per serving (1 roll with ¾ cup meat): 356 Cal, 10 g Fat, 2 g Sat Fat, 67 mg Chol, 813 mg Sod, 33 g Carb, 4 g Fib, 32 g Prot, 86 mg Calc. ***POINTS: 7.***

top tips

- This dish can be made with ground skinless chicken, ground lean beef, or, for a vegetarian version, textured vegetable protein crumbles, now found in the freezer case in most supermarkets. Just cook the crumbles according to the package directions and add them to the cooked vegetable mixture at step 2.
- If you'd like a little more heat, try adding 1 chopped jalapeño pepper to the vegetable mixture in Step 1, then stir in 2 tablespoons of chopped cilantro just before serving.

Turkey Sloppy Joes and Coleslaw

Grilled Duck Breasts with Orange-Balsamic Glaze

MAKES 8 SERVINGS

Remember Duck à l'Orange? The dish that was the height of elegance in the sixties soon became a culinary cliché. This thoroughly modern version brings it back in all its glory, using sophisticated flavorings and easy-to-cook duck breasts. Try it for a special-occasion meal.

- **1¼ cups orange juice**
- **½ cup balsamic vinegar**
- **1 whole (1¾-pound) boneless duck breast, trimmed of all skin and visible fat, and separated into 4 equal pieces**
- **2 small shallots, minced**
- **½ cup dry red wine or reduced-sodium chicken broth**
- **1 tablespoon grated orange zest**
- **¼ teaspoon salt**
- **Freshly ground white pepper**
- **1 bunch arugula, torn into bite-size pieces (optional)**

1. Combine 1 cup of the orange juice and ¼ cup of the vinegar in a large zip-close plastic bag; add the duck. Squeeze out the air and seal the bag; turn to coat the duck. Refrigerate, turning the bag occasionally, at least 2 hours or overnight. Drain and discard the marinade.
2. Spray the grill rack with nonstick spray; prepare the grill.
3. Meanwhile, to prepare the glaze, combine the shallots, wine or broth, the remaining ¼ cup each orange juice and vinegar, the orange zest, salt, and pepper in a medium saucepan; bring to a boil. Reduce the heat and simmer, watching carefully and stirring occasionally, until the mixture is reduced by half, about 15 minutes. Remove from the heat.
4. Grill the duck, turning once and basting with the glaze, until the juices run clear when pierced with a fork, about 8 minutes per side.
5. Transfer the duck to a carving board, let cool slightly. Thinly slice lengthwise. Arrange the slices on serving plates and drizzle with any leftover glaze. Serve each portion with ⅓ cup of the arugula, if using.

Per serving (3 ounces): 187 Cal, 9 g Fat, 3 g Sat Fat, 73 mg Chol, 130 mg Sod, 3 g Carb, 0 g Fib, 21 g Prot, 18 mg Calc. ***POINTS: 4.***

top tip

Duck breasts are now available at many supermarkets and from the butcher; however, they are very likely to be frozen. Be sure they are solidly frozen and haven't begun to thaw. If you're lucky enough to find them fresh, store them in the refrigerator in their original packaging and cook them within two days. If not previously frozen, duck can be stored in the freezer for up to six months, then thawed in the refrigerator overnight.

Weight Watchers taught me that there's no black and white in life, that nobody's perfect. There's no being 'on the Program' or 'off the Program.' You're always a member, even if you're not attending meetings, even if you've gained weight. You can always make mistakes and learn from what you do. There's no failure, only feedback.

—Carol Kramer, Manager, New Service Development and Training, Weight Watchers International

"When we start to lose weight, we think we have to cut out things—so people tend to stay away from fats and proteins. But once they realize that they can actually hinder their weight loss by doing this, the whole picture becomes clear. They realize they have choices, but there is plenty of structure and balance in the Program, too—what we call the 'right mix.' I love seeing the light bulb go on over people's heads when we talk about the right mix. I usually have a big turnaround after those meetings. People look at their journals and say, 'Duh!'"

—Susie Huebner, Leader, Des Moines

The Leaders are people who have gone through the same things the members go through—and they know that the best way to enjoy their weight loss is to give it away. That's the joy of it. You can't enjoy it by just looking in a mirror; you have to share it with others.

—Jean Nidetch

When someone asks me, 'If you inherited a million dollars, would you still work for Weight Watchers?' I tell them I'd still be working for Weight Watchers. I'd be handing out $100 bills along with the stars and the ribbons at meetings, but I'd still be working for Weight Watchers. That's how much I believe in it.

—Sharon Claye, Leader, Detroit

The Meat Goes On

1983

Flashdance, the film about a dancer with a dream and a great wardrobe, captivates the nation—and gets us all wearing leotards, leggings, and leg warmers (whether they flatter us or not).

1984

Weight Watchers introduces the At Work Program, giving members with busy work schedules a more convenient meeting option.

WEIGHT WATCHERS

THE AT WORK PROGRAM

1985

Noting that great results in the first weeks of a weight-loss program can help motivate people and keep them from giving up on their goals, Weight Watchers introduces Quick Start—a nutritionally sound program for initially quick, safe weight loss.

>>>

Individual Beef Wellingtons and Roasted-Garlic Mashed Potatoes

Individual Beef Wellingtons

MAKES 4 SERVINGS

In the sixties, Beef Wellington was a dish to aspire to, attempted only by a few home cooks. In the classic technique, expensive, fork-tender beef fillet is spread with either foie gras (fatty goose or duck liver) or duxelles (sautéed mushroom-shallot-herb paste), then wrapped in puff pastry and baked. We've made our updated version much simpler and lighter by topping individual filets with sautéed mushrooms and enclosing them in phyllo dough. The results are still divinely impressive.

- **4 (¼-pound) filets mignons, trimmed of all visible fat**
- **½ teaspoon salt**
- **¼ teaspoon freshly ground pepper**
- **1 teaspoon olive oil**
- **8 ounces sliced white mushrooms (about 2 cups)**
- **1 small onion, chopped**
- **1 teaspoon chopped thyme**
- **2 garlic cloves, minced**
- **¼ cup Madeira**
- **4 sheets phyllo dough, thawed, if frozen**

1. Preheat the oven to 400°F. Spray a baking sheet with nonstick spray. Sprinkle the filets with the salt and pepper.
2. Heat a large nonstick skillet over medium-high heat. Swirl in the oil, then add the filets. Cook until browned on both sides, about 4 minutes. Transfer to a warmed plate.
3. Return the skillet to the heat; add the mushrooms, onion, thyme, and garlic. Cook, stirring occasionally, until the mushrooms are softened, about 6 minutes. Add the Madeira and cook until liquid evaporates, 3 minutes. Remove from heat and let cool 5 minutes.
4. Cover the phyllo sheets with plastic wrap to keep them from drying out as you work. Place one sheet of phyllo on a work surface, with the long side closest to you. Spray with nonstick spray and top with another phyllo sheet. Spray the second sheet with nonstick spray, then cut the stack in half vertically. Place one filet in the center of the lower third of each half. Top each filet with ¼ cup of the mushroom mixture. Fold the short sides of the phyllo over the filets, and roll up the long end, jelly-roll style. Transfer to the baking sheet, and repeat with the remaining phyllo, filets, and mushroom mixture.
5. Spray the Wellingtons with nonstick spray and bake until the crust is golden and the filets are cooked to the desired doneness, 10–12 minutes for medium.

Per serving (1 Wellington): 288 Cal, 10 g Fat, 3 g Sat Fat, 65 mg Chol, 426 mg Sod, 20 g Carb, 2 g Fib, 28 g Prot, 21 mg Calc. ***POINTS: 6.***

top tip

Madiera, a rich-tasting fortified dry wine made on the Portuguese island of the same name, gives the Beef Wellingtons an incomparable, complex flavor. If you don't have any in your pantry, substitute dry sherry—or, for a less flavorful, teetotaling version, use reduced-sodium chicken broth instead (and subtract ½ ***POINT*** per serving).

Roasted Beef Tenderloin with Mushroom Sauce

MAKES 8 SERVINGS

The recent revival of steak house cuisine is proof: There's something really alluring about a good cut of beef. And few dishes, no matter how hard you've slaved over a hot stove, make the impression that a skillfully prepared beef tenderloin does. It's expensive, but it's easy to fix and definitely worth splurging on, if you can, for special occasions.

BEEF

- **1 (2-pound) beef tenderloin, trimmed of all visible fat**
- **½ cup dry red wine or reduced-sodium chicken broth**
- **¼ cup chopped flat-leaf parsley**
- **1 shallot, minced**
- **1 tablespoon balsamic vinegar**
- **1 teaspoon chopped thyme**
- **1 garlic clove, bruised**
- **¼ teaspoon salt**
- **Freshly ground pepper**

SAUCE

- **2 teaspoons olive oil**
- **1 (10-ounce) package sliced white mushrooms**
- **1 small onion, minced**
- **½ cup chopped flat-leaf parsley**
- **½ cup dry red wine or reduced-sodium chicken broth**
- **½ cup reduced-sodium beef broth**
- **¼ teaspoon red-wine vinegar or fresh lemon juice**
- **¼ teaspoon salt**
- **Freshly ground pepper**
- **Chopped flat-leaf parsley (optional)**

1. Remove the beef from the refrigerator and let stand at room temperature 1 hour before cooking. Place the oven rack on the bottom third of the oven. Preheat the oven to 450°F.
2. To prepare the beef, combine the wine, parsley, shallot, balsamic vinegar, thyme, and garlic in a small bowl. Place the meat on a rack in a large roasting pan. Brush with the wine mixture and sprinkle with the salt and pepper. Roast until an instant-read thermometer inserted in the center registers 140°F for medium-rare, about 45 minutes (subtract or add about 5 minutes for rare or well-done beef).
3. Meanwhile, to prepare the sauce, heat a large nonstick skillet. Swirl in the oil, then add the mushrooms and onion. Sauté until the mushrooms have released some of their liquid and the onion is soft, about 10 minutes. Add the parsley, wine, broth, and wine vinegar or lemon juice. Cook over medium-high heat, watching carefully, until thickened and reduced by one-third; stir in the salt and pepper. Set aside and keep warm.
4. Transfer the beef to a warmed platter; tent with foil and keep warm. Let rest 10 minutes, then cut into ½-inch slices. Serve with the sauce and the additional parsley, if using.

Per serving (3 ounces with 2 tablespoons sauce): 207 Cal, 9 g Fat, 3 g Sat Fat, 64 mg Chol, 182 mg Sod, 4 g Carb, 1 g Fib, 26 g Prot, 22 mg Calc. ***POINTS: 5.***

Beef Fajitas

MAKES 4 SERVINGS

Eighties eaters were passionate about all things Tex-Mex—especially sizzling fajitas. True to the primordial Texas recipe, we've made ours with flank steak. Though it needs a little time to marinate, it's loaded with beefy flavor and has a good chew. If you can't find it at your market, look for skirt steak, bottom round, or rump steak, and trim it well.

- **3 tablespoons fresh lime juice**
- **3 garlic cloves, minced**
- **1½ teaspoons ground cumin**
- **12 ounces flank steak, trimmed of all visible fat, thinly sliced on the diagonal**
- **1 small onion, thinly sliced**
- **1 red bell pepper, sliced into thin strips**
- **1 green bell pepper, sliced into thin strips**
- **1 jalapeño pepper, seeded and chopped**
- **1½ tablespoons reduced-sodium soy sauce**
- **1 tablespoon Worcestershire sauce**
- **1 teaspoon chili powder**
- **4 (8-inch) fat-free flour tortillas**
- **½ cup fat-free sour cream**
- **½ cup salsa**

1. Combine the lime juice, garlic, and cumin in a zip-close plastic bag; add the steak. Squeeze out the air and seal the bag; turn to coat the steak. Refrigerate, turning the bag occasionally, 20 minutes. Drain and discard the marinade.
2. Spray a large nonstick skillet with nonstick spray and set over medium-high heat. Add the onion, red and green bell peppers, and the jalapeño pepper; cook, stirring occasionally, until softened, 5 minutes. Add the steak and cook until lightly browned but still barely red in the center, 3–4 minutes. Add the soy sauce, Worcestershire sauce, and chili powder; cook 1 minute longer.
3. Warm the tortillas according to package directions. Place a tortilla on a work surface and place one-fourth of the beef mixture in a strip down the center, leaving a 1½-inch border at either end. Fold the bottom flap up over the filling, then fold over the sides to enclose; roll up to form a package. Repeat with the remaining tortillas and filling, and serve the fajitas at once with the sour cream and salsa.

Per serving (1 tortilla with 1 cup filling and 2 tablespoons each sour cream and salsa): 307 Cal, 7 g Fat, 2 g Sat Fat, 49 mg Chol, 632 mg Sod, 35 g Carb, 3 g Fib, 26 g Prot, 159 mg Calc. ***POINTS: 6.***

Stuffed Pork Chops and Braised Cabbage with Apples, Onions, and Raisins

Stuffed Pork Chops

MAKES 4 SERVINGS

Today's leaner pork isn't the juicy, fat-marbled meat it once was—good news for Weight Watchers, bad news for those who like their pork chops tender. We've solved the problem by starting our chops on the stove and finishing them in the oven, keeping all that great browned flavor without drying them out. And while the stuffing packs a whole lot of flavor and crispy texture, it's much leaner than the original.

- **4 (¼-pound) boneless loin pork chops, trimmed of all visible fat**
- **3 tablespoons plain dried bread crumbs**
- **½ celery stalk, finely chopped**
- **½ small onion, finely chopped**
- **2 tablespoons fat-free egg substitute**
- **1 tablespoon chopped flat-leaf parsley**
- **1 tablespoon chopped sage**
- **Freshly ground black pepper**

1. Cut a large, deep pocket in the side of each chop with a very sharp knife.
2. Combine the bread crumbs, celery, onion, egg substitute, parsley, sage, and pepper in a medium bowl. Fill the pocket of each chop with the mixture; skewer the edges with toothpicks to hold them together, if necessary.
3. Preheat the oven to 400°F. Spray a 1-quart shallow baking pan with nonstick spray.
4. Spray a large nonstick skillet with nonstick spray and set over medium heat. Add the stuffed chops and cook, turning once, until golden brown on each side. Transfer to the baking pan; cover with foil, and bake until the meat is no longer pink and the vegetables in the stuffing are tender, about 10 minutes. Remove the foil and continue baking until the stuffing is golden and slightly crispy, 10 minutes more.

Per serving (1 chop with 2 tablespoons stuffing): 208 Cal, 9 g Fat, 3 g Sat Fat, 70 mg Chol, 101 mg Sod, 5 g Carb, 1 g Fib, 26 g Prot, 28 mg Calc. ***POINTS: 5.***

"Many of the men in my meetings are parents. They want to be good role models, and they want to be active with their kids. One man came in when his wife got pregnant. He said, 'I want to be able to play ball with my child.' He lost the weight, and he's a great dad."

—Kristen Prentiss Trapasso, Leader, Syracuse, New York

The New Pork and Beans

MAKES 6 SERVINGS

In the early days of Weight Watchers, many types of beans were virtually verboten, but frankfurters weren't—resulting in such memorable recipes as Franks and Green Beans in the first *Weight Watchers Cookbook*. Today's version turns the tables, using richly flavored, slowly baked beans, with savory spiced pork medallions taking the place of the franks.

BAKED BEANS

- **1 pound dried navy beans, soaked according to package directions**
- **1 (14-ounce) can reduced-sodium chicken broth**
- **1 cup water**
- **1 medium onion, chopped**
- **⅓ cup light molasses**
- **5 teaspoons grainy mustard**
- **4–5 teaspoons Asian-style hot chile sauce**
- **2 bacon slices, chopped**

PORK MEDALLIONS

- **1 large garlic clove**
- **¾ teaspoon salt**
- **1½ pounds pork tenderloin, well trimmed and cut into 12 (1-inch-thick) rounds**
- **1 teaspoon paprika**
- **¼ teaspoon Chesapeake Bay seasoning**
- **1 teaspoon olive or vegetable oil**

1. Combine the soaked beans, broth, and water in an ovenproof bean pot or Dutch oven; bring to a boil. Reduce the heat and simmer until just tender, 30–40 minutes.
2. Arrange the oven racks to divide the oven into thirds. Preheat the oven to 300°F. Stir the onion, molasses, mustard, chile sauce, and bacon into the beans, and return to a boil. There should be just enough broth to reach the level of the beans; if necessary, add a little water. Bake, uncovered, on the lower rack, 2 hours. Increase the oven temperature to 400°F. Continue baking until the beans are tender but not mushy, and the liquid is thickened, about 1 hour and 15 minutes more.
3. About 20 minutes before the beans are finished, prepare the pork: Finely chop the garlic on a cutting board, and sprinkle on the salt; mash to a paste with the side of a large knife. Rub paste all over the pork. Combine the paprika and Bay seasoning in a small bowl or cup; sprinkle evenly onto all sides of pork rounds.
4. Heat the oil in a large ovenproof nonstick skillet over medium-high heat, add the pork rounds, and cook until browned, 1–2 minutes per side. Bake on the upper rack of the oven, until just cooked through, 8–10 minutes. To serve, top the beans with the pork.

Per serving (generous 1 cup of beans with 2 pork rounds): 505 Cal, 10 g Fat, 3 g Sat Fat, 72 mg Chol, 700 mg Sod, 61 g Carb, 13 g Fib, 42 g Prot, 178 mg Calc. ***POINTS: 10.***

top tips

- Chesapeake Bay seasoning is a special blend of spices containing celery salt, paprika, allspice, cayenne, and dozens of other flavors. Look for it in your supermarket. Our favorite brand is Old Bay.
- Don't have an ovenproof skillet? Transfer the pork slices to a broiler pan or baking sheet and bake as directed in Step 4.

Veal Marsala

MAKES 4 SERVINGS

This dish is one of those elegantly simple preparations that will never go out of style (though many of us had our first taste of it in classy restaurants in the sixties and seventies). It's just as wonderful made with chicken or turkey breast pounded to scaloppine-like thinness.

- **4 (¼-pound) veal leg cutlets or scaloppine slices, trimmed of visible fat**
- **½ teaspoon salt**
- **Freshly ground pepper**
- **3 teaspoons olive oil**
- **1 medium onion, chopped**
- **1 tablespoon all-purpose flour**
- **2 garlic cloves, minced**
- **8 ounces shiitake mushrooms, stemmed and sliced**
- **½ cup dry Marsala**
- **½ cup reduced-sodium beef broth**
- **2 plum tomatoes, seeded and chopped**
- **2 tablespoons chopped basil**

1. Sprinkle the veal with ¼ teaspoon of the salt and a grinding of the pepper.
2. Heat a large nonstick skillet over medium-high heat. Swirl in 2 teaspoons of the oil, then add the veal. Cook until lightly browned on both sides, about 3 minutes. Transfer to a plate and keep warm.
3. Return the skillet to the heat and swirl in the remaining 1 teaspoon oil. Add the onion, flour, and garlic; cook, stirring, 30 seconds. Add the mushrooms, the remaining ¼ teaspoon salt, and another grinding of the pepper. Cook until softened, about 3 minutes. Pour in the Marsala and broth; bring to a boil and continue cooking, stirring occasionally, until slightly thickened, 2 minutes. Add the veal and tomatoes; cook 1 minute, turning the veal once, until heated through, 1 minute. Remove from the heat and stir in the basil; serve at once.

Per serving (1 cutlet with 2–3 tablespoons sauce): 205 Cal, 8 g Fat, 2 g Sat Fat, 74 mg Chol, 381 mg Sod, 12 g Carb, 2 g Fib, 20 g Prot, 38 mg Calc. ***POINTS: 4.***

top tip

Marsala is Italy's most famous fortified wine, and to make this dish without it seems unthinkable. However, dry sherry or Madiera makes a pretty good substitute. For an alcohol-free version, substitute ¼ cup each of reduced-sodium chicken broth and tart apple cider for the Marsala.

Diner-Style Meatloaf

MAKES 8 SERVINGS

Diner food was big in the fifties and made an astounding comeback in the eighties, due in no small part to the 1982 film, *Diner*. The movement also merged well with the comfort-food craze—and meatloaf was prized in both camps. Our slimmed-down version substitutes ground turkey and ground turkey breast for the fattier beef-pork-veal combination served up at the corner diner. But omit the ketchup? Never!

- **1 medium onion, finely chopped**
- **1 red bell pepper, finely chopped**
- **1 pound lean ground turkey**
- **1 pound lean ground turkey breast**
- **1 cup ketchup**
- **½ cup seasoned dried bread crumbs**
- **1 large egg white**
- **2 tablespoons prepared mustard**
- **1 teaspoon Worcestershire sauce**
- **1 teaspoon garlic powder**
- **¼ teaspoon salt**
- **¼ teaspoon freshly ground pepper**

1. Preheat the oven to 400°F. Place the oven rack in the center of the oven. Spray a baking sheet with nonstick spray.
2. Spray a large nonstick skillet with nonstick spray and set over medium-high heat. Add the onion and bell pepper; cook, stirring occasionally, until softened, about 5 minutes. Remove from the heat and let cool 10 minutes.
3. Blend together the ground turkey and turkey breast, the onion mixture, ½ cup of the ketchup, the bread crumbs, egg white, mustard, Worcestershire sauce, garlic powder, salt, and pepper in a large bowl. Transfer the mixture to the baking sheet and shape into a 5 x 10-inch loaf, about 2½ inches thick. Spread the remaining ½ cup ketchup over the top of the meat loaf. Bake until a thermometer inserted into the center of the meatloaf registers 180°F, about 50 minutes. Remove from the oven and let stand 10 minutes before slicing.

Per serving (⅛ of loaf): 245 Cal, 8 g Fat, 2 g Sat Fat, 72 mg Chol, 615 mg Sod, 16 g Carb, 1 g Fib, 27 g Prot, 47 mg Calc. ***POINTS: 5.***

Diner-Style Meatloaf and Creamed Spinach

Veal Chops with Sage and White Wine

MAKES 4 SERVINGS

Veal chops are flavorful, elegant, and easy to prepare, making this is the perfect dish to serve for last-minute company. It's so good, in fact, that you may just want to treat yourself like company and prepare it often.

- **3 tablespoons all-purpose flour**
- **4 (5-ounce) boneless veal loin chops, trimmed of all visible fat**
- **4 teaspoons olive oil**
- **1½ tablespoons chopped sage**
- **½ cup dry white wine or reduced-sodium chicken broth**
- **¼ teaspoon salt**
- **Freshly ground white pepper**
- **Sage sprigs (optional)**

1. Place the flour on a sheet of wax paper. Dip the veal into the flour, coating on both sides and shaking off the excess. (Discard any leftover flour.)
2. Heat a large nonstick skillet over medium-high heat. Swirl in the oil, then add the veal chops and sage. Cook, turning once, until golden brown and cooked through, about 8 minutes. Transfer the chops to a warmed serving platter; keep warm.
3. Add the wine or broth, salt, and pepper to the skillet; bring to a boil and cook, scraping up the browned bits from the bottom of the pan, until the liquid has reduced to ¼ cup. Pour the wine mixture over the chops; garnish with the sage sprigs, if using, and serve at once.

Per serving (1 chop with 1 tablespoon sauce): 210 Cal, 10 g Fat, 3 g Sat Fat, 94 mg Chol, 227 mg Sod, 5 g Carb, 0 g Fib, 23 g Prot, 30 mg Calc. ***POINTS: 5.***

Lamb Chops with Mint Pesto

MAKES 4 SERVINGS

No wonder lamb and mint have long been partners; the sweet freshness of the herb complements the intense flavor of the meat. Only fresh mint will bring you the right flavor; if it's unavailable, save this recipe for another time.

- **4 (¼-pound) loin lamb chops, 1-inch thick, trimmed of all visible fat**
- **1½ cups packed flat-leaf parsley**
- **½ cup packed mint leaves**
- **¼ cup reduced-sodium chicken broth**
- **3 tablespoons chopped walnuts**
- **2 tablespoons freshly grated Parmesan cheese**
- **4 teaspoons olive oil**
- **1 garlic clove, chopped**
- **¼ teaspoon salt**
- **Freshly ground pepper**
- **1 lemon, cut into 4 wedges**
- **Mint sprigs (for garnish)**

1. Remove the lamb from the refrigerator 1 hour before cooking.
2. Spray the broiler rack with nonstick spray; preheat the broiler.
3. Pulse the parsley, mint, broth, walnuts, cheese, oil, garlic, salt, and pepper in a mini food processor, scraping the sides often, until the mixture forms a coarse paste.
4. Squeeze 1 lemon wedge over each lamb chop; broil the chops 4 inches from the heat, turning once, about 7 minutes on each side for medium (subtract or add 1–2 minutes per side for rare or well-done chops). Serve each chop with a dollop of the mint pesto, and garnish all with the mint sprigs.

Per serving (1 chop with 2 tablespoons pesto): 269 Cal, 17 g Fat, 4 g Sat Fat, 77 mg Chol, 306 mg Sod, 4 g Carb, 1 g Fib, 26 g Prot, 98 mg Calc. ***POINTS: 7.***

Lamb Kebabs

MAKES 4 SERVINGS

The term kebab comes from Turkey and means "spit-roasted meat." Recipes dating back to the ancient Greeks cite chunks of lamb soaking up flavor from marinades of lemon, olive oil, and herbs—not very different from the shish kebabs we enjoy today. In this simple recipe, a variety of vegetables provide a wonderful exchange of flavors and make this meal-on-a-stick great company fare. You'll need at least 12-inch skewers, and if you're using wooden or bamboo ones, be sure to soak them in hot water for 30 minutes first so they don't catch fire on the grill.

1 onion, chopped
¼ cup dry red wine or reduced-sodium chicken broth
Grated zest of 1 lemon
3 tablespoons fresh lemon juice
4 teaspoons olive oil
1 tablespoon chopped rosemary
1 tablespoon chopped thyme
1 tablespoon chopped oregano
1 tablespoon chopped mint
1 garlic clove, minced
⅛ teaspoon crushed red pepper
15 ounces boneless beef tenderloin or boneless leg of lamb, well trimmed and cut into 1-inch cubes
1 medium onion, cut into 8 wedges (remove the thick inner pieces and reserve for another use)
1 medium green bell pepper, seeded and cut into 8 (1-inch) squares
8 medium mushroom caps
8 cherry tomatoes
½ teaspoon salt

1. Puree the chopped onion, wine or broth, lemon zest, lemon juice, oil, rosemary, thyme, oregano, mint, garlic, and red pepper in a food processor. Place the mixture in a large zip-close plastic bag; add the meat. Squeeze out the air and seal the bag; turn to coat the meat. Refrigerate, turning the bag occasionally, 30 minutes. Let the meat stand at room temperature 30 minutes; drain and discard the marinade.
2. Spray the broiler rack with nonstick spray; preheat the broiler.
3. Thread the onion wedges, bell pepper, mushroom caps, tomatoes, and meat onto 4 long skewers, beginning and ending with the onions. Set the skewers on the rack. Broil, turning once, until the meat is browned on the outside and vegetables are charred on their edges, about 5 minutes per side. Sprinkle with the salt and serve at once.

Per serving (1 kebab): 208 Cal, 9 g Fat, 3 g Sat Fat, 61 mg Chol, 352 mg Sod, 7 g Carb, 2 g Fib, 24 g Prot, 20 mg Calc. ***POINTS: 5.***

"I hid a lot of my eating—candy wrappers in drawers, that sort of thing. I was hiding behind my weight. At my first meeting, my Leader told me, 'Heather, your card states that you're only 15 years old. You are way too young to be hiding under all those clothes, and your face is too pretty to be heavy like it is.' She said it, and it was true. I had packed on mascara to draw attention from my full cheeks, and I had been hiding my body, even from myself. It took me eight months to reach my goal weight, and I felt as if I'd graduated from college. My whole life changed—I became active! I went to the junior prom! Today, nobody can believe I was ever a fat person."

—Heather Haldeman, member, Pasadena, California

"The hardest thing to convey to people is that the Program is a lifestyle change, not a diet. Sometimes, even the most educated people, in the back of their minds, still believe that once they lose the weight, they can go back to their old way of eating again. Once they overcome that, they always succeed."

—Sharon Claye, Leader, Detroit

"People learn how to use their will power and drive to reach any goal they have. They see how they can apply our **Tools for Living** to other parts of their lives. They see that they can do anything. That's what makes Weight Watchers so powerful."

—Stephanie Del Valle, Leader and Area Trainer, New York City

"Just after my second marriage, I woke up one morning and looked at my new husband sleeping beside me. I said to myself, 'I love this man so much, and I'm being given a second chance in my life. I owe it to myself to lose this weight and stay healthy, for myself.' That's when I joined the Weight Watchers Program, and I lost 40 pounds. Nobody urged me—it was my decision. For once, it wasn't about trying to fit into a dress or to look good for someone. This time, it was for me."

—Wendy Brintnall, Leader, Omaha

By the Sea

fish and shellfish

1987

The National Cholesterol Education Program (logo, below) sponsored by the National Heart, Lung, and Blood Institute, releases its first set of treatment guidelines for cholesterol lowering. The Weight Watchers Program—low in fat and saturated fat—conforms to their recommendations.

1988

The Surgeon General's Report on Nutrition and Health is published—a groundbreaking attempt to distill current information on diet and health into usable guidelines for all Americans. It stresses the importance of healthy weight; the Weight Watchers Plan, again, is in sync.

1989

Jean Nidetch is honored by the Horatio Alger Association as an inspiration to all Americans. Also this year, talk-show host Oprah Winfrey loses 67 pounds after following a stringent liquid diet. By 1992, she gains back 80-some pounds and reaches her highest weight ever.

>>>

Baked Halibut with Lemon and Capers

MAKES 4 SERVINGS

A recipe for Halibut Broil in the first *Weight Watchers Cookbook* tried to re-create the pleasures of a time-honored way to cook fish: baking it with a crust of flavorful bread crumbs. The only thing missing was the bread crumbs! Our update brings the dish back to its original roots, with a savory herbed bread crumb topping. Use the freshest fish you can find; if halibut isn't available, flounder, sole, red snapper, catfish, and cod are also good choices.

4 (¼-pound) halibut fillets
¼ cup fresh lemon juice
4 teaspoons olive oil
2 tablespoons plain dried bread crumbs
2 tablespoons capers, drained
¼ teaspoon salt
Freshly ground pepper
½ cup minced flat-leaf parsley
4 lemon wedges

1. Preheat the oven to 350°F. Spray 9 x 13-inch baking dish with nonstick spray.
2. Place the fillets skin-side down in the baking dish; sprinkle them with the lemon juice. Brush each fillet with the oil, then sprinkle with the bread crumbs, capers, salt, and pepper.
3. Bake until the fish flakes easily when tested with a fork, 15–20 minutes, depending on the thickness of the fish. Spoon any pan juices over the fish and sprinkle with the parsley. Serve at once, with the lemon wedges.

Per serving (1 fillet): 168 Cal, 6 g Fat, 1 g Sat Fat, 60 mg Chol, 388 mg Sod, 5 g Carb, 1 g Fib, 22 g Prot, 40 mg Calc. ***POINTS: 4.***

Moroccan Monkfish with Couscous

MAKES 4 SERVINGS

Monkfish is a very firm-fleshed white fish that some people consider a close cousin to lobster in taste and texture. Its partner in this dish, couscous, is a staple of North African and Middle Eastern cuisines. Couscous' popularity keeps on growing in this country, thanks to our fascination with all things Mediterranean and all things quick-cooking. A pasta rather than a grain, it's made of tiny balls of semolina dough, which are steamed and then dried. It can be found in most supermarkets and cooks in just a few minutes.

4 teaspoons olive oil
1 onion, chopped
1 green bell pepper, chopped
4 (5-ounce) monkfish fillets
1 (14-ounce) can diced tomatoes
1 cup fish broth or bottled clam juice
Juice of 1 lemon
½ cup chopped flat-leaf parsley
1 teaspoon ground cumin
1 garlic clove, chopped
½ teaspoon turmeric
¼ teaspoon salt
Freshly ground black pepper
1 cup couscous
¼ cup dry white wine or reduced-sodium chicken broth

1. Heat a large nonstick skillet. Swirl in 2 teaspoons of the oil, then add the onion and green pepper. Sauté until wilted, about 5 minutes. Transfer to a heatproof plate and keep warm.
2. Return the skillet to the heat; swirl in the remaining 2 teaspoons oil, then add the monkfish. Cook, turning once, until lightly browned on each side. Place the onion-pepper mixture on top of the fish in the skillet; add the tomatoes, broth, lemon juice, parsley, cumin, garlic, turmeric, salt, and pepper. Stir gently, then cover and cook, stirring the vegetables and turning the fish occasionally, until the fish flakes when tested with a fork, about 12 minutes. Transfer the fish and vegetables to a warmed platter; keep warm.
3. Meanwhile, cook the couscous according to package directions.
4. Add the wine or broth to the remaining liquid in the skillet; cook over high heat, stirring, until thickened and reduced by half. Spoon over the fish and serve with the couscous.

Per serving (1 fillet with 1 cup couscous and ½ cup sauce): 396 Cal, 7 g Fat, 1 g Sat Fat, 80 mg Chol, 571 mg Sod, 46 g Carb, 5 g Fib, 36 g Prot, 93 mg Calc. ***POINTS: 8.***

Cajun Catfish and Sweet Potato Fritters

Cajun Catfish

MAKES 4 SERVINGS

No wonder we all fell in love with Cajun cuisine in the eighties. This fascinating hybrid of French and Southern culinary influences makes great use of crawfish, chicken, pork, and seasonal game. It also often includes filé powder (from the sassafras tree), parsley, bay leaves, cayenne, black pepper, and a variety of hot peppers as its signature spices. This recipe evokes some of those flavors. Although it calls for catfish, red snapper is an excellent alternative.

¼ cup all-purpose flour
¼ cup chopped flat-leaf parsley
2 teaspoons ground cumin
1 teaspoon dried oregano
1 teaspoon dried thyme
½ teaspoon cayenne
¼ teaspoon salt
¼ cup fat-free egg substitute
4 (6-ounce) catfish fillets
4 teaspoons vegetable oil
Chopped flat-leaf parsley (optional)

1. Combine the flour, parsley, cumin, oregano, thyme, cayenne, and salt on a sheet of wax paper. Place the egg substitute in a shallow dish.
2. Dip the fish first in the egg substitute, then coat lightly with the flour mixture and transfer to a plate. (Discard any leftover egg or flour mixture.) Cover the fish and refrigerate for 30 minutes.
3. Heat a large nonstick skillet over medium heat. Swirl in the oil, then add the fish. Cook, turning once, until it is golden brown and flakes easily when tested with a fork, about 10 minutes. Sprinkle with the additional chopped parsley, if using, and serve at once.

Per serving (1 fillet): 261 Cal, 7 g Fat, 1 g Sat Fat, 104 mg Chol, 330 mg Sod, 7 g Carb, 1 g Fib, 39 g Prot, 55 mg Calc. ***POINTS: 6.***

top tip

How long will the fish take to cook? Here's a good rule of thumb: Lay the fish flat and measure it at its thickest point. Count on approximately 10 minutes of cooking time for each inch of thickness.

Blackened Redfish with Remoulade

MAKES 4 SERVINGS

The eighties saw the arrival of Cajun cuisine on a national level. Paul Prudhomme, one of New Orleans's most famous chefs, brought the notion of blackening into our homes with his frequent television appearances—and Blackened Redfish remains one of his signature dishes. Be sure to serve this classic with some steamed brown rice or Cajun-style "dirty" rice.

- **6 tablespoons reduced-fat mayonnaise**
- **½ small onion, finely chopped**
- **2 tablespoons chopped parsley**
- **1 tablespoon fresh lemon juice**
- **2 teaspoons drained capers, chopped**
- **1 teaspoon Dijon mustard**
- **½ teaspoon sugar**
- **1 tablespoon Cajun seasoning mix**
- **2 teaspoons paprika**
- **2 teaspoons canola oil**
- **4 (6-ounce) red snapper fillets, skin left on**

1. To prepare the remoulade (a French cousin of tartar sauce), combine the mayonnaise, onion, parsley, lemon juice, capers, mustard, and sugar in a medium bowl; blend well and set aside.
2. Combine the Cajun seasoning and paprika on a piece of wax paper. Heat a large nonstick skillet over medium-high heat until hot; swirl in the oil. Dip the flesh side of each snapper fillet into the seasoning mixture, then immediately place flesh-side down into the hot skillet. Repeat with the remaining seasoning mixture and fillets. Cook, turning once, until the skin is blackened and the fish flakes easily with a fork, about 4 minutes. Serve immediately with the remoulade.

Per serving (1 fillet with 2 tablespoons remoulade): 259 Cal, 12 g Fat, 2 g Sat Fat, 97 mg Chol, 762 mg Sod, 4 g Carb, 1 g Fib, 32 g Prot, 34 mg Calc. ***POINTS: 6.***

top tip

If red snapper isn't available in your fish market, any small, firm-fleshed, mild fish will do, such as grouper, sea bass, or even catfish. The versatile blackening mix is also delicious and cooks beautifully on boneless skinless chicken breast halves, pork chops, or shrimp.

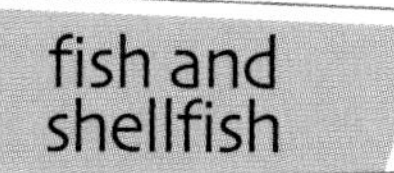

Salmon en Papillote

MAKES 4 SERVINGS

Doesn't Salmon en Papillote, which includes the classic French term for baking a dish in parchment or foil, sound a lot better than Boiled Fish in Paper? That recipe, from the first *Weight Watchers Cookbook*, needed an upgrade in both title and preparation. It called for soaking the fish in a salt solution, wrapping it in a foil bag with dehydrated onion flakes, parsley, lemon juice, and chopped pimiento, and cooking it in a kettle of boiling water. Our new version is a lot simpler: We just pop a packet of fish and fresh vegetables in the oven. And we're no longer afraid to use an oily fish like salmon, a rich source of heart-healthy omega-3 fatty acids. Serve this dinner-in-an-envelope with Asparagus en Papillote [page 196], and you've got yourself a virtually pot-and-pan-free dinner.

- **4 carrots, peeled and cut into matchstick-size pieces**
- **1 fennel bulb, cleaned and very thinly sliced**
- **1 leek, cleaned and thinly sliced**
- **2 medium (5-ounce) potatoes, peeled and cut into matchstick-size pieces**
- **4 (¼-pound) salmon fillets**
- **½ cup hot reduced-sodium vegetable broth**
- **4 tablespoons dry white wine**
- **4 teaspoons olive oil**
- **2 tablespoons chopped dill**
- **1 tablespoon grated peeled fresh ginger**
- **½ teaspoon salt**
- **Freshly ground pepper**
- **4 lemon slices**
- **Dill sprigs (optional)**

1. Preheat the oven to 425°F.
2. Combine the carrots, fennel, leek, and potatoes in a steamer basket; set in a saucepan over 1 inch of boiling water. Cover tightly and steam until slightly wilted but still crunchy, 2 minutes.
3. Tear off 4 (12-inch) squares of foil. Divide the vegetable mixture in half, then evenly divide one-half among the foil squares, placing the vegetables in the center of each square. Top with the salmon, then with another layer of the remaining vegetables. Spoon 2 tablespoons of the hot broth over each salmon-vegetable stack, then drizzle each with a tablespoon of wine and a teaspoon of oil. Sprinkle with the dill, ginger, salt, and pepper, then top with a lemon slice.
4. Fold the foil into packets, making a tight seal. Place the packets on a baking sheet and bake until just opaque in the center, about 15 minutes (watch for escaping steam as you open the foil to check). Place each packet on a serving plate. Standing back to avoid the steam, cut each packet open slightly in the center. Garnish with the dill sprigs, if using, and serve at once.

Per serving (1 fillet with 1 cup vegetables): 323 Cal, 11 g Fat, 3 g Sat Fat, 75 mg Chol, 454 mg Sod, 28 g Carb, 6 g Fib, 27 g Prot, 89 mg Calc. ***POINTS: 7.***

top tip

To clean the leek, trim the roots, leaving the root end intact to hold the layers together. Slice it in half lengthwise, fan open the layers, and swish them in a large bowl of cool water. Let stand a few minutes to allow the grit to fall to the bottom, then lift the leek halves out.

Tabbouleh Niçoise

MAKES 4 SERVINGS

It's an old Weight Watchers trick to find substitutes for potatoes, which were once a "limited" treat on the program. Here, we've used bulgur—steamed and dried cracked wheat—as a substitute for the boiled potatoes traditionally served in a Niçoise salad. The result? Chewier texture, nuttier flavor, and a lot more fiber and magnesium, to boot.

- **3 cups boiling water**
- **1 cup bulgur**
- **1 pound tuna steaks**
- **1 teaspoon salt**
- **½ teaspoon coarsely ground pepper**
- **½ red onion, thinly sliced**
- **2 tablespoons red-wine vinegar**
- **1 tablespoon extra-virgin olive oil**
- **¼ teaspoon sugar**
- **1 cup thinly sliced romaine lettuce**
- **1 cup halved grape or cherry tomatoes**
- **⅓ cup slivered basil leaves**
- **8 pitted kalamata olives, halved**

1. Pour the boiling water over the bulgur in a large heatproof bowl; cover and let stand 30 minutes. Drain well.
2. Meanwhile, sprinkle both sides of the tuna with ½ teaspoon of the salt and the pepper. Spray a nonstick skillet with nonstick spray and heat over high heat. Add the tuna and sear 1 minute per side for a red center, 2 minutes per side for medium. Cool and thinly slice.
3. Combine the onion, vinegar, oil, the remaining ½ teaspoon of the salt, and the sugar in a large bowl. Add the drained bulgur, the lettuce, tomatoes, basil and olives; toss to coat evenly. Arrange the salad on a platter and top with the tuna slices, fanned out into an attractive pattern.

Per serving (1¼ cups salad with about 3 ounces tuna): 343 Cal, 10 g Fat, 2 g Sat Fat, 43 mg Chol, 708 mg Sod, 32 g Carb, 8 g Fib, 32 g Prot, 46 mg Calc. ***POINTS: 7.***

"When I joined [Weight Watchers] I was 50 pounds overweight, and I had just overdosed on diet pills and was hospitalized. My doctor told me, 'If you take another diet pill, I won't be responsible for you.' That was the turning point for me."

—Florine Mark, Franchise Owner, Detroit

Tabbouleh Niçoise

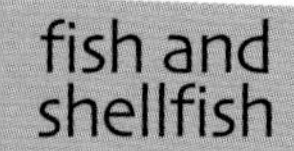

Soy-Sesame Grilled Tuna

MAKES 4 SERVINGS

In the Asian food–obsessed nineties, this flavorful dish would have been right at home on any elegant restaurant menu. It's simple—and impressive—to make at home too. If you prefer your tuna medium or rare, which some people do these days, just reduce the grilling time accordingly.

- **2 tablespoons reduced-sodium soy sauce**
- **2 tablespoons fresh lemon juice**
- **2 tablespoons dry white wine or reduced-sodium vegetable broth**
- **2 teaspoons sesame oil**
- **2 garlic cloves, minced**
- **Freshly ground pepper**
- **4 (6-ounce) tuna steaks, 1½ inches thick**

1. Combine the soy sauce, lemon juice, wine or broth, oil, garlic, and 2 grindings of the pepper in a large zip-close plastic bag; add the tuna. Squeeze out the air and seal the bag; turn to coat the tuna. Refrigerate, turning the bag once or twice, 30 minutes. Remove the tuna from the marinade; discard the marinade.
2. Spray the grill rack with nonstick spray; prepare the grill.
3. Grill the tuna 5 inches from the heat, turning once, until the outside is golden and the center is barely pink, about 13 minutes.

Per serving (1 steak): 226 Cal, 9 g Fat, 3 g Sat Fat, 101 mg Chol, 167 mg Sod, 1 g Carb, 0 g Fib, 33 g Prot, 20 mg Calc. ***POINTS: 5.***

top tips

- Add some extra flavor by tossing a handful of soaked fruitwoods, mesquite, or whole herb sprigs on the fire just before grilling the fish.
- You can also make this dish in the broiler: Spray the broiler rack with nonstick spray, and preheat the broiler. Broil 5 inches from the heat until barely pink in the center, about 6 to 7 minutes on each side.

Crab Cocktail with Homemade Cocktail Sauce

MAKES 4 SERVINGS

For those who believe that shrimp cocktail is the highlight of retro cuisine, we present an equally heavenly version, made with sweet crabmeat instead. For the best appearance, lump or jumbo-lump crabmeat is preferable to pasteurized canned or frozen crabmeat; look for it in fish markets or better supermarkets. Serve the cocktail plain or with melba toast rounds or water crackers.

- **½ cup ketchup-based chili sauce (such as Heinz)**
- **4 teaspoons prepared horseradish, drained**
- **5 teaspoons fresh lemon juice**
- **12 ounces jumbo-lump crabmeat, picked over**
- **1 celery stalk, finely chopped**
- **½ small red onion, finely chopped**
- **1 tablespoon chopped fresh parsley**

1. Combine the chili sauce, horseradish, and 3 teaspoons of the lemon juice in a small bowl.
2. Combine the crabmeat, celery, onion, the remaining 2 teaspoons lemon juice, and the parsley in a medium bowl; mix gently. Serve chilled with the cocktail sauce.

Per serving (½ cup with 2 tablespoons sauce): 126 Cal, 2 g Fat, 0 g Sat Fat, 85 mg Chol, 609 mg Sod, 10 g Carb, 1 g Fib, 18 g Prot, 105 mg Calc. ***POINTS: 2.***

> Ask anybody who's following a strict diet: Sometimes they just blow it. Then they go overboard the next day because they think it's all over. But there's no such thing as blowing it on the ***POINTS*** Food System.
>
> *—Felice Lippert, Cofounder, Weight Watchers International*

Crab Cakes with Tartar Sauce

MAKES 4 SERVINGS

These wonderful crab cakes are all about crab. We've made them without any bread-crumb filler so that each bite is pure seafood delight. Tartar sauce a taboo, you say? Not today, we say. Enjoy!

- **½ cup + ⅓ cup reduced-fat mayonnaise**
- **2 tablespoons chopped parsley**
- **2 tablespoons pickle relish**
- **1 tablespoon drained capers**
- **1 large egg, lightly beaten**
- **2 teaspoons Dijon mustard**
- **1 teaspoon Chesapeake Bay seasoning**
- **½ teaspoon Worcestershire sauce**
- **1 pound fresh, canned, or thawed frozen lump crabmeat, picked over**

1. Preheat oven to 400°F. Spray a baking sheet with nonstick spray.
2. To prepare the tartar sauce, combine ½ cup of the mayonnaise, the parsley, relish, and capers in a small bowl. Cover and refrigerate until ready to use.
3. Combine the remaining ⅓ cup mayonnaise, the egg, mustard, Chesapeake Bay seasoning, and Worcestershire sauce in a large bowl; mix well. Gently fold in the crabmeat until well combined. Cover and refrigerate 30 minutes.
4. Divide the crab mixture into 8 portions, and shape each into a ½-inch-thick patty. Spray a large nonstick skillet with nonstick spray and set over medium heat. Add 4 of the crab cakes and cook, turning once, until light golden, 4 minutes. Transfer to the baking sheet and repeat with the remaining crab cakes. Bake until the crab cakes until heated through, about 5 minutes. Serve with the tartar sauce.

Per serving (2 cakes with 3 tablespoons sauce): 300 Cal, 20 g Fat, 3 g Sat Fat, 183 mg Chol, 1,090 mg Sod, 4 g Carb, 0 g Fib, 25 g Prot, 133 mg Calc. ***POINTS: 8.***

top tips

- Chesapeake Bay seasoning, a special blend of spices containing celery salt, paprika, allspice, cayenne, and dozens of other flavors, gives these crab cakes authentic flavor and tang. Look for it in your supermarket spice section; Old Bay is the best-known brand.
- Crab cakes are a great do-ahead dish. Make the recipe up to shaping the patties, then wrap each patty individually in plastic wrap. Freeze the wrapped crab cakes in a zip-close freezer bag for up to a month. To use them, simply defrost the cakes in the refrigerator overnight, then proceed with the recipe at Step 4.

Mussels in White Wine with Garlic

MAKES 4 SERVINGS

This is one of those timeless dishes that always seems festive (even though mussels remain one of the best bargains in the fish market). In our version, we've doubled the satisfaction: After you've polished off your last mussel, there's still a delicious piece of toasted bread soaked with all that wonderful broth in the bottom of your dish to enjoy.

- **4 pounds mussels**
- **2 teaspoons olive oil**
- **1 medium shallot, chopped**
- **3 large garlic cloves, minced**
- **¼ cup dry white wine or reduced-sodium vegetable broth**
- **2 tablespoons chopped thyme**
- **4 (1-ounce) slices French or Italian bread, toasted**

1. Scrub the mussels well with a vegetable brush under cold running water. Pull off the hairy beards that may be attached to some of the mussel shells; if it's difficult, use a small knife. Place the mussels in a large pot of cold water; let them soak a few minutes to release any residual grit, then drain. Repeat for several changes of water, until no sand falls to the bottom of the pot.
2. Heat a large nonstick saucepan. Swirl in the oil, then add the shallot. Sauté until golden, 3 minutes. Add the garlic and sauté until just fragrant. Add the mussels, wine or broth, and thyme; cook, covered, shaking the pan occasionally, until the mussels open, about 5 minutes. Discard any that don't open.
3. Place a slice of the bread into each of 4 large soup bowls. Ladle the mussels with their shells and broth into the bowls and serve at once.

Per serving (about 30 mussels with 1 slice bread and ¼ cup broth): 203 Cal, 5 g Fat, 1 g Sat Fat, 45 mg Chol, 543 mg Sod, 19 g Carb, 1 g Fib, 20 g Prot, 97 mg Calc. ***POINTS: 4.***

top tip

If they're available at your fish market, farm-raised mussels are a more convenient choice for this dish. They tend to be cleaner and rarely have any beards, so they save you lots of prep time.

Prosciutto-Wrapped Scallops and Asparagus en Papillote

Prosciutto-Wrapped Scallops

MAKES 4 SERVINGS

Prosciutto is ham that has been salt-cured and air-dried rather than smoked, producing an incomparably sweet-tasting, firm-textured meat. Pairing it with sweet scallops is a match made in heaven. You don't have to buy the priciest, best prosciutto (which hails from Parma, Italy) for this recipe; domestic prosciutto is fine, as long as it is sliced paper-thin.

- **1 cup orange juice**
- **¼ cup balsamic vinegar**
- **1 teaspoon sugar**
- **1 teaspoon grated orange zest**
- **5 paper-thin proscuitto slices (about 2½ ounces)**
- **1 pound jumbo sea scallops (about 20)**

1. Preheat oven to 450°F. Spray a baking sheet with nonstick spray.
2. Combine the juice, vinegar, and sugar in a medium saucepan. Bring to a boil over high heat; continue boiling until syrupy, about 8 minutes. Remove from the heat and stir in the zest.
3. Place one slice of proscuitto on a cutting board; slice into 4 (¾ x 5-inch) strips. Repeat with the remaining proscuitto. Wrap each scallop in a proscuitto strip and place it, seam-side down, on the baking sheet. Bake the scallops 5 minutes; brush them with the orange-balsamic syrup and roast until cooked through, 2–3 minutes more. Brush the scallops with any remaining syrup just before serving.

Per serving (5 scallops): 148 Cal, 2 g Fat, 1 g Sat Fat, 33 mg Chol, 425 mg Sod, 11 g Carb, 0 g Fib, 21 g Prot, 94 mg Calc. ***POINTS: 3.***

Spicy Grilled Shrimp and Scallops

MAKES 4 SERVINGS

Served hot or at room temperature, as an hors d'oeuvre, appetizer, or entrée, this fare from the deep blue is a real crowd pleaser. Adjust the cayenne and paprika up or down ¼ teaspoon, depending on how hot or mild you like your food.

- **4 teaspoons olive oil**
- **2 teaspoons fresh lemon juice**
- **2 garlic cloves, minced**
- **½ teaspoon paprika**
- **½ teaspoon kosher salt**
- **¼ teaspoon cayenne**
- **½ pound medium shrimp, peeled and deveined**
- **½ pound bay scallops, rinsed and patted dry with paper towels**
- **4 lemon wedges**

1. Spray the broiler rack with nonstick spray; preheat the broiler.
2. Combine the oil, lemon juice, garlic, paprika, salt, and cayenne in a medium bowl. Toss with the shrimp and scallops, then place them on the broiler rack. Broil until golden brown on both sides, turning once, 6–8 minutes. Serve at once with the lemon wedges.

Per serving (4 ounces): 116 Cal, 5 g Fat, 1 g Sat Fat, 65 mg Chol, 349 mg Sod, 3 g Carb, 1 g Fib, 14 g Prot, 59 mg Calc. ***POINTS: 3.***

top tips

- Bay scallops are small (about ½- to ¾-inch diameter) and have a wonderfully sweet flavor. They're rather pricey but worth the splurge. The larger, somewhat less tender sea scallops can be used if you prefer, but cut them into halves or quarters, depending on their size. And pass up those tiny calico scallops, which can become rubbery during cooking.
- Why kosher salt? Thanks to its larger crystalline structure, kosher salt retains a little crunchiness as it coats the shrimp. It also contains fewer crystals per teaspoon than table salt, so you'll get a little less sodium. Use table salt if you prefer, but use less: A heaping ¼ teaspoon or so should deliver the same amount of saltiness.

Paella Valenciana

MAKES 6 SERVINGS

Paella is arguably Spain's most beloved dish—and in the sixties it was the ultimate dinner-party entrée. Nowadays, it's easier to find its core ingredients, but the dish hasn't lost any of its glamour. Our streamlined version is still perfect for serving to company or for a Sunday family dinner.

- **16 littleneck clams**
- **1 tablespoon extra-virgin olive oil**
- **8 ounces skinless boneless chicken thighs, trimmed of visible fat and cut into 1-inch chunks**
- **2 medium red bell peppers, chopped**
- **1 medium yellow onion, chopped**
- **4 ounces turkey kielbasa, sliced ¼ inch thick**
- **4 garlic cloves, chopped**
- **½ teaspoon saffron threads, crushed**
- **1 cup reduced-sodium chicken broth**
- **¾ cup long-grain white rice**
- **½ cup frozen peas**
- **½ pound large shrimp, peeled and deveined**
- **1 (15-ounce) can quartered artichoke hearts, drained**

1. Scrub the clams well with a vegetable brush under cold running water. Place them in a large pot of cold water; let them soak a few minutes to release any residual grit, then drain. Repeat for several changes of water until no sand falls to the bottom of the pot.
2. Heat a large nonstick skillet over medium-high heat. Swirl in the oil, then add the chicken, peppers, onion, kielbasa, garlic, and saffron. Cook, stirring occasionally, until the vegetables begin to soften, 2–3 minutes. Add the broth, rice, and peas; bring to a boil. Reduce the heat to medium-low, cover, and simmer 15 minutes.
3. Add the clams, shrimp, and artichoke hearts to the skillet; cover and cook until the clams open and the shrimp are pink and opaque, about 10 minutes longer. Serve at once.

Per serving (1½ cups): 286 Cal, 6 g Fat, 1 g Sat Fat, 80 mg Chol, 491 mg Sod, 33 g Carb, 5 g Fib, 25 g Prot, 76 mg Calc. ***POINTS: 5.***

top tip

Saffron, the key flavoring and coloring element of this dish, is the world's most expensive spice. But cheaper substitutes just won't do for an authentic paella. Saffron strands are the stigmas of a small purple crocus, and each flower only yields three stigmas. The stigmas must be painstakingly harvested by hand, then dried. To make 1 ounce of saffron it takes close to 15,000 stigmas! Luckily, a little goes a long way in imparting its distinctive flavor to the dish. Look for saffron threads (not the inferior powdered form) in gourmet stores and better supermarkets.

Tuna Noodle Casserole

MAKES 6 SERVINGS

One reason this sixties classic is so timeless is its convenience. Designed to use canned and frozen ingredients and pantry staples, it's one of those meals you can assemble on a dime. We've given it a fresher spin, with fresh herbs and sautéed mushrooms, but kept the beloved potato-chip topping.

- **6 cups extra-wide egg noodles**
- **1 (10-ounce) can reduced-fat condensed cream of mushroom soup**
- **1 cup low-fat (1%) milk**
- **2 tablespoons unsalted light butter**
- **2 garlic cloves, minced**
- **2 cups sliced white mushrooms (8 ounces)**
- **4 scallions, chopped**
- **1 cup frozen peas**
- **2 teaspoons chopped thyme**
- **2 teaspoons chopped rosemary**
- **2 (6-ounce) cans solid white tuna in water, rinsed, drained, and flaked**
- **¼ cup chopped parsley**
- **1 ounce reduced-fat baked potato chips, lightly crushed (about 1 cup)**

1. Preheat the oven to 350°F. Spray an 8-inch-square baking pan with nonstick spray. Cook the noodles according to package directions; drain and keep warm.
2. Combine the soup and milk in a large bowl; set aside.
3. Melt the butter in a large nonstick skillet over medium-high heat. Add the garlic and sauté until fragrant, 30 seconds. Stir in the mushrooms, scallions, peas, thyme, and rosemary; cook, stirring occasionally, until the mushrooms are softened, about 5 minutes. Stir into the soup mixture. Add the noodles, tuna, and parsley; toss well. Transfer to the baking pan and sprinkle with the potato chips. Bake until bubbly and the top is golden, 30–35 minutes.

Per serving (generous 1 cup): 314 Cal, 7 g Fat, 3 g Sat Fat, 58 mg Chol, 462 mg Sod, 40 g Carb, 3 g Fib, 22 g Prot, 104 mg Calc. ***POINTS: 6.***

Tuna Noodle Casserole

California Rolls

MAKES 8 SERVINGS

Most Americans became acquainted with sushi through a Japanese-American creation known as the California roll. With cooked crabmeat (or its close cousin, surimi) rather than raw fish in its center, it was a good gateway dish for the timid. But even sushi aficionados love these beautiful, flavorful easy-to-make rolls. Serve them the traditional way, if you like, with a little reduced-sodium soy sauce for dipping, a dab of wasabi paste, thin slices of pink, pickled ginger—and of course, chopsticks.

- **2 cups water**
- **1½ cups short-grain rice**
- **3 tablespoons rice vinegar**
- **1 tablespoon sugar**
- **¼ teaspoon salt**
- **8 sheets nori**
- **1 teaspoon prepared wasabi paste**
- **1 Hass avocado, peeled, pitted, and cut into 16 long, thin strips**
- **10 ounces surimi (imitation crabmeat), cut into long, thin strips**
- **2 teaspoons toasted sesame seeds**

1. Combine the water and rice in a medium saucepan. Bring to a boil, reduce the heat to medium-low, and simmer, covered, until the water evaporates, about 20 minutes. Remove from the heat and let stand 10 minutes. Meanwhile, combine the vinegar, sugar, and salt in a small bowl. Stir into the rice, tossing gently with a spatula to combine, and let cool 15 minutes.
2. Place a bamboo sushi mat on a work surface so that the slats run horizontally. Put a nori sheet, with a long side facing you, on top of the mat. With moistened hands, spread ½ cup of the vinegared rice onto it, leaving a 1-inch border along the top edge. Spread ⅛ teaspoon of the wasabi paste horizontally across the center of the rice. Arrange 2 avocado slices end to end in a horizontal line over the wasabi, and top with one-eighth of the surimi. Sprinkle with ¼ teaspoon of the sesame seeds. Grasp the edges of the nori and the mat closest to you. Roll the nori evenly and tightly away from you, pressing down slightly with each quarter turn. Seal the roll with a few drops of water on the far edge of the nori, being sure to press the seam closed. Repeat with the remaining rice, wasabi, avocado, surimi, and sesame seeds to make 8 rolls. If not serving immediately, cover the rolls with plastic wrap and refrigerate up to 6 hours.
3. Just before serving, place the rolls on a cutting board. With a serrated knife dipped in hot water, cut each roll crosswise into 6 pieces.

Per serving (1 (6-piece) roll): 212 Cal, 4 g Fat, 1 g Sat Fat, 11 mg Chol, 399 mg Sod, 35 g Carb, 3 g Fib, 9 g Prot, 26 mg Calc. ***POINTS: 4.***

"When I went to the [New York City Department of Health Obesity] Clinic, it was the first time in my life I'd seen a diet that didn't start with the words, 'Do not eat the following.' Instead, it started with, 'You must eat.' Imagine that—you must eat the following!"

—Jean Nidetch

"One woman joined with her husband about a year and a half ago. She had so many health problems—she was in a wheelchair, she had back pain, she had been on oxygen for a period of time...and for the first month, even though she did everything right, she gained weight. Yet she stuck with it, and now she's lost more than 100 pounds (her husband just became a Lifetime Member). Now she's walking, and she and her husband are active together. Not everyone loses weight right away, but we can all succeed."

—Kristen Prentiss Trapasso, Leader, Syracuse, New York

"One of my member's husband told her, 'If you don't lose 90 pounds, I'm out of here.' And she did—she made her goal. Two weeks later, she came in and told me he had left her. 'But that's OK,' she said. 'I'm back to hunting weight.' She knew he had given her an ultimatum he had expected her to fail, and he'd lost."

—Wendy Brintnall, Leader, Omaha

"I remember a man who had lost 100 pounds or so. He found a bulge on his chest. His wife said, 'Oh, that's just a bone—we couldn't see it before because you were so heavy.' But he went to the doctor anyway—and it turned out that he had a very rare form of breast cancer. His doctor wrote us to say that if he hadn't lost that weight and found that lump, he probably would have been dead within a year."

—Florine Mark, Franchise Owner, Detroit

It's Easy Being Green

1990

McDonald's McLean, a new reduced-fat (12 grams) hamburger, arrives on the fast-food scene—and departs after several years of lackluster sales.

The Department of Health and Human Services releases its "Healthy People 2000" health objectives; Weight Watchers is a major sponsor of the national launch in Washington, D.C.

1992

The USDA releases the Food Guide Pyramid, which emphasizes eating more grains, fruits, and vegetables, and less meat, dairy products, and fats.

Weight Watchers sponsors Women and Weight: The Risks, the Reason, Resolutions for Empowerment, a major health communications symposium.

1993

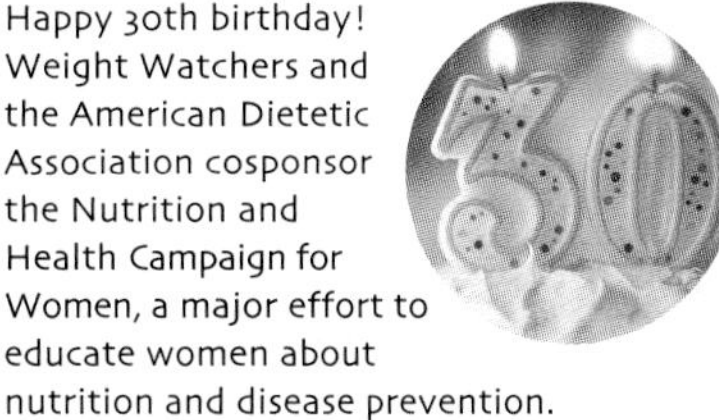

Happy 30th birthday! Weight Watchers and the American Dietetic Association cosponsor the Nutrition and Health Campaign for Women, a major effort to educate women about nutrition and disease prevention.

>>>

Cauliflower Casserole, Pizza-Style

MAKES 6 SERVINGS

In the distant Weight Watchers past, many a "pizza" was made using cauliflower as the "crust" and cooked-down tomato juice as the "sauce." Today's version packs a lot more flavor and cheesy goodness but still keeps the inspiration. Use marinara sauce from a jar, or try our easy recipe [see page 78].

- **1 medium (2-pound) cauliflower head, trimmed and separated into florets**
- **2 cups low-fat marinara sauce**
- **¼ cup seasoned dried bread crumbs**
- **1 cup shredded part-skim mozzarella cheese**
- **2 tablespoons freshly grated Parmesan cheese**

1. Preheat the oven to 350°F.
2. Fill a medium saucepan two-thirds full with water and bring to a boil; add the cauliflower. Reduce the heat and simmer until the cauliflower is tender-crisp, 8–10 minutes; drain.
3. Spread 1 cup of the sauce in the bottom of an 8-inch-square baking dish or 9-inch pie plate. Add the cauliflower, then sprinkle with the bread crumbs. Pour the remaining sauce evenly over, then sprinkle with the mozzarella and Parmesan cheeses. Cover with foil and bake until the cauliflower is soft and the cheese is melted, about 30 minutes.

Per serving (¾ cup): 139 Cal, 6 g Fat, 3 g Sat Fat, 12 mg Chol, 566 mg Sod, 14 g Carb, 3 g Fib, 9 g Prot, 217 mg Calc. ***POINTS: 3.***

> "Back in the old days of Weight Watchers, we used a lot of cauliflower, and I still do today. We used it the way some people now use tofu; it's a great extender. You can make it into a sauce, blend it into a soup, or add it to a meat loaf—you don't even know it's there, and it doesn't add any ***POINTS***."
>
> *—Carol Kramer, Manager, New Service Development and Training (and former Leader), Weight Watchers International*

Cheese Sauce

MAKES 6 SERVINGS

Even the earliest *Weight Watchers Cookbook* included a recipe for cheese sauce; then, as now, it was a great way to top vegetables deliciously. Try this rich, creamy version on cauliflower, broccoli, or asparagus. It just may get you to eat more vegetables!

- **½ cup evaporated fat-free milk**
- **3 tablespoons all-purpose flour**
- **¾ cup low-fat (1%) milk**
- **2 teaspoons Dijon mustard**
- **½ teaspoon salt**
- **½ cup shredded reduced-fat sharp cheddar cheese**
- **¼ teaspoon ground pepper**

1. Whisk together the evaporated milk and flour in a small saucepan until smooth. Whisk in the low-fat milk, mustard, and salt. Bring to a simmer and cook, stirring frequently, until the sauce is slightly thickened, 4 minutes.
2. Stir in the cheddar cheese and pepper. Remove from the heat and stir until the cheese has just melted and the sauce is smooth. Serve at once.

Per serving (3 tablespoons): 72 Cal, 2 g Fat, 1 g Sat Fat, 7 mg Chol, 305 mg Sod, 7 g Carb, 0 g Fib, 6 g Prot, 171 mg Calc. ***POINTS: 2.***

top tip

Today, it's easy to find reduced-fat cheeses in the supermarket dairy section. To get the most flavor, look for sharp cheddar, with the fat reduced by 50 percent (cheddar with a greater fat reduction tends to be too rubbery). You can also find reduced-fat cheddar preshredded and sold in plastic bags.

Green Bean Casserole

Green Bean Casserole

MAKES 4 SERVINGS

This beloved dish comes straight out of the fifties: Made with canned and/or frozen components, it epitomizes that era's penchant for convenience food in all forms. Yet it still finds a place on our tables today, especially around the holidays. We've found a way to capture that same convenience (and that irresistible crunch of those canned French-fried onions) without blowing the ***POINTS*** budget. Life is good!

- **4 cups frozen cut green beans**
- **1 medium onion, chopped**
- **1 teaspoon sugar**
- **1 (12-ounce) can reduced-fat condensed cream of mushroom soup**
- **¾ cup reduced-fat shredded sharp cheddar cheese**
- **1 teaspoon Worcestershire sauce**
- **½ teaspoon garlic powder**
- **½ cup French-fried onions**

1. Preheat the oven to 350°F. Spray an 8-inch-square baking pan with nonstick spray.
2. Cook the green beans according to package directions on the stovetop or in the microwave. Drain and transfer to a large bowl.
3. Spray a small nonstick skillet with nonstick spray and set over medium-high heat. Add the onion and sugar, cook, stirring, until starting to brown, 5–6 minutes. Transfer the onion to the bowl with the green beans. Stir in the soup, cheese, Worcestershire sauce, and garlic powder. Pour into the baking pan.
4. Bake 25 minutes; sprinkle with the French-fried onions and bake until bubbly, 5 minutes longer.

Per serving (1 cup): 173 Cal, 8 g Fat, 3 g Sat Fat, 13 mg Chol, 514 mg Sod, 18 g Carb, 4 g Fib, 8 g Prot, 231 mg Calc. ***POINTS: 3.***

Grits with Cheese

MAKES 4 SERVINGS

Thanks to the awakened interest in American regional cooking during the eighties, grits are no longer just a Southern secret. (A note to non-Southerners: Grits are made from ground hominy—dried corn kernels from which the hull and germ have been removed.) In our version, they're spiked with creamy cheeses and other flavorings to make an anything-but-boring side dish. Make sure to use the quick-cooking grits, which cook in half the time.

1¾ cups water
3 scallions, chopped
¼ teaspoon salt
¼ teaspoon dried thyme
½ cup quick-cooking grits
½ cup shredded reduced-fat cheddar cheese
3 tablespoons freshly grated Parmesan cheese
¼ teaspoon ground pepper

Bring the water, scallions, salt, and thyme to a boil in a medium saucepan. Slowly stir in the grits and reduce the heat to medium-low. Cover and cook, stirring occasionally, until thickened, 9 minutes. Remove from the heat and stir in the cheddar and Parmesan cheeses, and the pepper. Serve hot.

Per serving (½ cup): 138 Cal, 4 g Fat, 2 g Sat Fat, 11 mg Chol, 310 mg Sod, 17 g Carb, 1 g Fib, 8 g Prot, 182 mg Calc. ***POINTS: 3.***

"My favorite foods are cheese, chocolate (dark only!) and pastry. But I've been able to stay within goal-weight range for 19 years. I often count ***POINTS*** in my head. My lifesavers are carrots and grapefruit juice. If I'm feeling peckish, I eat carrot sticks, and if I crave sweets, I try a sip of grapefruit juice first."

—Linda Huett, President and CEO, Weight Watchers International

Tortilla-Cheese Casserole

MAKES 6 SERVINGS

Corn lovers rejoiced when Weight Watchers removed this tasty vegetables from the "forbidden" list. Here, luxurious-tasting but fat-free creamed corn lends a touch of sweetness and creamy texture to this easy-to-make casserole. Don't worry about the pepper sauce; use a mild, flavorful type like Frank's Red Hot to add a spicy tang without a lot of heat.

- **4 (6-inch) corn tortillas**
- **1 large sweet onion, chopped**
- **1 green bell pepper, chopped**
- **1½ teaspoons ground cumin**
- **¾ teaspoon dried marjoram**
- **1 (15-ounce) can creamed corn**
- **2 large eggs**
- **3 egg whites**
- **⅔ cup shredded reduced-fat cheddar cheese**
- **2 tablespoons chopped cilantro or parsley**
- **2 tablespoons mild pepper sauce**
- **¾ cup salsa**

1. Place the oven rack in the center of the oven; preheat the oven to 375°F. Spray a 1½-quart casserole dish with nonstick spray. Stack the tortillas and cut crosswise into 1-inch strips. Place the tortilla strips on a baking sheet in a single layer. Bake until lightly golden, 6 minutes.
2. Spray a large nonstick skillet with nonstick spray and set over medium heat. Add the onion and pepper and cook, stirring occasionally, until just tender, 12 minutes. Stir in the cumin and marjoram; remove from the heat and let cool in the pan.
3. Meanwhile, stir together the creamed corn, eggs, egg whites, ⅓ cup of the cheese, the cilantro or parsley, and the pepper sauce in a large bowl until blended. Stir in the cooled vegetable mixture. Spoon about half of the mixture into the prepared dish. Arrange half of the tortilla strips on top. Spoon on the remaining egg mixture and arrange the remaining strips on top. (You can stand a few rounded strips along the edges for a scalloped effect, if you like.) Bake until golden and set in the center, 35–40 minutes. Serve with the salsa.

Per serving (⅙ of casserole with 2 tablespoons salsa): 186 Cal, 5 g Fat, 2 g Sat Fat, 78 mg Chol, 581 mg Sod, 27 g Carb, 4 g Fib, 11 g Prot, 162 mg Calc. ***POINTS: 3.***

Ratatouille au Gratin

MAKES 4 SERVINGS

Anyone who says she doesn't like vegetables has never tasted a good ratatouille. A staple in the south of France (and in the kitchens of seventies gourmet cooks), this medley of Mediterranean vegetables is a tasty addition to just about any meal. Here, we've topped it with a crunchy Parmesan crust for extra impact. Got leftovers? They're even more delicious the next day.

4 teaspoons olive oil
1 large onion, chopped
2 garlic cloves, minced
1 yellow bell pepper, cut into ½-inch strips
1 green bell pepper, cut into ½-inch strips
1 cup water
1 medium (1¼-pound) eggplant, peeled and chopped
1 medium (8-ounce) zucchini, chopped
1 (14-ounce) can diced tomatoes, with juice
1 cup tomato juice
1 tablespoon chopped basil, or 1 teaspoon dried
1 tablespoon chopped oregano, or 1 teaspoon dried
1 tablespoon chopped thyme, or 1 teaspoon dried
¼ teaspoon salt
Freshly ground pepper
¼ cup freshly grated Parmesan cheese
¼ cup plain dried bread crumbs
Fresh parsley (optional)

1. Heat a large nonstick skillet over medium heat. Swirl in the oil, then add the onion and garlic. Cook, stirring occasionally, until fragrant, about 2 minutes.
2. Add the yellow and green peppers and ½ cup of the water; cook, stirring frequently, until the liquid has evaporated and the peppers are wilted. Add the eggplant, zucchini, and the remaining ½ cup water; cook, stirring frequently, until the liquid has evaporated and the eggplant and zucchini are wilted. Add the tomatoes, tomato juice, basil, oregano, thyme, salt, and pepper. Cook, stirring occasionally, until the liquid has evaporated and the vegetables are tender, 15–20 minutes.
3. Meanwhile, preheat the broiler. Spray a 2-quart shallow baking dish with nonstick spray.
4. Transfer the ratatouille to the baking dish. Combine the cheese and bread crumbs in a small bowl; sprinkle the mixture over the ratatouille. Broil 5 inches from the heat, watching carefully, until the top is golden brown, about 2 minutes. Sprinkle with the parsley, if using.

Per serving (1 cup): 191 Cal, 8 g Fat, 2 g Sat Fat, 5 mg Chol, 708 mg Sod, 27 g Carb, 6 g Fib, 7 g Prot, 170 mg Calc. ***POINTS: 4.***

Soyful Scalloped Potatoes

MAKES 6 SERVINGS

Heart-healthy soy is de rigueur these days, and here, in the form of tofu, it lends creamy richness to a classic potato dish. Tofu haters will never know it's there, thanks to the sweet, caramelized onions and buttery cheese. Be sure to use imported Swiss Gruyère; its rich flavor goes a long way.

- **½ pound firm tofu, cut into ½-inch slices**
- **3 teaspoons unsalted butter**
- **1 large sweet onion, sliced into very thin wedges**
- **1 teaspoon minced fresh rosemary, or ½ teaspoon dried**
- **½ teaspoon salt**
- **¼ teaspoon freshly ground pepper**
- **1¾ pounds Yukon Gold potatoes, peeled and cut into ¼-inch slices**
- **½ cup coarsely shredded Gruyère cheese**
- **1¼ cups reduced-sodium chicken broth**

1. To press some of the moisture out of the tofu, line a baking sheet with a double layer of paper towels. Arrange the tofu in a single layer and then top with another double layer of towels. Cover with another baking sheet and weight with 2 large cans. Let stand 15 minutes, then pat tofu dry with more paper towels.
2. Meanwhile, preheat the oven to 400°F. Spray a 2-quart shallow baking dish with nonstick spray.
3. Melt 2 teaspoons of the butter in a large nonstick skillet over medium heat. Add the onion and cook, stirring occasionally, until tender, 20 minutes. Add the rosemary, increase the heat to medium-high, and cook until slightly crisped and golden, 5–7 minutes more. Sprinkle with the salt and pepper and toss.
4. Arrange half the potatoes in the baking dish, overlapping them slightly. Crumble the pressed tofu on top, then scatter over half of the onions and ¼ cup of the cheese. Repeat to make a second layer of potatoes, onion, and cheese on top of that. Pour in the broth and dot with the remaining 1 teaspoon butter. Cover and bake 45 minutes. Uncover and continue baking until the potatoes are tender and the cheese is melted and slightly golden, about 15 minutes more.

Per serving (about ¾ cup): 228 Cal, 8 g Fat, 3 g Sat Fat, 13 mg Chol, 330 mg Sod, 28 g Carb, 4 g Fib, 12 g Prot, 183 mg Calc. ***POINTS: 4.***

Curried Vegetable Stew

MAKES 8 SERVINGS

Like some of the most beloved Weight Watchers recipes, this one is a delicious way to enjoy lots of *POINTS*-free vegetables. Don't be put off by the long list of ingredients; the stew is one of those throw-everything-together-in-a-pot dishes that makes a great family meal, company dish, or contribution to a potluck supper. Serve it with rice, pita bread, or perhaps Tandoori-Marinated Turkey Breast [see page 121]. And don't be afraid to add or substitute other veggies.

4 teaspoons vegetable oil
2 teaspoons curry powder
2 onions, chopped
1 tablespoon minced peeled fresh ginger
2 garlic cloves, minced
1 (14-ounce) can diced tomatoes, with juice
1 cup reduced-sodium vegetable broth
1 medium (1¼-pound) eggplant, peeled and chopped
1 medium (8-ounce) zucchini, chopped
1 (10-ounce) box frozen cut green beans
4 carrots, sliced ¼-inch thick
1 (5-ounce) potato, chopped
1 cup hot water
1 (10-ounce) box frozen cauliflower florets
1 (15-ounce) can chickpeas, rinsed and drained
½ teaspoon salt
Freshly ground pepper
¼ cup chopped cilantro

1. Heat a large nonstick saucepan. Swirl in the oil, then add the curry powder. Cook, stirring constantly, until fragrant, about 30 seconds. Add the onions, ginger, and garlic; sauté until the onions are wilted and the garlic is fragrant, about 2 minutes.
2. Add the tomatoes and broth; simmer over low heat until heated through. Add the eggplant, zucchini, green beans, carrots, potato, and water. Cover and simmer, stirring occasionally, until the vegetables are tender, about 20 minutes. Add the cauliflower, chickpeas, salt, and pepper; simmer, covered, until heated through, about 15 minutes. Sprinkle with the cilantro and serve.

Per serving (1¼ cups): 168 Cal, 4 g Fat, 1 g Sat Fat, 0 mg Chol, 367 mg Sod, 30 g Carb, 8 g Fib, 6 g Prot, 82 mg Calc. ***POINTS: 3.***

Curried Vegetable Stew

Bulgur Pilaf

MAKES 6 SERVINGS 

The growing interest in ethnic foods—which blossomed in the eighties and continues to the present—inspired this Mediterranean version of a Middle Eastern rice pilaf. Because the dish is simmered, it works best with coarse bulgur, not the finer stuff used for tabbouleh. Look for coarse bulgur in health-food stores, but don't worry if you can't find it. The recipe will work just as well with regular bulgur but will have a softer texture and cook 5 to 10 minutes faster. Use scissors to easily snip the figs into small pieces.

- **1 tablespoon olive oil**
- **2 shallots, finely chopped**
- **1 cup coarse bulgur**
- **1 large garlic clove, finely chopped**
- **1 teaspoon cumin seeds**
- **1 (14-ounce) can reduced-sodium chicken broth**
- **½ teaspoon salt**
- **¼ teaspoon cinnamon**
- **1 (15-ounce) can chickpeas, drained and rinsed**
- **7 dried mission figs, cut into small pieces**
- **3 tablespoons finely chopped cilantro**

Heat a medium saucepan over medium heat. Swirl in the oil, then add the shallot. Sauté until translucent, 3 minutes. Add the bulgur, garlic, and cumin; toast, stirring occasionally, 3 minutes. Stir in the broth, salt, and cinnamon; reduce the heat, cover, and simmer until the liquid is absorbed, 15–18 minutes. Remove from the heat and let stand 5 minutes. Add the chickpeas, figs, and cilantro, fluffing with a fork.

Per serving (¾ cup): 246 Cal, 4 g Fat, 1 g Sat Fat, 0 mg Chol, 449 mg Sod, 4 g Carb, 9 g Fib, 9 g Prot, 78 mg Calc. ***POINTS: 4.***

"In the seventies we did a survey: We asked members which foods they missed the most when they were on the Weight Watchers Program. I expected answers like ice cream or chocolate. But the number one response was—peanut butter! We were finding that people would be able to lose the weight, but then they wouldn't know how to add back the foods they had missed without going overboard. So the Program became more flexible, including more foods, even wine."

—Felice Lippert, Cofounder, Weight Watchers International

Quinoa Pilaf

MAKES 4 SERVINGS

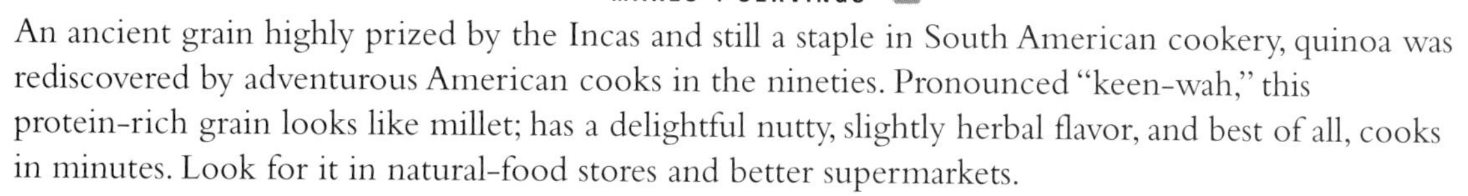

An ancient grain highly prized by the Incas and still a staple in South American cookery, quinoa was rediscovered by adventurous American cooks in the nineties. Pronounced "keen-wah," this protein-rich grain looks like millet; has a delightful nutty, slightly herbal flavor, and best of all, cooks in minutes. Look for it in natural-food stores and better supermarkets.

- **1 tablespoon olive oil**
- **1 medium fennel bulb, finely chopped**
- **1 onion, finely chopped**
- **1 celery stalk, finely chopped**
- **1 carrot, finely chopped**
- **2 garlic cloves, minced**
- **½ teaspoon salt**
- **¼ teaspoon lightly crushed fennel seeds**
- **⅛ teaspoon freshly ground pepper**
- **1 cup quinoa, well rinsed**
- **1½ cups reduced-sodium chicken broth**
- **¼ cup chopped parsley**
- **1 tablespoon chopped tarragon**

1. Heat a large saucepan over medium heat. Swirl in the oil, then add the fennel, onion, celery, carrot, garlic, salt, fennel seeds, and pepper; cook, stirring occasionally, until softened, about 5 minutes.
2. Stir in the quinoa and cook, stirring, 2 minutes. Add the broth and bring to a boil; reduce the heat to medium-low, cover, and simmer until the liquid is absorbed, about 15 minutes. Remove from the heat, let stand 5 minutes. Fluff with a fork, and stir in the parsley and tarragon.

Per serving (1 cup): 246 Cal, 7 g Fat, 1 g Sat Fat, 0 mg Chol, 530 mg Sod, 39 g Carb, 6 g Fib, 9 g Prot, 87 mg Calc. ***POINTS: 5.***

top tips

Like all grains, quinoa should be rinsed well to remove any impurities or dirt. Place it in a sieve set into a large pot; pour in enough cold water to cover by several inches. Swirl the grains with your fingers, allowing any debris to rise to the top. Pour off the debris, then drain well. Repeat until the water is clear.

Crushing the fennel seeds helps release their fragrance. Here's how: Place the seeds on a work surface and press down on them gently and firmly with the flat side of a heavy knife.

Black Bean and Corn Cakes

MAKES 6 SERVINGS

These savory pancakes, with their southwestern flavorings, are a wonderful brunch treat. They're also the perfect accompaniment to grilled or roasted meat or poultry.

- **1 cup all-purpose flour**
- **1 teaspoon baking powder**
- **½ teaspoon ground cumin**
- **½ teaspoon ground coriander**
- **½ teaspoon salt**
- **¼ teaspoon baking soda**
- **⅛ teaspoon cayenne**
- **3 large eggs**
- **¾ cup low-fat buttermilk**
- **1 tablespoon corn oil**
- **1 cup cooked black beans**
- **1 cup cooked or thawed frozen corn kernels**
- **¾ cup salsa**
- **6 tablespoons fat-free sour cream**

1. Combine the flour, baking powder, cumin, coriander, salt, baking soda, and cayenne in a large bowl.
2. Whisk together the eggs, buttermilk, and oil in a medium bowl; gently stir into the flour mixture until well combined. Fold in the beans and corn.
3. Spray a large nonstick skillet or griddle with nonstick spray; set over medium heat until a drop of water sizzles. Spoon the batter by ¼-cup measures into the skillet. Cook until the tops are just covered with bubbles and the edges of the cakes look cooked, 2–3 minutes. Flip and cook until lightly browned, about 1½ minutes more. Transfer to a warmed plate and repeat with the remaining batter. Serve with the salsa and sour cream.

Per serving (2 cakes with 2 tablespoons salsa and 1 tablespoon sour cream): 230 Cal, 6 g Fat,1 g Sat Fat, 108 mg Chol, 493 mg Sod, 35 g Carb, 4 g Fib, 11 g Prot, 170 mg Calc. ***POINTS: 4.***

Chickpea Croquettes with Roasted Tomato Sauce

MAKES 4 SERVINGS

Chickpeas, like many legumes, used to be relegated to the "no more than once a week" category in the Weight Watchers Program. These days we know better. Besides being deliciously nutty tasting, chickpeas are a high-fiber and virtually fat-free protein source. Here, we've pureed them into a tasty croquette reminiscent of the Spanish tapas treat known as croquetas.

- **10 medium very ripe plum tomatoes, halved**
- **2 large garlic cloves**
- **½ teaspoon salt**
- **¼ teaspoon freshly ground pepper**
- **3 teaspoons olive oil**
- **1 medium onion, chopped**
- **1 tablespoon sesame seeds**
- **1 teaspoon cumin seeds**
- **1 (15-ounce) can chickpeas, drained and rinsed**
- **½ small jalapeño pepper, chopped, with seeds**
- **1 large egg, separated (room temperature)**
- **¼ teaspoon baking powder**
- **1 egg white (room temperature)**
- **3 tablespoons all-purpose flour**

1. To prepare the sauce, preheat the oven to 450°F. Spray a broiler pan with nonstick spray. Arrange the tomatoes, cut-side up, spray the tops with nonstick spray, and roast until charred on the bottoms, 15 minutes. Puree the tomatoes (with their charred skins), garlic, ¼ teaspoon of the salt, and the pepper in the food processor until smooth.
2. Heat a large nonstick skillet over medium heat. Swirl in 1 teaspoon of the oil, then add the onion. Sauté until lightly browned, about 8 minutes, adding the sesame and cumin seeds in the last minute of cooking time. Transfer to a food processor.
3. Add the chickpeas, jalapeño pepper, the egg yolk, baking powder, and remaining ¼ teaspoon of the salt to the processor. Pulse until a chunky paste forms and transfer to a medium bowl.
4. With an electric mixer on high speed, whip the 2 egg whites in a medium bowl until soft peaks form. Fold half of the whipped whites into the chickpea mixture; sprinkle the flour over the top and fold it in lightly, then add the remaining whipped whites and fold in until just combined.
5. Return the skillet to medium-high heat; swirl in ½ teaspoon of the oil. Drop 10 tablespoonfuls of the batter into the pan, flattening them slightly to form croquettes. Cook until golden, about 1½ minutes, then turn. Add another ½ teaspoon oil to the pan, swirling pan gently to distribute. Cook until croquettes are golden, 1–1½ minutes more. Transfer to a platter; keep warm; repeat to make 10 more croquettes. Serve immediately, with the sauce.

Per serving (5 croquettes with a scant ⅓ cup sauce): 243 Cal, 8 g Fat, 1 g Sat Fat, 53 mg Chol, 532 mg Sod, 34 g Carb, 6 g Fib, 11 g Prot, 82 mg Calc. ***POINTS: 5.***

Vegetable Quesadillas

Vegetable Quesadillas

MAKES 4 SERVINGS

Once Americans discovered quesadillas in the eighties, there was no turning back. Our version is baked in the oven, making it an extra-easy choice for a weeknight supper. Make the vegetable mixture in advance, if you like—just assemble and cook in minutes. If you'd rather not heat up the oven, prepare the quesadillas one at a time in a nonstick skillet sprayed with nonstick spray.

- **8 (6-inch) flour tortillas**
- **½ teaspoon olive oil**
- **1 medium red onion, thinly sliced**
- **1 large red bell pepper, thinly sliced**
- **1 cup frozen corn kernels**
- **1 teaspoon ground cumin**
- **¾ teaspoon dried oregano**
- **¼ cup chopped cilantro**
- **1 tablespoon fresh lime juice**
- **1½ cups shredded reduced-fat Monterey Jack or cheddar cheese**
- **1⅓ cups salsa**
- **¼ cup reduced-fat sour cream**

1. Adjust the oven racks to divide the oven into thirds; preheat the oven to 375°F. Arrange 4 of the tortillas on a baking sheet.
2. Heat a nonstick skillet over medium heat. Swirl in the oil, then add the onion and pepper. Sauté until softened, 6 minutes. Stir in the corn, cumin, and oregano; cook until the vegetables are tender-crisp, 4 minutes more. Remove from the heat; stir in the cilantro and lime juice.
3. Sprinkle half of the cheese evenly over the tortillas on the baking sheet, leaving a ½-inch border. Spoon the vegetable mixture on top, dividing evenly among the tortillas and spreading level. Sprinkle on the remaining cheese and top with the 4 remaining tortillas, pressing lightly on top.
4. Bake until golden brown and the cheese is melted, 10 minutes, rotating the baking sheet halfway through. Cut each quesadilla into 8 wedges and serve with the salsa and sour cream.

Per serving (1 quesadilla with ⅓ cup salsa and 1 tablespoon sour cream): 368 Cal, 14 g Fat, 6 g Sat Fat, 29 mg Chol, 685 mg Sod, 45 g Carb, 5 g Fib, 19 g Prot, 442 mg Calc. ***POINTS: 8.***

Warm Lentils with Escarole

MAKES 4 SERVINGS

All good seventies cookbooks included a recipe for lentil soup, but it wasn't until the nineties that these wonderful legumes got their just due in sophisticated recipes. Here, the earthy-tasting beans are paired with slightly bitter escarole, a classic combination. Cook the lentils in gently boiling water and start taste-testing after 12 minutes: The older they are, the longer they'll take to cook. For this dish, they should be just tender and holding their shape.

- **3 cups water**
- **1 cup brown lentils**
- **1 small carrot, diced (⅓ cup)**
- **½ bunch escarole, coarsely chopped (about ½ pound)**
- **1 teaspoon olive oil**
- **2 large garlic cloves, minced**
- **½ medium red onion, diced**
- **¼ cup reduced-sodium chicken broth**
- **2 tablespoons sherry vinegar**
- **½ teaspoon salt**
- **¼ teaspoon freshly ground pepper**

1. Bring the water and lentils to a boil in a medium saucepan; reduce the heat and simmer gently until the lentils are tender but still retain their shape, 12–20 minutes. Just before the lentils are finished, add the carrot and cook 30 seconds. Drain in a colander, rinsing briefly with cold water to stop cooking. Transfer to a medium bowl.
2. Meanwhile, heat a large nonstick skillet over medium-high heat. Add the escarole, with water still clinging to the leaves; cover and cook until wilted, 3–4 minutes. Drain, if necessary, and add to the lentils; wipe out the skillet and return it to the stove over medium heat.
3. Swirl the oil in the center of the skillet; drop in the garlic and heat until it begins to sizzle. Add the onion and sauté 1 minute. Add the broth, vinegar, salt, and pepper; let the mixture bubble about 5 seconds. Pour over the lentil mixture and toss gently.

Per serving (about ¾ cup): 196 Cal, 2 g Fat, 0 g Sat Fat, 0 mg Chol, 341 mg Sod, 33 g Carb, 13 g Fib, 14 g Prot, 66 mg Calc. ***POINTS: 3.***

Pasta Primavera

MAKES 6 SERVINGS

Invented in the seventies at New York's legendary Le Cirque restaurant, this "springtime pasta" traditionally showcases delicate spring vegetables in all their glory. In our version, we get a big flavor boost from sun-dried tomatoes. A little unorthodox...but wonderful nonetheless!

- **2 cups boiling water**
- **10 sun-dried tomato halves (not oil-packed)**
- **3¼ cups farfalle (bow-tie pasta)**
- **2 tablespoons extra-virgin olive oil**
- **4 garlic cloves, sliced**
- **1 medium fennel bulb, chopped (about 1 cup)**
- **½ pound asparagus, trimmed and cut into 1-inch pieces**
- **1 medium onion, chopped**
- **1 cup thawed frozen peas**
- **½ cup dry white wine**
- **½ teaspoon salt**
- **¼ teaspoon freshly ground pepper**
- **½ cup freshly grated Parmesan cheese (preferably Parmigiano-Reggiano)**
- **½ cup chopped parsley**
- **⅓ cup chopped basil**

1. Combine the boiling water and the tomato halves in a heatproof bowl; let stand until the tomatoes are softened, 6 minutes. Drain, discarding the water; when cool enough to handle, slice the tomatoes into thin strips.
2. Cook the farfalle according to package directions; drain and keep warm.
3. Heat a large nonstick skillet over medium-high heat. Swirl in the oil, then add the garlic. Sauté until fragrant, 30 seconds. Add the fennel, asparagus, onion, and the tomato slices; cook, stirring occasionally, 5 minutes. Stir in the peas, wine, salt, and pepper; reduce the heat to medium-low, cover, and simmer 2 minutes. Remove from the heat and stir in the farfalle; toss to coat. Add the cheese, parsley, and basil; toss and serve immediately or at room temperature.

Per serving (generous 1 cup): 274 Cal, 8 g Fat, 2 g Sat Fat, 7 mg Chol, 441 mg Sod, 39 g Carb, 4 g Fib, 11 g Prot, 161 mg Calc. ***POINTS: 5.***

I asked the [Weight Watchers] Leader, 'Please teach me how to feed myself, because I already know how to diet.' After that day, I never missed a meeting for 68 pounds. I finally decided not to walk out on myself this time.

—Sandy Foley, Leader, Long Island, New York

Orechiette with Broccoli Rabe, Garlic, and Red Pepper Flakes

MAKES 4 SERVINGS

We all fell in love with pasta in the eighties, but by the nineties we became increasingly adventurous with pasta shapes and sizes. Orechiette ("little ears") are perfect for this dish, as their shape catches and holds the flavorful bits of broccoli. If they're not available, small shells make a good substitute. And if you can't find broccoli rabe—broccoli's delightfully bitter Italian cousin—plain broccoli will work nicely.

- **1 pound broccoli rabe, thick stems removed, chopped**
- **1¼ teaspoons salt**
- **1⅓ cups orechiette**
- **5 teaspoons extra-virgin olive oil**
- **6 garlic cloves, thinly sliced**
- **¼ teaspoon crushed red pepper**
- **¾ cup reduced-sodium chicken broth**
- **¼ cup freshly grated Parmesan cheese**

1. Bring a large pot of water to a boil. Add the broccoli and 1 teaspoon of the salt; cook until bright green, 2 minutes, and remove with a slotted spoon. Rinse in a colander under cold running water to stop cooking; squeeze out the excess water and reserve.
2. Return the pot to a boil and cook the orechiette according to package directions. Drain and transfer to a large serving bowl; keep warm.
3. Heat a large nonstick skillet over medium-high heat. Swirl in the oil, then add the garlic and red pepper. Cook, stirring, until the garlic just begins to brown, 1 minute. Add the broth and continue cooking 1 minute. Stir in the broccoli rabe and heat through. Add to the bowl with the orechiette; stir in the cheese and the remaining ¼ teaspoon salt, tossing well to combine. Serve hot or at room temperature.

Per serving (1¼ cups): 330 Cal, 9 g Fat, 2 g Sat Fat, 5 mg Chol, 722 mg Sod, 50 g Carb, 4 g Fib, 13 g Prot, 140 mg Calc. ***POINTS: 7.***

Pad Thai

MAKES 4 SERVINGS

The national dish of Thailand, Pad Thai is a delectable mix of hot, sour, salty, and sweet flavors as well as chewy and crunchy textures. A key ingredient is Thai fish sauce (*nam pla*), a clear brown, subtly fishy flavoring made from fermented fish; it's easy to find in today's global marketplace. Look for it, and the rice noodles, in the international section of your supermarket or in Asian groceries. A bottle of fish sauce will last for several years in the pantry.

- **8 ounces flat rice noodles or pad thai noodles**
- **6 tablespoons ketchup**
- **3 tablespoons Thai fish sauce**
- **2 tablespoons packed dark brown sugar**
- **1 teaspoon chili garlic paste**
- **2 tablespoons peanut oil**
- **2 eggs, lightly beaten**
- **3 garlic cloves, minced**
- **12 ounces reduced-fat firm tofu, pressed and cut into ½-inch cubes**
- **4 scallions, cut into ½-inch pieces**
- **2 tablespoons chopped unsalted peanuts**
- **2 cups bean sprouts**
- **4 lemon wedges**

1. Bring a large pot of water to a boil. Add the noodles and cook until tender, 6–8 minutes; drain in a colander under cold running water to stop cooking. Set aside.
2. Combine the ketchup, fish sauce, sugar, and chili paste in a small bowl; set aside.
3. Heat a large nonstick skillet over medium-high heat. Swirl in 1 tablespoon of the oil. Add the eggs and cook, stirring occasionally, 2 minutes. Transfer the eggs to a bowl; return the skillet to the heat, and swirl in the remaining 1 tablespoon oil. Add the garlic and sauté until fragrant, 30 seconds. Stir in the tofu; cook until hot, about 3 minutes. Add the scallions and the cooked eggs; cook, stirring, 1 minute. Add the reserved noodles and the ketchup mixture; cook, tossing, until just heated through, 3 minutes. Transfer to a serving platter. Sprinkle with the peanuts, and serve with the bean sprouts and lemon wedges.

Per serving (1½ cups): 404 Cal, 15 g Fat, 3 g Sat Fat, 106 mg Chol, 896 mg Sod, 15 g Carb, 4 g Fib, 18 g Prot, 98 mg Calc. ***POINTS: 9.***

top tips

- To press the tofu, place it between two plates and weight the top with a heavy can. Let stand until some of the liquid is pressed out, 20 to 30 minutes. Drain off the liquid and pat tofu dry with a paper towel.
- Chili garlic paste, a condiment made from hot red chiles, vinegar, and plenty of garlic, can be found in Asian groceries and some supermarkets. Beware: Its pungent, fiery-hot flavor is addictive! If it's unavailable, you can substitute 2 to 3 teaspoons of your favorite brand of hot pepper sauce.

Lemon Risotto with Spring Vegetables

MAKES 8 SERVINGS

A well-made risotto is creamy yet never mushy; it's probably the most sophisticated comfort food in the universe. We've flavored this one with delicate spring vegetables and fresh lemon; try it at your next dinner party. For the creamiest, most luscious texture, be sure to use Arborio or another Italian medium-grain rice with a high starch content, such as Carnaroli or Vialone Nano. They're available in better supermarkets and gourmet stores.

- **1 pound asparagus, trimmed and cut into 1-inch pieces**
- **1 teaspoon salt**
- **5½ cups reduced-sodium chicken broth**
- **1 tablespoon olive oil**
- **2 leeks, cleaned and chopped**
- **3 garlic cloves, minced**
- **1 teaspoon chopped thyme**
- **1½ cups Arborio rice**
- **⅓ cup dry white wine**
- **1 cup thawed frozen baby peas**
- **3 tablespoons fresh lemon juice**
- **1 teaspoon grated lemon zest**
- **½ cup freshly grated Parmesan cheese**
- **¼ teaspoon freshly ground pepper**

1. Bring a large pot of water to a boil. Add the asparagus and salt, and cook just until bright green, 2 minutes. Drain and rinse the asparagus in a colander under cold running water to stop cooking; set aside.
2. Bring the broth to a gentle simmer in a large saucepan over medium-low heat; reduce the heat and keep at a simmer.
3. Heat the oil in a large nonstick skillet. Sauté the leeks, garlic, and thyme until the leeks begin to soften, about 3 minutes. Add the rice and cook, stirring, until the outer shell is translucent, about 1 minute. Stir in the wine and cook, stirring constantly, until it is absorbed. Add the broth 1 cup at a time, stirring until it is absorbed before adding more, until the rice is just tender but still slightly toothy. Add the asparagus, peas, lemon juice, and lemon zest with the last (½-cup) addition of broth. The cooking time from the first addition of broth should be about 22 minutes. Stir in the cheese and pepper; serve immediately.

Per serving (1 cup): 241 Cal, 5 g Fat, 2 g Sat Fat, 5 mg Chol, 532 mg Sod, 37 g Carb, 3 g Fib, 11 g Prot, 134 mg Calc. ***POINTS: 5.***

top tips

- To clean the leeks, trim the roots, leaving the root ends intact to hold the layers together. Slice them lengthwise, fan open the layers, and swish them in a large bowl of cool water. Let stand a few minutes to allow the grit to fall to the bottom, then lift them out.
- For an alcohol-free risotto, substitute nonalcoholic dry white wine and a tablespoon of white vinegar for the wine, or omit it altogether and increase the chicken broth to 6 cups.

Lemon Risotto with Spring Vegetables

Barley Mushroom "Risotto"

MAKES 6 SERVINGS

In this delightful homage to risotto, we've used pearl barley instead of the traditional Arborio rice. It too becomes lusciously creamy when cooked, and offers a delightful chewy texture.

- **1 ounce dried porcini mushrooms**
- **2 cups hot water**
- **2 tablespoons extra-virgin olive oil**
- **1 medium onion, chopped**
- **8 ounces shiitake or oyster mushrooms (or a combination), stemmed and sliced**
- **3 garlic cloves, minced**
- **2 teaspoons chopped fresh thyme**
- **2 teaspoons chopped fresh rosemary**
- **1 cup pearl barley**
- **4 cups reduced-sodium chicken broth**
- **½ teaspoon salt**
- **¼ teaspoon freshly ground pepper**
- **⅓ cup chopped parsley**
- **⅓ cup freshly grated Parmesan cheese**

1. Rinse the porcini in several changes of water to remove any dirt or grit. Place in a heatproof bowl and cover with the hot water; let soak until softened, about 15 minutes. Remove the porcini from the liquid, squeeze them gently and coarsely chop.
2. Strain the porcini liquid into a small saucepan. Bring to a boil and cook until it is reduced to ½ cup, 8–10 minutes; set aside.
3. Heat a large nonstick saucepan over medium-high heat. Swirl in the oil, then add the onion. Cook, stirring often, until beginning to soften, 4–5 minutes. Add the fresh mushrooms and porcini; cook, stirring occasionally, until golden, about 8 minutes. Stir in the garlic, thyme, and rosemary and cook 1 minute. Add the barley and cook, stirring, 1 minute.
4. Pour in 3 cups of the broth, the reserved porcini liquid, the salt, and pepper. Bring to a boil, reduce the heat to medium, and simmer, covered, until the liquid is almost absorbed and the barley is almost tender, about 30 minutes. Add the remaining 1 cup broth and cook uncovered, stirring occasionally, until the barley is tender, 12–15 minutes. Remove from the heat, stir in the parsley and cheese, and serve at once.

Per serving (¾ cup): 232 Cal, 8 g Fat, 2 g Sat Fat, 4 mg Chol, 626 mg Sod, 32 g Carb, 6 g Fib, 10 g Prot, 109 mg Calc. ***POINTS: 5.***

top tip

Porcini mushrooms, also called cèpes, are brown wild mushrooms with a robust, earthy flavor. Most commonly imported from Italy or France, they are easiest to find in their dried form. Look for them in gourmet stores and better supermarkets; they're pricey but worth every penny, since their intense flavor goes a long way. Choose specimens that have the largest, freshest looking-pieces, and avoid those with a lot of dust or fragments in the package.

Creamy Polenta with Mushroom Ragu

MAKES 6 SERVINGS

Polenta, made from cornmeal and similar to mush, is Italian comfort food at its highest level. Served creamy or firm, polenta can be eaten plain or topped with any number of boldly flavored, chunky sauces such as this one. Experiment with different types of mushrooms, if you like, depending on what looks good in the produce aisle.

- **1 tablespoon extra-virgin olive oil**
- **2 shallots, chopped**
- **8 ounces shiitake mushrooms, sliced (4 cups)**
- **8 ounces cremini mushrooms, sliced (4 cups)**
- **1 teaspoon chopped thyme**
- **¼ cup dry sherry**
- **½ cup reduced-sodium beef broth**
- **1 tablespoon reduced-sodium soy sauce**
- **3 cups low-fat (1%) milk**
- **2 cups water**
- **½ teaspoon salt**
- **¼ teaspoon freshly ground pepper**
- **1 cup instant polenta**
- **½ cup freshly grated Parmesan cheese**

1. Heat a large nonstick skillet over medium-high heat. Swirl in the oil, then add the shallots. Cook, stirring occasionally, 1 minute. Add the shiitake and cremini mushrooms, and the thyme; cook, stirring occasionally, until the mushrooms soften, about 5 minutes. Add the sherry and continue cooking until it is just absorbed. Add the broth and soy sauce; cook until slightly thickened, 2–3 minutes. Remove from the heat and keep warm.
2. Combine the milk, water, salt, and pepper in a large saucepan over medium-high heat. Bring to a boil; then pour the polenta into the saucepan in a slow steady stream, whisking constantly, until smooth. Cook, stirring constantly, 5 minutes, until the polenta is thick and creamy. Stir in the cheese. Divide the polenta among 6 plates; top each with ⅓ cup of the mushroom sauce and serve immediately.

Per serving (⅔ cup polenta, with 1/3 cup sauce): 225 Cal, 7 g Fat, 3 g Sat Fat, 11 mg Chol, 530 mg Sod, 30 g Carb, 3 g Fib, 12 g Prot, 280 mg Calc. ***POINTS: 4.***

top tip

Cremini mushrooms are brown Italian mushrooms, similar in size and shape to white mushrooms, with a slightly earthier flavor. If they're unavailable, substitute white mushrooms.

Portobello Burgers

MAKES 4 SERVINGS

Portobello mushrooms look like ordinary brown mushrooms on steroids. They became a restaurant staple in the nineties and still dominate menus today. Their earthy flavor and chewy texture make them a great meat alternative. With their large caps, they also look great on a grill. Here, we've copied a standard restaurant technique, serving them up like classic burgers.

- **4 large portobello mushroom caps (about 1 pound)**
- **4 tablespoons + 2 teaspoons fat-free balsamic vinaigrette dressing**
- **¼ teaspoon salt**
- **¼ teaspoon freshly ground pepper**
- **4 multigrain hamburger rolls**
- **1 cup mixed baby greens**
- **1 medium tomato, cut into 4 thick slices**
- **1 small sweet onion, cut into 4 thick slices**
- **2 ounces goat cheese, softened**

1. Prepare the grill for a hot fire; spray a grill rack with nonstick spray. (Or, if you have one, spray a ridged grill pan with nonstick spray and set over medium-high heat until hot.)
2. Brush the portobellos with 2 tablespoons of the balsamic dressing, then sprinkle with the salt and pepper. Grill, turning once, until softened, about 12 minutes.
3. Layer the bottom half of each roll with a portobello cap, ¼ cup of the greens, and a slice each of the tomato and onion. Drizzle each "burger" with 2 teaspoons of the remaining balsamic dressing. Spread one-fourth of the goat cheese on the top half of each roll, place on top of the burgers, and serve at once.

Per serving (1 burger): 220 Cal, 6 g Fat, 3 g Sat Fat, 13 mg Chol, 664 mg Sod, 36 g Carb, 5 g Fib, 9 g Prot, 142 mg Calc. ***POINTS: 4.***

Barley Waldorf Salad

MAKES 6 SERVINGS

Talk about retro! This sweet, crunchy salad was created at the turn of the last century at the famed Waldorf-Astoria Hotel in New York City, but remained popular through the ages. Here, we've updated its profile by adding oh-so-trendy barley.

- **3 cups water**
- **⅔ cup pearl barley**
- **¾ teaspoon salt**
- **¼ cup plain low-fat yogurt**
- **3 tablespoons diced sweet onion**
- **2 tablespoons reduced-fat mayonnaise**
- **1 tablespoon fresh lemon juice**
- **1 tablespoon fresh tangerine or orange juice**
- **½ teaspoon sugar**
- **1 large, slightly tart apple, such as Braeburn, Gala, or Mutsu, cored, seeded, and cut into ½-inch cubes**
- **1 cup halved green seedless grapes**
- **⅓ cup pecan halves, toasted and finely chopped**

1. Combine the water, barley, and salt in a medium saucepan; bring to a boil. Reduce the heat, cover, and simmer until tender, about 30 minutes. Drain in a colander, rinsing briefly with cold water to stop the cooking.
2. Stir together the yogurt, onion, mayonnaise, lemon juice, tangerine juice, and sugar in a large bowl. Add the barley, apple, and grapes; toss gently to coat evenly. Sprinkle the top with the pecans.

Per serving (generous ¾ cup): 205 Cal, 6 g Fat, 1 g Sat Fat, 1 mg Chol, 85 mg Sod, 35 g Carb, 6 g Fib, 4 g Prot, 37 mg Calc. ***POINTS: 4.***

top tip

To toast the pecan halves, place them in a dry nonstick skillet over medium heat. Cook, shaking the pan often to prevent burning, until they become fragrant and only slightly darkened (watch for burning), about 3 minutes.

Best Side Story

1994

A Center for Science in the Public Interest survey shows that a large bucket of seemingly harmless movie-theatre popcorn contains six Big Mac's worth of fat and saturated fat.

Broadcast journalist Kathleen Sullivan is Weight Watchers new spokesperson.

 = x6

1995

Weight Watchers Magazine publishes the results of its groundbreaking sex survey of 6,000 readers. Not only do most respondents report having sex more frequently than the national average, a full 76 percent claim that their partners are attracted to them at their current weight.

1996

Progress (not): Studies report that Americans' fat intake declined since the sixties, from about 42 percent of calories to 34 percent in 1994. But because we were eating about 100 calories more per day, on average, the amount of fat we ate actually rose—from 81 grams per day in the sixties to 83 grams per day in the early nineties.

>>>

Asparagus en Papillote

MAKES 4 SERVINGS

En papillote, meaning "in an envelope or twist of paper" in French, is a simple, elegant way to prepare asparagus. The foil packet seals in all the flavor and nutrients and…there's one less pot to wash.

1 (1-pound) bunch asparagus, trimmed
2 teaspoons olive oil
2 teaspoons fresh lemon juice
¼ teaspoon salt
Freshly ground pepper

1. Preheat oven to 400°F. Cut a 24-inch sheet of heavy-duty foil.
2. Place the asparagus in the center of the foil; fold the foil into a packet, rolling and crimping the foil on all sides to make a tight seal. Bake until the asparagus is tender but still bright green, 20–30 minutes (watch for escaping steam as you open the foil to check).
3. Carefully open the packet, avoiding the steam, and transfer the asparagus with tongs to a serving platter. Drizzle with the oil and lemon juice, then sprinkle with the salt and pepper. Serve hot, cold, or at room temperature.

Per serving (4–6 spears): 37 Cal, 3 g Fat, 0 g Sat Fat, 0 mg Chol, 148 mg Sod, 3 g Carb, 1 g Fib, 2 g Prot, 15 mg Calc. ***POINTS: 1.***

top tip

If you prefer, you can use baking parchment instead of foil; look for it in kitchenware stores and some supermarkets.

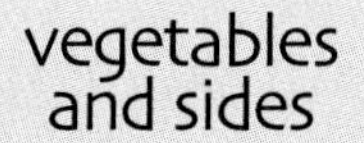

Broccoli Rabe with Lemon and Garlic

MAKES 4 SERVINGS

The first *Weight Watchers Cookbook* included a recipe for Lemon Broccoli—cooked broccoli tossed with a little lemon juice and sugar substitute. We've improved on the original by adding a holy trio that makes any green vegetable taste better: lemon, garlic, and a little olive oil. Try this recipe with broccolini, Swiss chard, spinach, or just plain broccoli.

- **1 bunch broccoli rabe, trimmed of tough stalks, and coarsely chopped**
- **4 teaspoons olive oil**
- **½ cup reduced-sodium chicken broth**
- **4 garlic cloves, minced**
- **¼ teaspoon salt**
- **¼ teaspoon crushed red pepper**
- **2 tablespoons fresh lemon juice**
- **4 lemon wedges (optional)**

1. Put the broccoli in a steamer basket; set it in a saucepan over 1 inch of boiling water. Cover tightly and steam until barely tender, 3–5 minutes.
2. Heat a large nonstick skillet. Swirl in the oil, then add the broccoli. Cook, stirring, 1 minute; add the broth, garlic, salt, and pepper. Cook, stirring frequently, until the broccoli is tender but still bright green and the liquid has evaporated, about 5 minutes. Add the lemon juice and toss to coat. Serve with the lemon wedges, if using.

Per serving (½ cup): 80 Cal, 5 g Fat, 1 g Sat Fat, 0 mg Chol, 236 mg Sod, 7 g Carb, 3 g Fib, 4 g Prot, 58 mg Calc. ***POINTS: 1.***

> "People say that nutrition information keeps changing. But I think we all know what a healthy diet is. It is the Weight Watchers Program, with menu suggestions and guidelines: Eat a variety of foods, in moderation. Weight Watchers teaches people to add fruits and vegetables to their diet, and it reaches their children and families. It is truly a public health approach."
> *—Reva Frankle, M.S., Ed.D., former Director of Nutrition, Weight Watchers International*

Brussels Sprouts with Dried Cranberries and Lemon

MAKES 4 SERVINGS

Brussels sprouts used to be counted as a "limited" vegetable in the Weight Watchers program, to be eaten sparingly and only at dinner. To some, that may not have been much of a hardship—but then, they hadn't tasted this colorful sweet-and-sour side dish. It pairs perfectly with roasted meat or fowl; try it at Thanksgiving.

- **1 (10-ounce) package Brussels sprouts**
- **½ cup dried cranberries**
- **2 tablespoons fresh lemon juice**
- **4 teaspoons olive oil**
- **¼ teaspoon salt**
- **¼ teaspoon ground pepper**

1. Trim the tough outer leaves from the Brussels sprouts; slice off the stem end and cut a small x in the bottom of each sprout.
2. Put the sprouts in a steamer basket; set it in a saucepan over 2 inches of boiling water. Cover tightly and steam until the sprouts are tender but still bright yellow-green, 10–15 minutes.
3. Combine the cranberries, lemon juice, oil, salt, and pepper in a medium bowl. Add the Brussels sprouts and toss to coat. Serve hot or at room temperature.

Per serving (¾ cup): 118 Cal, 5 g Fat, 1 g Sat Fat, 0 mg Chol, 163 mg Sod, 19 g Carb, 4 g Fib, 3 g Prot, 19 mg Calc. ***POINTS: 2.***

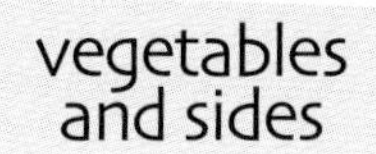

Cauliflower Puree

MAKES 4 SERVINGS

Once upon a time, when *potatoes* were a bad word in the Weight Watchers Program, members were encouraged to whip up some Mock Mashed Potatoes—or pureed cooked cauliflower—whenever they craved the real thing. Our update is creamier and more flavorful, but it's still a great substitute for mashed potatoes.

- **1 medium (2-pound) cauliflower head, trimmed and separated into florets**
- **⅓ cup fat-free half-and-half**
- **½ teaspoon salt**
- **⅛ teaspoon nutmeg**
- **Pinch white pepper**

Fill a medium saucepan two-thirds full with water and bring to a boil; add the cauliflower. Reduce the heat and simmer until the cauliflower is soft, about 15 minutes; drain. Pulse the cauliflower in a food processor to a smooth puree. Add the half-and-half, salt, nutmeg, and pepper; pulse to blend. Serve at once.

Per serving (½ cup): 45 Cal, 0 g Fat, 0 g Sat Fat, 0 mg Chol, 345 mg Sod, 9 g Carb, 3 g Fib, 3 g Prot, 379 mg Calc. ***POINTS: 0.***

top tip

You can also turn the puree into a creamy soup. Just thin it with a (15-ounce) can of reduced-sodium chicken broth to make four (1-cup) servings.

Braised Red Cabbage with Apples, Onions, and Raisins

MAKES 4 SERVINGS

The sweet-and-sour tanginess of this side dish is a terrific partner for beef, ham, or pork. And try it on leftover-meat sandwiches, Reuben-style. It's best served a day or two after it's made.

- **2 teaspoons vegetable oil**
- **1 large red onion, chopped**
- **1 small red cabbage, coarsely chopped**
- **1 cup hot water**
- **1 apple, peeled, cored, and chopped**
- **¼ cup raisins**
- **3 tablespoons firmly packed dark brown sugar**
- **3 tablespoons cider vinegar**
- **½ teaspoon caraway seeds**
- **¼ teaspoon salt**
- **Freshly ground pepper**
- **¼ cup chopped flat-leaf parsley (optional)**

1. Heat a large nonstick skillet. Swirl in the oil, then add the onion. Sauté over medium heat until golden, about 10 minutes.
2. Stir in the cabbage, water, apple, raisins, sugar, vinegar, caraway seeds, salt, and pepper. Reduce the heat to low; cook, covered, stirring occasionally, until the cabbage is tender but still crunchy, about 10 minutes. Uncover and cook, stirring occasionally, until the cabbage is very tender and the liquid has evaporated, about 10 minutes more. Sprinkle with the parsley, if using, or cover tightly and refrigerate until ready to serve.

Per serving (1 cup): 159 Cal, 3 g Fat, 0 g Sat Fat, 0 mg Chol, 178 mg Sod, 34 g Carb, 5 g Fib, 3 g Prot, 94 mg Calc. ***POINTS: 3.***

top tip

To save time, buy the shredded cabbage and sliced red onion at your supermarket's salad bar. You'll need about 1½ pounds of cabbage and ¼ pound of onions.

Coleslaw

MAKES 4 SERVINGS  

Were Weight Watchers members satisfied by the 1966 recipe for Coleslaw, in which shredded cabbage was tossed with a dressing that included mustard, nonfat dry-milk powder, and a little artificial sweetener? We may never know, but we're certain of how tangy and authentic-tasting this twenty-first-century version is. If you want to prepare it ahead of time, add the onion just before serving—or omit it.

1 tablespoon + 1 teaspoon reduced-fat mayonnaise
¼ cup + 2 tablespoons white-wine or cider vinegar
3 tablespoons sugar
3 tablespoons plain fat-free yogurt
1 tablespoon vegetable oil
1 teaspoon prepared mustard
½ teaspoon celery seeds
¼ teaspoon salt
Freshly ground pepper
1 small (1-pound) green cabbage, shredded (4 cups)
2 carrots, peeled and grated
1 small onion, minced (optional)

Whisk the mayonnaise, vinegar, sugar, yogurt, oil, mustard, celery seeds, salt, and pepper in a large nonreactive bowl. Add the cabbage, carrots, and onion, if using, to the bowl; toss to coat evenly. Serve at once, or cover and refrigerate up to 3 hours (add the onion just before serving).

Per serving (1½ cups): 133 Cal, 6 g Fat, 1 g Sat Fat, 0 mg Chol, 237 mg Sod, 21 g Carb, 3 g Fib, 3 g Prot, 84 mg Calc. ***POINTS: 3.***

Stir-fried Baby Bok Choy with Snow Peas, Shiitake Mushrooms, and Ginger

MAKES 4 SERVINGS

Stir-frying is the answer to a vegetable lover's prayers. Thanks to the larger cooking surface of a wok or large skillet and just a little oil, vegetables cook in a flash and retain their flavor and crunchiness. Be daring and create your own stir-fry veggie combinations, adding small pieces of meat, chicken, or shrimp. Even with the additions, you'll get a lot of eating pleasure for relatively few ***POINTS***.

- **1 tablespoon vegetable oil**
- **4 (¼-pound) heads baby bok choy, trimmed, and sliced**
- **½ cup reduced-sodium vegetable broth**
- **1 onion, cut into 16 wedges**
- **12 shiitake mushroom caps, sliced**
- **¼ pound snow peas, trimmed and thinly sliced on the diagonal**
- **1 tablespoon reduced-sodium soy sauce**
- **1 teaspoon sesame oil**
- **1 teaspoon grated peeled fresh ginger**
- **2 garlic cloves, finely chopped**
- **½ teaspoon crushed red pepper**

Heat a large nonstick skillet or wok over high heat until a drop of water skitters. Pour in the vegetable oil; swirl to coat the pan. Add the bok choy and broth; cover and steam 1 minute. Uncover and stir in the onion and mushroom caps; stir-fry another 2–3 minutes. Add the snow peas, soy sauce, sesame oil, ginger, garlic, and pepper. Cook, stirring continuously, until the vegetables are tender-crisp and the liquid has evaporated, 3–4 minutes.

Per serving (1 cup): 100 Cal, 11 g Fat, 1 g Sat Fat, 0 mg Chol, 255 mg Sod, 11 g Carb, 3 g Fib, 5 g Prot, 135 mg Calc. ***POINTS: 2.***

top tips

- Baby bok choy is a smaller, more tender (and some say sweeter) version of Chinese bok choy. It's available in Asian groceries and some supermarkets. If unavailable, substitute 1 head of regular bok choy.
- Freeze the ginger in a zip-close freezer bag for up to three months. When you need some, just scrape off an inch or so of its tough brown outer skin and grate it in its frozen state.

Stir-fried Baby Bok Choy with Snow Peas, Shiitake Mushrooms, and Ginger

Steamed Cauliflower with Raisins and Pine Nuts

MAKES 4 SERVINGS

Here's a surprising trio! The cabbage-y taste and softness of the cauliflower are complemented by the sweetness and chewiness of the raisins. And then there's that extra crunch from the pine nuts (also known as pignoli). This dish might just convert a cauliflower hater. Or you could prepare it with almost any lightly cooked vegetable. Try broccoli or Brussels sprouts, or chopped sturdy greens like kale, cabbage, or collards.

½ cup raisins
1 medium (2-pound) cauliflower head, trimmed and separated into florets
¼ cup pine nuts
4 teaspoons olive oil
¼ teaspoon salt
Freshly ground white pepper
4 lemon wedges

1. Put the raisins in a small bowl of hot water until plump and soft, about 10 minutes; drain and set aside.
2. Put the cauliflower in a steamer basket; set it in a saucepan over 1 inch of boiling water. Cover tightly and steam until tender but not mushy, 6–8 minutes.
3. Meanwhile, toast the pine nuts in a small, dry nonstick skillet over medium-low heat; slide the pan gently back and forth over the heat so the nuts cook evenly. As soon as they begin to turn golden, remove the pan from the heat and transfer the nuts to a heatproof plate to cool.
4. Toss the cauliflower with the raisins, pine nuts, oil, salt, and pepper in a serving bowl. Serve with the lemon wedges.

Per serving (1¼ cups): 175 Cal, 9 g Fat, 1 g Sat Fat, 0 mg Chol, 191 mg Sod, 24 g Carb, 5 g Fib, 4 g Prot, 41 mg Calc. ***POINTS: 3.***

Corn, Zucchini, and Green Bean Succotash

MAKES 4 SERVINGS

Succotash is a traditional Southern dish made from lima beans, corn, and red or green bell peppers. In our version, we've given it a little more crunch (and *POINTS*-free veggies) with the addition of zucchini and green beans.

- **½ pound green beans, trimmed and cut into 1½-inch lengths**
- **2 tablespoons unsalted butter**
- **1 medium onion, chopped**
- **1 garlic clove, minced**
- **1 medium (8-ounce) zucchini, quartered lengthwise and cut into ½-inch pieces**
- **2 plum tomatoes, seeded and chopped**
- **2 cups cooked or thawed frozen corn kernels**
- **½ teaspoon salt**
- **⅛ teaspoon nutmeg**
- **⅛ teaspoon cayenne**

1. Bring a large pot of water to a boil. Add the beans; return to a boil and cook until just bright green, 3 minutes. Drain in a colander under cold water to stop cooking.
2. Melt the butter in a large nonstick skillet over medium-high heat. Stir in the onion and garlic; cook until starting to soften, 3 minutes. Add the zucchini and tomatoes, and sauté until softened, 3 minutes. Stir in the green beans, corn, salt, nutmeg, and cayenne; cook until heated through, about 3 minutes.

Per serving (1¼ cups): 151 Cal, 6 g Fat, 4 g Sat Fat, 16 mg Chol, 304 mg Sod, 24 g Carb, 5 g Fib, 4 g Prot, 43 mg Calc. ***POINTS:* 3.**

top tip

This recipe also makes a great summer salad. Just follow the recipe, substituting 1 tablespoon of extra-virgin olive oil for the butter and omitting the nutmeg. Let the succotash cool, then stir in ¼ cup slivered basil leaves and 1 tablespoon of balsamic vinegar.

Green Beans with Tomato and Oregano

MAKES 4 SERVINGS

Those who remember the old days of Weight Watchers fondly recall the exotic-sounding recipe, Cold String Bean Stew (*Loob-yee ib Zayt*). Consisting of frozen string beans, onions, and tomatoes cooked in chicken stock, it had to be made with French-style green beans, which didn't contain the (then considered high-calorie) beans in their pods. After you've tried this twenty-first-century version—including whole green beans jazzed up with oregano—you'll make it your new favorite.

1 pound green beans, trimmed
4 teaspoons olive oil
1 onion, chopped
4 plum tomatoes, chopped
1 tablespoon chopped oregano, or 1 teaspoon dried
¼ teaspoon salt
Freshly ground pepper
Fresh oregano sprigs (optional)

1. Put the green beans in a steamer basket; set it in a saucepan over 1 inch of boiling water. Cover tightly and steam the beans until tender but still bright green, about 8 minutes. Rinse in a colander under cold water to stop the cooking; set aside.
2. Heat a large nonstick skillet. Swirl in the oil, then add the onion. Sauté until golden brown, 10–12 minutes. Add the tomatoes and sauté until they release some of their moisture, about 2 minutes.
3. Add the green beans, oregano, salt, and pepper to the skillet; cook over low heat, stirring occasionally, until heated through. Garnish with the oregano sprigs, if using, and serve at once.

Per serving (1½ cups): 89 Cal, 5 g Fat, 1 g Sat Fat, 0 mg Chol, 160 mg Sod, 11 g Carb, 4 g Fib, 2 g Prot, 59 mg Calc. ***POINTS: 1.***

top tips

- A 1-pound bag of frozen green beans can be substituted for the fresh ones. Cook according to package directions, then proceed with the recipe at Step 2.
- Got leftover oregano? Freeze the whole leaves (washed and thoroughly dried) in a zip-close freezer bag for up to three months. Once frozen, the oregano can be used (unthawed) in any recipe in which it is cooked.

Baked Vidalia Onions Balsamico

MAKES 4 SERVINGS

Is this a side dish, or a dessert? Two culinary discoveries of the eighties and nineties—sweet Vidalia onions and rich, caramel-like balsamic vinegar—combine to make a delightfully sweet, complex dish.

2 (8-ounce) Vidalia onions, peeled, trimmed, and sliced ¼-inch thick
¼ cup water
2 teaspoons olive oil
2 tablespoons balsamic vinegar
2 teaspoons sugar
½ tablespoon chopped thyme
¼ teaspoon salt
Freshly ground pepper
Fresh thyme sprigs (optional)

1. Preheat the oven to 425°F. Spread the onions evenly in a 9 x 13-inch baking dish; pour in the water. Drizzle with the oil and vinegar; sprinkle with the sugar, thyme, salt, and pepper. Cover and bake until tender, about 30 minutes.
2. Uncover and continue baking, adding water ¼ cup at a time as needed to keep the onions moist, basting occasionally, until the onions are golden brown and caramelized, about 25 minutes. Garnish with the fresh thyme sprigs, if using.

Per serving (½ onion): 69 Cal, 3 g Fat, 0 g Sat Fat, 0 mg Chol, 149 mg Sod, 12 g Carb, 2 g Fib, 1 g Prot, 24 mg Calc. ***POINTS: 1.***

"A man came to one of my meetings with a huge chip on his shoulder. The next week he came in furious because he hadn't lost any weight. I said, 'Well, if you'd followed the Program, you would have.' He was angry, but I got through to him. A week later, he came back, having lost 15 pounds. After that, he never missed a meeting. I watched his transformation—clothes, hair, attitude—and finally, he lost nearly 200 pounds. His biggest problem was wondering what to do with all the attention he was getting from women. I told him that was one area I couldn't help him with!"

—Wendy Brintnall, Leader, Omaha

Cheddar Corn Pudding

MAKES 6 SERVINGS

Ultra creamy and rich tasting, you'll never believe this casserole doesn't contain a speck of cream! And knowing that corn used to be a "forbidden" food on the Weight Watchers program just makes it even more satisfying. The perfect side dish for a holiday meal, it can be made ahead and reheated at Medium power in the microwave.

- **1½ tablespoons all-purpose flour**
- **1 cup low-fat (1%) milk**
- **2 cups frozen corn kernels**
- **2 scallions, chopped**
- **2 teaspoons sugar**
- **¼ teaspoon salt**
- **¼ teaspoon poultry seasoning or dried thyme**
- **¼ teaspoon ground pepper**
- **1 large egg**
- **1 egg white**
- **½ cup shredded reduced-fat cheddar cheese**

1. Place the oven rack in the center of the oven; preheat the oven to 350°F. Spray a 1-quart baking dish with nonstick spray.
2. Place the flour in a medium saucepan. Gradually whisk in the milk. Add the corn, scallions, sugar, salt, poultry seasoning or thyme, and pepper. Bring to a simmer over medium heat, whisking frequently; cook until slightly thickened, 2 minutes.
3. Beat the egg and egg white in a small bowl. Gradually beat in some of the hot milk mixture, whisking constantly. Whisk the egg mixture back into the saucepan. Reserve 2 tablespoons of the cheese; stir the remaining cheese into the corn mixture. Spoon into the prepared baking dish and sprinkle the reserved cheese on top.
4. Pull the oven rack partly out. Place a large roasting pan on the rack; place the corn casserole inside it. Carefully pour enough hot water into the roasting pan to fill it one-third of the way up the side of the casserole. Bake until the pudding is just set in the center, about 35 minutes. Remove from the water bath and serve.

Per serving (⅙ of casserole): 115 Cal, 3 g Fat, 2 g Sat Fat, 42 mg Chol, 190 mg Sod, 16 g Carb, 2 g Fib, 7 g Prot, 130 mg Calc. ***POINTS: 2.***

Oven-Fried Onion Rings

MAKES 4 SERVINGS

Through the years, Weight Watchers has learned many a thing about faux frying—and these crispy rings are proof. Though they're baked in the oven, they've got all the flavor and crunch of the rings served at your favorite steak house or pub, minus the greasiness. They're sure to become a family favorite with everything from burgers to broccoli.

2 tablespoons all-purpose flour
¼ teaspoon salt
Freshly ground pepper
⅓ cup plain dried bread crumbs
¼ cup fat-free egg substitute
2 large (8-ounce) onions, peeled, sliced ¼-inch thick, and separated into double rings

1. Adjust the oven racks to divide the oven in half. Preheat the oven to 400°F. Spray a nonstick baking sheet with nonstick spray. On a sheet of waxed paper, combine the flour, salt, and pepper. Place the bread crumbs on another sheet of wax paper. Place the egg substitute in a shallow dish.
2. Coat each double onion ring on both sides with the flour mixture, shaking off the excess; dip into the egg substitute, then coat lightly with the bread crumbs. Arrange the rings on the baking sheet (save any broken or small inner rings or pieces for another use), and spray the tops with nonstick spray. Discard the excess flour mixture, egg, and bread crumbs.
3. Bake on the top oven rack until browned, 10 minutes. Turn carefully and bake until browned, 5 minutes. Serve at once.

Per serving (1 cup): 95 Cal, 1 g Fat, 0 g Sat Fat, 0 mg Chol, 245 mg Sod, 19 g Carb, 3 g Fib, 4 g Prot, 47 mg Calc. ***POINTS: 1.***

top tip

Chop and freeze the unused parts of the onions in a zip-close freezer bag. Then you'll have them on hand when you need chopped onions in a recipe (don't bother thawing first).

Cranberry Holiday Mold

MAKES 8 SERVINGS 

A retro-recipe collection simply has to include a gelatin-based fruit salad. This one would look great on a Thanksgiving table, when old-fashioned recipes are a must. For a more beautiful look, use a fancy 6-cup mold or kugelhopf pan to mold the salad, but any 6-cup bowl will do nicely. Garnish the mold, if you like, with whole strawberries and unshelled walnuts, or with fresh herb sprigs. If it's your preference, you can substitute strawberry or raspberry gelatin for the cranberry-flavored variety.

- **2 cups boiling water**
- **2 (3-ounce) packages cranberry-flavored gelatin**
- **1½ cups cold mandarin orange–flavored sparkling water**
- **1 tablespoon grated orange zest**
- **10 strawberries, stemmed and halved**
- **1 Granny Smith apple, peeled, cored, and cut into ½-inch cubes**
- **⅓ cup walnuts, chopped**

1. Spray a 6-cup bundt pan or bowl with nonstick spray.
2. Combine the boiling water and gelatin in a medium heatproof bowl, stirring until completely dissolved. Stir in the sparkling water and orange zest. Refrigerate until thickened but not set, 1½–2 hours.
3. Stir in the strawberries, apple, and walnuts. Transfer the mixture to the bundt pan or bowl and refrigerate until the mold has set, at least 4 hours or overnight.
4. To unmold, dip the pan or bowl in a large bowl of warm water for 15–20 seconds. Wet a spoon with water, then gently loosen the gelatin from the sides of the pan with the spoon. Place a serving plate on top of the pan, then invert. Shake slightly to help free the gelatin, and gently lift off the pan.

Per serving (¾ cup): 128 Cal, 3 g Fat, 0 g Sat Fat, 0 mg Chol, 64 mg Sod, 24 g Carb, 1 g Fib, 3 g Prot, 12 mg Calc. ***POINTS: 3.***

Cranberry Holiday Mold

Pureed Peas with Mint

MAKES 4 SERVINGS

"Delicious used as a stuffing for 1 cup baked mushroom caps," suggests the *Weight Watchers Program Cookbook* (1972) for its Puree of Peas recipe—cooked frozen peas pureed with a little onion powder and chopped chives. We'd rather serve our updated version, with its fresh-mint flavor, as a side dish or sauce, or as a quick soup, thinned with a little reduced-sodium chicken broth. It's especially good with lamb.

- **1 (10-ounce package) frozen peas, or 1½ pounds fresh peas, shelled (about 2 cups)**
- **2 tablespoons chopped mint**
- **1 tablespoon unsalted butter**
- **¼ teaspoon salt**
- **Freshly ground white pepper**
- **2–3 tablespoons reduced-sodium vegetable broth, heated**
- **Mint leaves or small sprigs (optional)**

1. Cook the peas according to package directions. (If using fresh peas, steam them over 1 inch of boiling water until just tender and bright green, 3–6 minutes, depending on their freshness.)
2. Puree the peas with the mint, butter, salt, and pepper in a food processor; add the broth, one tablespoon at a time, until the mixture has a thick, creamy consistency. Garnish with the mint leaves or sprigs, if using.

Per serving (¼ cup): 75 Cal, 3 g Fat, 2 g Sat Fat, 8 mg Chol, 63 mg Sod, 9 g Carb, 4 g Fib, 3 g Prot, 19 mg Calc. ***POINTS: 1.***

Creamed Spinach

MAKES 4 SERVINGS 

The second *Weight Watchers Program Cookbook* came up with a clever way of re-creating the creamy goodness of this classic steak house side dish, using a puree of braised onions, chicken broth, and nonfat dry-milk powder. Now that steak houses are enjoying a renaissance, we decided to revisit the dish—with creamier, tastier results!

- **1 (1-pound) bag triple-washed fresh spinach, trimmed and torn**
- **1 onion, minced**
- **½ tablespoon all-purpose flour**
- **¼ teaspoon salt**
- **Freshly ground white pepper**
- **Pinch ground nutmeg**
- **¼ cup fat-free milk**
- **¼ cup tub-style light cream cheese, softened**

1. Put the spinach in a steamer basket; set it in a large pot over 1 inch of boiling water (the leaves will be tightly packed but will reduce as they start to wilt). Cover tightly and steam until just wilted, about 2 minutes. Drain in a colander; when cool enough to handle, squeeze out the excess moisture and coarsely chop.
2. Spray a medium nonstick skillet with nonstick spray and set over medium heat. Add the onion; sauté until translucent, 3–5 minutes.
3. Combine the flour, salt, pepper, and nutmeg in a small bowl; stir into the onion. Add the milk and cream cheese; cook one minute, stirring constantly with a whisk, until blended. Add the spinach; cook, stirring constantly, until just heated through.

Per serving (½ cup): 71 Cal, 2 g Fat, 1 g Sat Fat, 6 mg Chol, 300 mg Sod, 0 g Carb, 4 g Fib, 5 g Prot, 148 mg Calc. ***POINTS: 1.***

top tip

If you buy bagged baby spinach in a microwavable bag (check the label), you can speed through Step 1: Following the directions on the spinach bag, microwave the spinach. Carefully cut a slit in the top of the spinach bag (watch out for escaping steam), and transfer the cooked greens to a colander. When cool enough to handle, squeeze out the excess moisture and coarsely chop.

Sautéed Swiss Chard and Onion

MAKES 4 SERVINGS

The natural sweetness of onions is one reason why they were once considered a "limited" vegetable in the early days of Weight Watchers. Here, we've used that sweet onion flavor to tame the natural bitterness of earthy chard. This trick works for any leafy green, by the way.

- **4 teaspoons olive oil**
- **1 onion, chopped**
- **1 bunch Swiss chard, coarsely chopped**
- **¼ teaspoon salt**
- **Freshly ground pepper**
- **4 lemon wedges (optional)**

Heat a large nonstick skillet. Swirl in the oil, then add the onion. Sauté until golden, 8–10 minutes. Stir in the chard and continue cooking until the chard is tender but still a vivid dark green, about 7 minutes. Remove from the heat and sprinkle with the salt and pepper. Serve hot or at room temperature with the lemon wedges, if using.

Per serving (½ cup): 68 Cal, 5 g Fat, 1 g Sat Fat, 0 mg Chol, 299 mg Sod, 6 g Carb, 2 g Fib, 2 g Prot, 56 mg Calc. ***POINTS: 1.***

top tip

Here's a quick way to slice the chard: Hold a few stalks together and slice into 1-inch pieces; then stack a few leaves together, roll them up, and slice them.

Roasted Root Vegetables

MAKES 4 SERVINGS

Everybody fell in love with their roasting pans in the nineties, especially health-conscious cooks. What better tool to help turn humble vegetables into something glorious? In this very autumnal and colorful dish, carrots, potatoes, and turnip form a medley of roasted earthiness. Serve it with meat or poultry.

2 carrots, peeled and cut into chunks
2 medium (5-ounce) potatoes, peeled and cut into chunks
1 white turnip, peeled and cut into chunks
1 shallot, peeled and separated into cloves
4 teaspoons olive oil
1 tablespoon chopped fresh rosemary, or 1 teaspoon dried
1 tablespoon chopped fresh thyme, or 1 teaspoon dried
¼ teaspoon salt
Freshly ground pepper

1. Preheat the oven to 400°F.
2. Combine the carrots, potatoes, turnip, and shallot in a large nonstick roasting pan; drizzle with the oil and sprinkle with the rosemary, thyme, salt, and pepper. Spread the vegetables evenly in the pan.
3. Roast, stirring occasionally, until the shallots are caramelized and the vegetables are browned and tender, about 40 minutes.

Per serving (½ cup): 119 Cal, 5 g Fat, 1 g Sat Fat, 0 mg Chol, 177 mg Sod, 19 g Carb, 3 g Fib, 2 g Prot, 32 mg Calc. ***POINTS: 2.***

"At Weight Watchers, people learn how to use their will power and drive to reach any goal they have. They see how they can apply our Tools for Living to other parts of their lives. They see that they can do anything. That's what makes Weight Watchers so powerful."

—Stephanie Del Valle, Leader and Area Trainer, New York City

Carrots with Toasted Sesame–Ginger Dressing

MAKES 4 SERVINGS

A tasty and satisfying break from traditional green salads, this Asian-inspired combination is a great partner for shrimp, pork, or chicken. It's also a real crowd pleaser at a buffet supper.

- **8 large carrots, peeled and thinly sliced on the diagonal (about 2 pounds)**
- **½ cup water**
- **2 tablespoons rice-wine or cider vinegar**
- **1 tablespoon vegetable oil**
- **1 teaspoon grated peeled fresh ginger**
- **1 teaspoon sesame oil**
- **½ teaspoon ground cumin**
- **½ teaspoon sugar**
- **¼ teaspoon salt**
- **Freshly ground pepper**
- **2 tablespoons sesame seeds**
- **2 tablespoons chopped cilantro (optional)**

1. Put the carrots in a steamer basket; set it in a saucepan over 2 inches of boiling water. Cover tightly and steam until tender, about 10 minutes. Set aside to cool to room temperature.
2. To prepare the dressing, puree ½ cup of the carrots, the water, vinegar, vegetable oil, ginger, sesame oil, cumin, sugar, salt, and pepper in a food processor.
3. To toast the sesame seeds, place them in a small nonstick skillet over medium-low heat; slide the pan constantly and gently back and forth over the heat so the seeds move around. As soon as they begin to turn golden, remove the pan from the heat and transfer to a heatproof plate to cool.
4. Toss the remaining carrots with the dressing and the sesame seeds in a large bowl. Sprinkle with the cilantro, if using, and serve at once.

Per serving (1 cup): 164 Cal, 7 g Fat, 1 g Sat Fat, 0 mg Chol, 225 mg Sod, 24 g Carb, 7 g Fib, 3 g Prot, 70 mg Calc. ***POINTS: 3.***

top tip

You can make this salad up to four days in advance—just cover and refrigerate—but wait until serving time to sprinkle on the cilantro.

Greek-Style Twice-Baked Potatoes

MAKES 4 SERVINGS

Twice-baked potatoes were *the* trendy dish of the eighties. Today we've updated them with a Greek twist. If you prefer a classic version, use shredded extra-sharp cheddar in place of the feta cheese.

- **4 (5-ounce) Idaho potatoes, scrubbed**
- **⅓ cup crumbled feta cheese, room temperature**
- **⅓ cup plain low-fat (1%) yogurt, room temperature**
- **1 tablespoon melted butter**
- **1 tablespoon snipped fresh chives**

1. Preheat the oven to 425°F. Bake the potatoes on the oven rack until a knife can easily pierce the center of each potato, about 45 minutes. Remove the potatoes and let cool slightly on a rack; reduce the oven heat to 375°F.
2. Split the potatoes in half horizontally (use oven mitts to protect your hands). Scoop out the flesh from each potato half, leaving a ¼-inch-thick layer still in the shell. Transfer the potato flesh to a medium bowl.
3. Add the feta, yogurt, butter, and chives to the potato flesh and mash well. Stuff the filling into the shells and arrange filling-side up on a baking sheet. Bake until the filling is hot in the center and the edges are lightly browned, about 12 minutes.

Per serving (2 potato halves): 194 Cal, 6 g Fat, 4 g Sat Fat, 20 mg Chol, 181 mg Sod, 31 g Carb, 3 g Fib, 6 g Prot, 113 mg Calc. ***POINTS: 4.***

Oven-Fried Onion Rings and Idaho Fries with Vinegar

Idaho Fries with Vinegar

MAKES 4 SERVINGS 

Who can resist fries? This version allows you to indulge in one of the most adored foods in America. A fairly hot oven, with the rack near the hot oven bottom, guarantees a crisp potato. Eat them hot, with a splash of malt vinegar instead of ketchup, as the Brits do.

- **4 (5-ounce) Idaho potatoes, scrubbed**
- **1 tablespoon olive or vegetable oil**
- **¼ teaspoon salt**
- **¼ teaspoon freshly ground pepper**
- **2 tablespoons malt or white vinegar**

1. Adjust the oven rack to the lowest position in the oven. Preheat the oven to 450°F.
2. Cut the potatoes lengthwise into eighths to form wedges. Toss the potatoes with the oil on a heavy baking sheet or jelly-roll pan, and arrange them flat in a single layer. Bake the potatoes without turning, until the bottoms are deep golden and crisp, 20 minutes; turn the potatoes to the opposite cut side. Bake 10 minutes more until crisp. Remove from the oven and immediately sprinkle with the salt and pepper, then the vinegar. (You can also serve the vinegar in a small bowl on the side, for dipping.)

Per serving (8 fries): 154 Cal, 3 g Fat, 0 g Sat Fat, 0 mg Chol, 155 mg Sod, 29 g Carb, 3 g Fib, 3 g Prot, 13 mg Calc. ***POINTS: 3.***

top tip

A different flavored vinegar will give these crispy fries even more pizzazz. Try white wine or tarragon vinegar—or even a fruit-infused version, such as pear or raspberry vinegar.

Roasted-Garlic Mashed Potatoes

MAKES 8 SERVINGS

The term "comfort food" was coined in the eighties, and we can think of no better homage to these words than mashed potatoes. We've chosen rich-tasting, yellow-fleshed Yukon Gold potatoes in our version to create the illusion of lots of butter—and added mellow, fat-free flavor with a whole head of sweet roasted garlic. No one will miss the butter and cream!

- **1 head garlic, top third sliced off**
- **3 pounds Yukon Gold potatoes, peeled and cut into 1-inch pieces**
- **⅔ cup low-fat (1%) milk**
- **¼ cup (½ stick) unsalted butter**
- **1½ teaspoons salt**
- **¼ teaspoon freshly ground pepper**

1. Preheat the oven to 400°F. Wrap the garlic with foil and place directly on the oven rack; roast until soft, 50–60 minutes. Remove from the oven and let cool completely. Squeeze the pulp from each clove and reserve; discard the skins.
2. Combine the potatoes in a large pot with enough cold water to cover them by 3 inches. Bring to a boil over high heat; simmer until tender, about 20 minutes. Drain the potatoes and return them to the pot. Mash the potatoes with a potato masher or fork until fairly smooth.
3. Meanwhile, combine the milk, the reserved garlic, the butter, salt, and pepper in a medium saucepan. Cook over medium heat, stirring occasionally, until the butter melts and the mixture is heated through. Stir into the potatoes and serve at once.

Per serving (¾ cup): 196 Cal, 6 g Fat, 4 g Sat Fat, 16 mg Chol, 455 mg Sod, 33 g Carb, 3 g Fib, 4 g Prot, 45 mg Calc. ***POINTS: 4.***

German Hot Potato Salad

MAKES 4 SERVINGS

It's still a favorite after all these years, but this one is not verboten, as we've lightened up the fat considerably. Upgrading the ingredients for twenty-first-century palates, we use Yukon Gold potatoes for their buttery richness, as well as premium-quality grainy mustard and sherry vinegar.

- **1½ pounds Yukon Gold potatoes, peeled**
- **1 slice bacon**
- **1–1½ teaspoons olive oil**
- **¾ red onion, very thinly sliced**
- **¼–½ teaspoon crushed red pepper**
- **¼ cup reduced-sodium chicken broth**
- **2 tablespoons grainy mustard**
- **1 tablespoon sherry vinegar**
- **1 teaspoon sugar**

1. Combine the potatoes and enough water to cover by 1 inch in a medium saucepan; bring to a boil and cook until fork-tender, about 20 minutes. Drain and let cool to just warm. Cut into bite-size chunks and place in a large bowl.
2. Meanwhile, cook the bacon in a medium nonstick skillet until crisp; pat dry with paper towels, and finely chop. Measure the pan drippings, and add enough oil to equal 2 teaspoons; return the skillet to the heat.
3. Add the onion and red pepper; sauté over medium heat until tender, 2 minutes. Stir in the broth, mustard, vinegar, and sugar; bring to a simmer. Pour over the potatoes; toss gently and let stand 2–3 minutes to absorb some of the dressing. Sprinkle with the chopped bacon.

Per serving (1 cup): 181 Cal, 4 g Fat, 1 g Sat Fat, 2 mg Chol, 162 mg Sod, 34 g Carb, 3 g Fib, 4 g Prot, 24 mg Calc. ***POINTS: 3.***

top tip

You can make this dish with cold leftover cooked potatoes, too—just skip Step 1. Be sure to warm the potatoes in a microwave before pouring the hot dressing over them; the warmth helps them absorb the dressing.

Potato Salad with Tarragon-Chive Dressing

MAKES 6 SERVINGS

On a summer evening, this salad is the perfect accompaniment to anything grilled. It's best made ahead of time and left at room temperature, as it loses its fresh taste once refrigerated.

- **1¾ pounds Yukon Gold potatoes, peeled and quartered**
- **2 tablespoons minced chives**
- **2 tablespoons white-wine or cider vinegar**
- **4 teaspoons olive oil**
- **1 tablespoon chopped tarragon**
- **1 tablespoon chopped parsley**
- **1 tablespoon dry white wine or reduced-sodium chicken broth**
- **¼ teaspoon salt**
- **Freshly ground pepper**
- **Small handful whole chives (optional)**
- **2–3 tarragon sprigs (optional)**
- **2–3 parsley sprigs (optional)**

1. Combine the potatoes and enough water to cover by 1 inch in a medium saucepan; bring to a boil and cook until fork-tender, about 20 minutes. Drain and let cool to just warm. Cut into bite-size chunks.
2. Combine the chives, vinegar, oil, tarragon, parsley, wine or broth, salt, and pepper in a large bowl; add the still-warm potatoes and toss to coat evenly. Garnish with the whole chives, tarragon sprigs, and/or parsley sprigs, if using. Let stand at least 30 minutes, and up to 3 hours, before serving.

Per serving (½ cup): 133 Cal, 3 g Fat, 0 g Sat Fat, 0 mg Chol, 104 mg Sod, 25 g Carb, 2 g Fib, 2 g Prot, 16 mg Calc. ***POINTS: 3.***

Sweet Potato Fritters

MAKES 4 SERVINGS

Using the (very) Petite Potato Pancakes in the 1972 *Weight Watchers Program Cookbook* as a starting point, we've updated the recipe with sweet potatoes, global flavors, and best of all, a satisfying portion size. Serve these pleasantly sweet fritters alongside saucy dishes like chili and curry, or with roasted pork, beef, or turkey—even our Cajun Catfish [see page 149].

2 (8-ounce) sweet potatoes
¼ cup low-fat (1%) milk
1 large egg, separated
4 teaspoons sugar
½ teaspoon grated fresh ginger
¼ teaspoon salt
⅛ teaspoon cinnamon
¼ cup all-purpose flour
½ teaspoon baking powder

1. Preheat oven to 425°F. Line a baking sheet with foil. Pierce the potatoes in several places with a fork and place on the baking sheet. Bake until a knife can pierce them easily, 40 minutes. When cool enough to handle, peel off and discard the skins.
2. Rice or mash the potatoes, using a potato ricer or potato masher, in a medium bowl. Whisk in the milk, egg yolk, sugar, ginger, salt, and cinnamon. Combine the flour and baking powder in a cup or small bowl.
3. With an electric mixer on medium speed, beat the egg white to soft peaks in a medium bowl. Gently fold into the potato mixture. Sprinkle the flour mixture over the top and fold in until smooth.
4. Spray a large nonstick skillet with nonstick spray; heat over medium heat. Drop the batter into the skillet by slightly rounded tablespoonfuls, flattening them slightly to form 6 (2-inch) patties. Cook until golden and set, about 1½ minutes per side. Transfer to a warmed plate, cover loosely with foil, and continue with the remaining potato mixture to make 24 fritters. Serve immediately.

Per serving (6 fritters): 147 Cal, 2 g Fat, 1 g Sat Fat, 54 mg Chol, 237 mg Sod, 28 g Carb, 2 g Fib, 4 g Prot, 80 mg Calc. ***POINTS: 3.***

Confetti Rice Salad

MAKES 4 SERVINGS

The Rice Salad Bowl in the second *Weight Watchers Program Cookbook* made a little bit of white rice go a long way, with tomatoes, artichoke hearts, scallions, and capers. Our update takes it to a new level by using green soybeans (edamame) and a mixed brown-rice combination that includes the reddish-hued Wehani rice, black japonica rice, and long-grain brown rice. If you can't find it at your supermarket, make your own blend of any other brown rices that strike your fancy; you'll need one cup total. Cook the rice according to package directions, and proceed with the recipe at Step 2, adding all the oil at once.

- **1 cup Wehani-japonica-brown-rice blend, or other brown rice**
- **2 cups water**
- **3 teaspoons olive oil**
- **1 small red bell pepper, diced**
- **1 small yellow bell pepper, diced**
- **½ cup cooked green soybeans (edamame)**
- **⅓ red onion, finely chopped**
- **1 tablespoon rice-wine vinegar**
- **1 tablespoon fresh lime juice**
- **1 teaspoon finely chopped cilantro**
- **½ teaspoon sugar**

1. Rinse the rice to remove any impurities; drain. Add the water and 1 teaspoon of the oil. Bring to a boil, cover, reduce the heat, and simmer until the liquid is absorbed, about 45 minutes. Remove from the heat and let stand, covered, 30 minutes. (This helps reduce starchiness, giving the rice grains a better texture for salad.) Fluff with a fork.
2. Combine the red pepper, yellow pepper, soybeans, onion, vinegar, lime juice, the remaining 2 teaspoons oil, the cilantro, and sugar in another bowl; add to the rice and toss.

Per serving (generous 1 cup): 237 Cal, 5 g Fat, 1 g Sat Fat, 0 mg Chol, 10 mg Sod, 41 g Carb, 5 g Fib, 6 g Prot, 36 mg Calc. ***POINTS: 4.***

> "I still follow the Weight Watchers Program; I always have. Now I use the ***POINTS*** Food System. It's the best plan we've ever created; it's all about portion control and common sense. I eat out quite a bit, and it's easy for me to make decisions using ***POINTS***."
>
> *—Felice Lippert, Cofounder, Weight Watchers International*

Fried Rice

MAKES 6 SERVINGS

Fried rice was one of the first dishes to convert Westerners to the pleasures of Chinese take-out, and it's actually very easy to make at home. The key is to use cold cooked rice; make it at least an hour ahead to give it time to chill thoroughly. Remember that pint of take-out white rice in your fridge from a few nights ago? Use it—it's perfect.

- **1 tablespoon peanut or vegetable oil**
- **¼ pound snow peas, thinly sliced**
- **1 large celery stalk, diced**
- **1 large carrot, coarsely shredded**
- **1 large shallot, finely chopped**
- **2 teaspoons grated fresh ginger**
- **¼ teaspoon crushed red pepper**
- **2½ cups cold cooked rice**
- **3 tablespoons reduced-sodium soy sauce**
- **1 tablespoon rice vinegar**
- **1 teaspoon sugar**
- **⅓ cup sliced scallion, green part only**

1. Heat a large nonstick skillet over high heat; swirl in the oil and add the snow peas, celery, carrot, shallot, ginger, and red pepper. Stir-fry 2 minutes; add the rice, stirring well to remove any clumps, and stir-fry until hot, 3–4 minutes.
2. Combine the soy sauce, vinegar, and sugar in a small bowl; sprinkle over the rice, along with the scallion, and stir-fry just to heat through, 2 minutes more. Serve immediately.

Per serving (3/4 cup): 135 Cal, 3 g Fat, 0 g Sat Fat, 0 mg Chol, 316 mg Sod, 25 g Carb, 2 g Fib, 3 g Prot, 31 mg Calc. ***POINTS: 3.***

Any Way You Slice It

1997

Weight Watchers introduces 1-2-3 Success® and the ***POINTS*** Food System, with more freedom in food choices than ever. To kick off the program is new spokesperson, Sarah Ferguson, Duchess of York.

1999

H. J. Heinz sells Weight Watchers International to Artal Luxembourg. Vice President of Operations for Weight Watchers UK (and former Leader) Linda Huett is named President.

The National Health and Nutrition Examination Survey finds that one out of eight children is now overweight.

2000

We now consume more sugar than ever: an astonishing 34 teaspoons per day, on average.

>>>

Multigrain Loaf with Flaxseeds

MAKES 12 SERVINGS

The back-to-the-land movement of the late sixties and seventies got us all baking our own bread—the more grains, the better. Here's a modern take on the concept, with food-processor speed and some newly trendy ingredients: flaxseed, a powerhouse of fiber and heart-healthy omega-3 fatty acids; and spelt, a nutty-tasting cousin of wheat that's high in protein. Both can be found in health-food stores.

- **1¼ cups hot (120°F–130°F) water**
- **2 tablespoons honey**
- **4 tablespoons flaxseed**
- **1 cup spelt flour**
- **1 cup whole-wheat flour**
- **1 cup unbleached all-purpose flour**
- **1 (¼-ounce) envelope quick-rise yeast**
- **1 teaspoon salt**
- **½ tablespoon cornmeal**
- **1 egg, lightly beaten**

1. Stir together the water, honey, and 2 tablespoons of the flaxseed in a measuring cup.
2. Combine the spelt flour, whole-wheat flour, all-purpose flour; yeast, and salt in a food processor. With the machine running, pour the water-honey mixture through the feed tube; pulse until the dough forms a smooth ball, about 1 minute.
3. Spray a large bowl with nonstick spray; put the dough in the bowl. Cover lightly with plastic wrap, and let the dough rise in a warm spot until doubled in size, about 30–40 minutes.
4. Punch down the dough. Kneading lightly, form the dough into a loaf. Spray a 5 x 9-inch loaf pan with nonstick spray; sprinkle the bottom and sides with the cornmeal. Place dough in the pan; Cover and let rise in a warm spot until doubled in size, 30 minutes.
5. Preheat the oven to 400°F. Gently brush the top of the loaf with the egg; sprinkle with the remaining 2 tablespoons flaxseed. Bake the bread until deep golden, 18–20 minutes. Cover the top loosely with a sheet of foil; bake 15–17 minutes more, or until an instant-read thermometer inserted into the center registers 210°F. Loosen the sides of the bread with a knife, and unmold the bread onto a rack to cool.

Per serving (¾-inch slice): 139 Cal, 2 g Fat, 0 g Sat Fat, 9 mg Chol, 199 mg Sod, 27 g Carb, 4 g Fib, 5 g Prot, 19 mg Calc. ***POINTS: 2.***

top tip

To make the bread by hand, use warm (105°F–115°F) rather than hot water. Combine the water, honey, and yeast in a large bowl; set aside until foamy. Stir in the spelt flour, whole-wheat flour, all-purpose flour, salt, and 2 tablespoons of the flaxseeds until the dough starts to gather around the spoon. Turn out the dough onto a lightly floured counter; knead until the dough is smooth and elastic, about 10 minutes. Proceed with the recipe at Step 3.

Bubble Bread with Herbs and Sun-Dried Tomatoes

MAKES 12 SERVINGS

Remember the fun of pulling off bubbles of tasty bread from a knobby bubble ring? While the terminology plants this recipe firmly in the sixties, our version is decidedly and deliciously modern.

- **1 cup warm (105°F–115°F) water**
- **Pinch sugar**
- **1 envelope active dry yeast**
- **¾ cup milk**
- **2 tablespoons unsalted butter, diced**
- **1 tablespoon honey**
- **4¾–5¼ cups unbleached all-purpose flour**
- **1½ teaspoons salt**
- **2 large eggs**
- **1 tablespoon minced fresh herbs (try rosemary and thyme, or dill)**
- **1 tablespoon drained minced oil-packed sun-dried tomatoes**

1. Combine the water and sugar in a small bowl. Sprinkle in the yeast and let stand until foamy, 5 minutes. Meanwhile, warm the milk, butter, and honey in a large microwavable measuring cup on High, until just warm and butter is nearly melted, 30–40 seconds.
2. Combine 4¾ cups of the flour with the salt in a food processor. With the machine running, scrape the yeast mixture and then milk mixture through feed tube, followed by one egg; pulse about 1 minute, until dough forms a smooth ball, adding only enough of remaining ½ cup flour, if needed, to form a ball.
3. Spray a large bowl with nonstick spray; put dough in bowl and lightly spray top with nonstick spray. Cover with plastic wrap and let dough rise in a warm spot until it doubles in size, about 1 hour.
4. Combine the herbs and sun-dried tomatoes in a small bowl. Punch down the dough. Sprinkle about one-third of the herb mixture on the surface of the dough. Fold the dough in half over the herbs and repeat twice more, folding the dough a few more times to incorporate the herb mixture completely.
5. Spray a 12-cup tube pan with nonstick spray. Pull off a piece of dough about the size of a golf ball and roll into a ball between your palms; drop it into the pan. Repeat, spacing the balls about ½ inch apart and covering the bottom evenly, until the pan is evenly filled with 2 layers of balls. Cover and let the dough rise until doubled in size, 45 minutes.
6. Preheat the oven to 375°F. Bake the bread until lightly golden, 20 minutes. Lightly beat remaining egg in a small bowl, and lightly brush it onto the top of the bread. Continue baking until deep golden, 10–12 minutes more. Carefully remove bread from the pan and cool on a rack. Serve warm or at room temperature.

Per serving (1⁄12 of loaf): 220 Cal, 3 g Fat, 2 g Sat Fat, 32 mg Chol, 310 mg Sod, 40 g Carb, 2 g Fib, 7 g Prot, 32 mg Calc. ***POINTS: 4.***

Pumpkin Rolls

MAKES 12 SERVINGS

With their crunchy poppy seed topping, these subtly spiced rolls are all-purpose: They give a special flavor boost to breakfast or lunch, and make uniquely elegant dinner rolls.

- **3 cups unbleached all-purpose flour**
- **½ cup whole-wheat flour**
- **1 envelope quick-rise yeast**
- **1 tablespoon sugar**
- **¾ teaspoon salt**
- **½ teaspoon ground ginger**
- **½ teaspoon cinnamon**
- **¾ cup milk**
- **½ cup pumpkin puree**
- **2 tablespoons butter, diced**
- **2 large eggs**
- **1 tablespoon poppy seeds**

1. Combine the all-purpose flour, whole-wheat flour, yeast, sugar, salt, ginger, and cinnamon in a food processor.
2. Whisk the milk and pumpkin in a microwavable bowl and stir in the butter. Microwave on High until the butter is melted and the milk registers 120°F–130°F on an instant-read thermometer, 50–70 seconds. With machine running, scrape the milk mixture through the feed tube, followed by one of the eggs; pulse about 1 minute, until dough forms a smooth ball, adding 1–2 tablespoons extra all-purpose flour only if needed to form a ball.
3. Spray a large bowl with nonstick spray; put the dough in the bowl. Cover lightly with plastic wrap and let the dough rise in a warm spot until doubled in size, about 40 minutes.
4. Punch down the dough. Spray a 12-cup muffin pan with nonstick spray. Roll the dough into a cylinder, then cut it into 12 equal pieces. Roll each piece between your palms to form smooth balls, dropping each into a muffin cup. Cover lightly with plastic wrap and let the dough rise in a warm spot until doubled in size, about 20 minutes.
5. Preheat the oven to 350°F. Beat the remaining egg in a small bowl; lightly brush the tops of the rolls with the beaten egg, and sprinkle evenly with the poppy seeds. Bake until golden, 20 minutes. Transfer to a rack to cool.

Per serving (1 roll): 176 Cal, 3 g Fat, 2 g Sat Fat, 32 mg Chol, 176 mg Sod, 31 g Carb, 2 g Fib, 6 g Prot, 43 mg Calc. ***POINTS: 3.***

top tip

To make the rolls ahead of time, wrap each cooled roll in foil, then freeze them in zip-close freezer bags for up to a month. The rolls can be defrosted in the microwave, or overnight on the counter. To thaw in the microwave, wrap each roll individually in paper towels and microwave on High about 15 to 30 seconds. Or place the unwrapped frozen rolls on a baking sheet and heat in a 350°F oven 8 to 10 minutes.

Zucchini Corn Bread

MAKES 12 SERVINGS

Don't let the long ingredients list stop you; this recipe can be made in one bowl. Adding zucchini to the batter—an innovation inspired by the zucchini breads of the seventies—makes it deliciously moist.

- **1½ bacon slices**
- **1½ small zucchini, coarsely shredded (1 cup)**
- **1 cup low-fat buttermilk**
- **1 (8-ounce) can creamed corn**
- **½ cup shredded extra-sharp cheddar cheese**
- **2 large eggs, room temperature**
- **2 scallions, minced**
- **3 tablespoons sugar**
- **1 tablespoon butter, melted**
- **1½ teaspoon salt**
- **¼ teaspoon cayenne**
- **1¼ cups yellow cornmeal**
- **1 cup all-purpose flour**
- **1 tablespoon baking powder**
- **¼ teaspoon baking soda**

1. Cook the bacon in a large cast-iron skillet over medium heat until crisp; remove and finely chop, leaving the drippings in the skillet. Preheat the oven to 375°F.
2. Combine the bacon with the zucchini, buttermilk, creamed corn, cheese, eggs, scallions, sugar, butter, salt, and cayenne in a large bowl, using a wooden spoon. Toss together the cornmeal, flour, baking powder, and baking soda on a sheet of wax paper; stir into the zucchini mixture until just combined.
3. Heat the skillet until very hot, about 2–3 minutes, then remove from the heat. Scrape the batter into the skillet and even the top with a spatula. Bake until lightly browned around the edges and a toothpick inserted into the center comes out clean, about 25 minutes. Use a knife to loosen the bread around the edges of the skillet, and carefully transfer the bread to a rack. Let cool at least 10 minutes. Cut into 12 wedges, and serve warm or at room temperature.

Per serving (1⁄12 of bread): 183 Cal, 5 g Fat, 3 g Sat Fat, 45 mg Chol, 405 mg Sod, 28 g Carb, 2 g Fib, 6 g Prot, 126 mg Calc. ***POINTS: 4.***

top tip

If you plan to use only portions of the bread at a time, wrap large wedges of bread in plastic wrap, then place in zip-close freezer bags. Defrost in the microwave on Low power or the Defrost setting, still wrapped, until just softened and slightly warmed, 30 to 40 seconds.

Sausage Focaccia

MAKES 12 SERVINGS

Like so many formerly "forbidden" ingredients, a little sausage can provide a lot of flavor—and pleasure. Try this chewy, satisfying bread as a soup mate or an appetizer.

- **1⅔ cups warm (105°F–115°F) water**
- **¼ teaspoon sugar**
- **1 envelope quick-rise yeast**
- **3 teaspoons olive oil**
- **3¾–4 cups all-purpose flour**
- **2¼ teaspoons kosher salt**
- **1½ links (6 ounces) Italian-style turkey sausage, casing removed**
- **1 tablespoon drained minced oil-packed sun-dried tomatoes**
- **1 tablespoon minced fresh rosemary**

1. Combine the water and sugar in a small bowl. Sprinkle in the yeast and let stand until just beginning to foam, about 2 minutes. Add 2 teaspoons of the oil.
2. Combine the flour and 2 teaspoons of the salt in a large bowl. Make a well in the center; add the yeast mixture, and begin stirring the flour into the liquid with a wooden spoon until well incorporated and the dough begins wrapping around the spoon. Scrape the sides of the bowl and turn the dough out onto a lightly floured work surface. Knead the dough gradually, adding only enough of the remaining flour to stop it from sticking, until smooth and elastic, 8–9 minutes. (The dough should remain soft and pliable; flour your hands frequently instead of adding flour to the dough, when possible.)
3. Spray a large bowl with nonstick spray; put the dough in the bowl and lightly spray the top with nonstick spray. Cover lightly with plastic wrap, and let the dough rise in a warm spot until it doubles in size, about 40 minutes.
4. Meanwhile, cook the sausage in a nonstick skillet over medium-high heat, breaking up the large pieces with a wooden spoon, until deep brown, 4 minutes. Let cool.
5. Preheat the oven to 450°F. Spray a large (10½ x 15½-inch) jelly-roll pan with nonstick spray. Punch down the dough. Sprinkle one third of the sausage, tomato, and rosemary on the surface of dough, spreading with fingertips. Fold dough in half over the mixture and repeat twice more, folding the dough a few more times to fully incorporate ingredients. Press dough evenly into the pan. Cover and let stand until just slightly puffed, about 10 minutes. Bake until crisp-edged and golden, 20–22 minutes. Immediately brush the top with the remaining 1 teaspoon oil and sprinkle with the remaining ¼ teaspoon salt.

Per serving (1⁄12 of loaf): 183 Cal, 3 g Fat, 1 g Sat Fat, 10 mg Chol, 455 mg Sod, 30 g Carb, 1 g Fib, 7 g Prot, 11 mg Calc. ***POINTS: 4.***

Sausage Focaccia

How Sweet It Is

2001

The attacks of September 11 make the whole country seem suddenly vulnerable. People seek comfort in one another—and in food. Weight Watchers grows considerably, as members return to find healthier ways to cope and care for themselves and their families.

2002

Weight Watchers announces a worldwide attendance record.

The IRS recognizes that obesity is a disease in its own right—and begins allowing certain weight-loss expenses to be tax-deductible (if documented medical necessity is shown).

2003

Weight Watchers turns 40, with no signs of a midlife crisis in sight.

Ambrosia

MAKES 6 SERVINGS

A timeless Southern favorite, our Ambrosia contains that once-forbidden fruit, grapes! To make the salad just right for *you,* feel free to vary the fruits to your liking. But to keep it authentically Southern, be sure to include the coconut and pecans. (We're breaking tradition, however, by omitting the maraschino cherries.)

- **3 tablespoons honey**
- **2 navel oranges**
- **¼ medium pineapple, trimmed, cored, and cubed (1½ cups)**
- **1 tart green or red apple, cored and chopped**
- **1 cup seedless red or green grapes, (halved, if large)**
- **¼ cup sweetened shredded coconut**
- **½ ounce pecan halves, toasted and finely chopped (about 2 tablespoons)**

1. Place the honey in a large bowl. Trim the rind and white pith from the oranges, then cut each orange in half lengthwise. Slice the orange halves crosswise into ¼-inch thick half rounds; place in the bowl, along with any of the juices. Add the pineapple, apple, grapes, and coconut, tossing to combine. (The salad can be made ahead up to this point up to 1 day in advance, then covered and refrigerated.)
2. When ready to serve, toss the fruit mixture gently and place it in a serving dish. Sprinkle with the toasted pecans and serve at once.

Per serving (about ½ cup): 139 Cal, 3 g Fat, 1 g Sat Fat, 0 mg Chol, 12 mg Sod, 29 g Carb, 3 g Fib, 1 g Prot, 27 mg Calc. ***POINTS: 2.***

top tip

To toast the pecans, place them in a dry nonstick skillet over medium heat. Cook, shaking the pan often to prevent burning, until they become fragrant and only slightly darkened (watch for burning), about 3 minutes.

Baked Apples

MAKES 4 SERVINGS

Once upon a time, diet ginger ale and a small apple were all you needed to make a Weight Watchers Baked Apple. But the recipe doesn't work with today's aspartame-sweetened diet sodas, since the sweetener loses its potency with heat. Here's a new version that's still easy—and so delicious. It's wonderful plain, and even better with a scoop of low-fat vanilla ice cream. For best results, choose apples that hold their shape during baking, such as McIntosh or Granny Smith.

- **4 medium apples, peeled and cored**
- **¼ cup raisins or dried cranberries**
- **1 tablespoon reduced-calorie pancake syrup**
- **1 tablespoon unsalted butter, softened**
- **¼ teaspoon cinnamon**
- **½ cup apple cider**

1. Preheat the oven to 350°F. Place the apples in a small baking dish or pie plate. Trim the bottoms, if necessary, to stand the apples upright.
2. Combine the raisins or cranberries, syrup, butter, and cinnamon in a small bowl. Spoon 1 tablespoon of the butter mixture into each apple's cavity. Pour the cider over, cover with foil, and bake until the apples are soft, about 30 minutes. Serve with the cooking juices spooned over each baked apple.

Per serving (1 apple): 150 Cal, 3 g Fat, 2 g Sat Fat, 8 mg Chol, 11 mg Sod, 32 g Carb, 3 g Fib, 1 g Prot, 15 mg Calc. ***POINTS: 3.***

"On September 11, I was at our Liberty Street location [across the street from the World Trade Center]. When the first plane hit, I didn't really know what had happened. But when I looked up, I could see that the World Trade Center was on fire. I just knew I had to get to my next meeting uptown, so I started walking.... I heard the second tower fall behind me, and first I ran, along with everyone else; then I just kept walking. When I finally reached the building, it was locked. That's when it really hit me. I had been at the very last meeting of the Liberty Street Center. A few days later, when the manager was allowed to go back to the site, there was nothing left standing except the flip chart that had been used at that last meeting. It read, The Power of the Group."

—Stephanie Del Valle, Leader and Area Trainer, New York City

Cranberry-Stuffed Apples

MAKES 4 SERVINGS

Both fresh and dried cranberries—and a hint of ginger—give a spirited tang to this comfort-food specialty. Since apple sizes vary considerably, you may have a little leftover filling. Add the leftover filling to the liquid in the pan before baking. You can serve it with the sauce or simply mound it on top of the baked apples.

- **⅓ cup packed light brown sugar**
- **1 cup cranberry juice**
- **4 large baking apples (1½ pounds), such as Jonagold, McIntosh, or Gala**
- **½ cup fresh or frozen cranberries, coarsely chopped**
- **¼ cup dried cranberries**
- **¼ cup golden raisins or chopped mixed dried fruit**
- **2 tablespoons chopped crystallized ginger**
- **½ teaspoon ground cinnamon**
- **¼ teaspoon ground allspice**
- **3 tablespoons reduced-fat sour cream**
- **1 tablespoon confectioners' sugar**
- **½ teaspoon vanilla extract**

1. Place the oven rack in the center of the oven; preheat the oven to 375°F. Reserve 2 tablespoons of the brown sugar for the filling. Combine the remaining brown sugar and the cranberry juice in the bottom of a 1½-quart baking dish.
2. Using a melon baller, cut out the cores of the apples without cutting all the way through to the bottom. Peel the top halves of the apples. Trim the bottoms, if necessary, to stand apples upright.
3. Combine the fresh and dried cranberries, the raisins, ginger, the reserved 2 tablespoons brown sugar, the cinnamon, and allspice in a small bowl. Pack the mixture into the cavities of the apples. Place the apples in the baking dish and cover loosely with foil. Bake, occasionally spooning the pan juices over the apples, until the apples are just tender when pierced with a knife, 40–45 minutes. Cool on a rack.
4. Meanwhile, stir together the sour cream, confectioners' sugar, and vanilla in a small bowl until smooth. Just before serving, baste the apples with the pan juices. Serve with the pan juices on the side and a dollop of the sour cream mixture.

Per serving (1 apple with 2½ tablespoons juices and 2 teaspoons cream): 323 Cal, 2 g Fat, 1 g Sat Fat, 4 mg Chol, 30 mg Sod, 80 g Carb, 6 g Fib, 1 g Prot, 56 mg Calc. ***POINTS: 6.***

Campari-Poached Grapefruit

MAKES 4 SERVINGS

Campari, that oh-so-chic sixties aperitif, is the perfect match for grapefruit: Both have a similar ying-yang flavoring of tart and sweet. Serve this fruit mixture in goblets or dessert dishes as a refreshing summer dessert or for an elegant brunch treat.

- **1¼ cups water**
- **½ cup sugar**
- **5 (3-inch) strips orange zest**
- **2 star anise or 4 whole cloves**
- **3 medium pink grapefruit**
- **3 tablespoons Campari or pomegranate juice**

1. Combine the water, sugar, orange zest, and anise or cloves in a large skillet. Cover, bring to a simmer, and cook 10 minutes.
2. Meanwhile, trim off the rind and white pith from the grapefruit, then cut each grapefruit into 8 wedges. Add the grapefruit pieces to the simmering liquid, and remove from the heat. Stir in the Campari or pomegranate juice; transfer to a serving bowl, then set aside to cool. Cover and refrigerate up to 4 days. Serve chilled or at room temperature.

Per serving (about ¾ cup): 189 Cal, 0 g Fat, 0 g Sat Fat, 0 mg Chol, 1 mg Sod, 44 g Carb, 2 g Fib, 1 g Prot, 25 mg Calc. ***POINTS: 3.***

top tip

Pomegranate juice, with its refreshingly tart sweetness, is a nice substitute for the Campari. Look for it in Middle Eastern markets and gourmet stores—or if you prefer, you can make it yourself in pomegranate season, which peaks in December. Be sure to use rubber gloves and wear an apron to prevent staining. To make the juice: Cut the crown end off the pomegranate with a sharp knife. Lightly score the rind in several places. Immerse the fruit in a bowl of water; soak for 5 minutes. Hold the fruit under water and break the sections apart, separating the seeds from the membrane. The seeds will sink, while the rind and membrane float. Skim off and discard the membranes and rind with a slotted spoon. Pour the seeds into a colander; drain and pat dry, then wrap the seeds in a damp cloth and squeeze them hard into a bowl. You should have about ½ cup of juice.

Spiced Plum-and-Port Compote

MAKES 6 SERVINGS

If you have fond memories of stewed prunes—one of the most delightful, old-fashioned desserts ever—you'll love this modern version. It's made with fresh plums, ginger for zing, and a splash of ruby port. If you prefer an alcohol-free version, try substituting fresh orange juice for the port.

- **2 cinnamon sticks**
- **4 slices peeled fresh ginger**
- **8 black peppercorns**
- **5 whole cloves**
- **½ cup packed brown sugar**
- **½ cup ruby port**
- **½ cup cranberry juice**
- **1½ pounds fresh plums (about 9 medium), halved and pitted**
- **1 tablespoon fresh lemon juice**

1. Place the cinnamon, ginger, peppercorns, and cloves in the center of a 5-inch square of cheesecloth. Gather up the edges of the cheesecloth and tie them together with kitchen string. Place in a medium saucepan, along with the sugar, port, and cranberry juice. Cover and bring to simmer over medium heat; reduce the heat to low and simmer 10 minutes.
2. Meanwhile, slice each plum half into thirds. Add to the saucepan, return to a simmer and cook, covered, until the plums are soft, 10–12 minutes. Remove from the heat, stir in the lemon juice and let cool in the pan. Refrigerate for at least 2 hours or up to 5 days. Serve cool or at room temperature.

Per serving (scant ½ cup): 171 Cal, 1 g Fat, 0 g Sat Fat, 0 mg Chol, 10 mg Sod, 37 g Carb, 2 g Fib, 1 g Prot, 22 mg Calc. ***POINTS: 3.***

Spiced Plum-and-Port Compote

Grilled Tropical Fruit with Lime Syrup

MAKES 8 SERVINGS

Here's a glamorous dessert that won't leave you feeling stuffed; it's a perfect finish to an outdoor dinner party. When you grill the fruit, the sugars on the surface concentrate and caramelize, adding smoky-sweet depth to the flavors.

- **¼ cup sugar**
- **3 tablespoons water**
- **3 tablespoons fresh lime juice**
- **1 teaspoon grated lime zest**
- **1 teaspoon grated orange zest**
- **1 pineapple, trimmed, cored, and cut lengthwise into 16 (½-inch-thick) slices**
- **2 mangoes, pitted, peeled, and cut into 8 (½-inch-thick) slices**

1. Combine the sugar and water in a small saucepan. Bring to a boil over medium-high heat; continue cooking until syrupy, 2 minutes more. Stir in the lime juice, lime zest, and orange zest; set aside.
2. Prepare the grill for a medium fire, or preheat the broiler.
3. Spray the pineapple and mango slices with nonstick spray on both sides. Grill or broil, turning once, until softened, about 4 minutes. Brush the slices with the lime syrup and turn the fruit over; grill or broil 1 minute more. Brush again with the syrup, turn, and grill or broil until the syrup has caramelized slightly, 1 minute longer. Transfer the fruit to a serving platter and brush with the remaining syrup. Serve warm, at room temperature, or chilled.

Per serving (2 pineapple slices and 1 mango slice): 88 Cal, 0 g Fat, 0 g Sat Fat, 0 mg Chol, 3 mg Sod, 24 g Carb, 2 g Fib, 1 g Prot, 10 mg Calc. ***POINTS: 1.***

Fruit-and-Nut Granola

MAKES 12 SERVINGS

Though it has always had a California-hippie provenance, one of granola's most important introductions was at the famed 1969 Woodstock Music and Arts Festival in upstate New York, where it was served to thousands of concertgoers. For many, it was their first introduction to the now-ubiquitous crunchy cereal.

- **4 cups old-fashioned rolled oats**
- **½ cup slivered almonds**
- **¼ cup sesame seeds**
- **1 teaspoon cinnamon**
- **¼ teaspoon salt**
- **⅛ teaspoon nutmeg**
- **6 tablespoons maple syrup**
- **⅓ cup honey**
- **2 tablespoons warm water**
- **2 tablespoons canola oil**
- **1 teaspoon vanilla extract**
- **1 cup golden raisins**
- **1 cup dried cranberries**

1. Preheat oven to 300°F. Spray a jelly-roll pan with nonstick spray.
2. Combine the oats, almonds, sesame seeds, cinnamon, salt, and nutmeg in a large bowl. Combine the syrup, honey, water, oil, and vanilla in a separate bowl. Pour the syrup mixture over the oats mixture and toss to combine. Evenly spread into the pan and bake, stirring and breaking up the clumps every 10 minutes, until lightly toasted, 45–55 minutes.
3. Remove from the oven, and stir in the raisins and cranberries; let cool completely. Store in an airtight container for up to 5 days or up to 1 month in the refrigerator.

Per serving (½ cup): 296 Cal, 8 g Fat, 1 g Sat Fat, 0 mg Chol, 54 mg Sod, 52 g Carb, 5 g Fib, 7 g Prot, 48 mg Calc. ***POINTS: 6.***

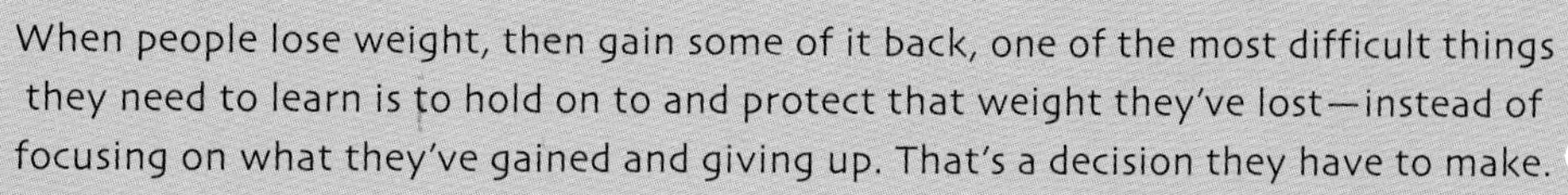

Raspberry-Peach Cobbler

Raspberry-Peach Cobbler

MAKES 6 SERVINGS

Bubbling sweetened fruit topped with crumbly biscuits—this old-fashioned dessert was retro before retro was cool! Make it at the height of peach season, and substitute apples or pears in winter. Though it's not necessary, you can peel the peaches if you like [see our easy method below].

- **½ cup raspberry jam**
- **⅓ cup peach nectar or cranberry juice**
- **1 tablespoon cornstarch**
- **½ teaspoon cinnamon**
- **¼ teaspoon ground nutmeg or allspice**
- **1½ pounds (about 5 medium) firm-ripe peaches or nectarines, peeled, if desired, halved, pitted, and thinly sliced**
- **1 cup all-purpose flour**
- **3 tablespoons sugar**
- **1 teaspoon baking powder**
- **¼ teaspoon baking soda**
- **½ cup low-fat buttermilk**
- **2 tablespoons melted unsalted butter or margarine**

1. Place the oven rack in the center of the oven; preheat the oven to 375°F. Whisk together the jam, nectar or cranberry juice, cornstarch, cinnamon, and nutmeg or allspice in a 9-inch deep-dish microwavable pie plate or casserole dish until blended. Stir in the peaches or nectarines to coat well. Microwave on High, stirring occasionally,until the mixture begins to bubble, 6–7 minutes.
2. Meanwhile, whisk together the flour, 2 tablespoons of the sugar, the baking powder, and baking soda in a medium bowl; make a well in the center. Pour the buttermilk and melted butter into the center. Quickly combine the dry ingredients with the wet, stirring just until combined.
3. Drop the mixture onto the hot fruit by the tablespoonful. Sprinkle the remaining tablespoon of sugar over the topping. Bake until the biscuits are golden and fruit mixture is bubbly, 25 minutes. Serve warm.

Per serving (⅙ of cobbler): 247 Cal, 4 g Fat, 3 g Sat Fat, 11 mg Chol, 167 mg Sod, 51 g Carb, 3 g Fib, 4 g Prot, 85 mg Calc. ***POINTS: 5.***

top tip

To peel the peaches, plunge them in boiling water just long enough to loosen their skins, about 1 to 3 minutes. Remove to a bowl of ice water; when cool enough to handle, peel off the skin with your fingers. You can also use a swivel-bladed apple peeler, but you'll lose some of the delicious peach flesh beneath.

No-Bake Strawberry-Rhubarb Crisp

MAKES 6 SERVINGS

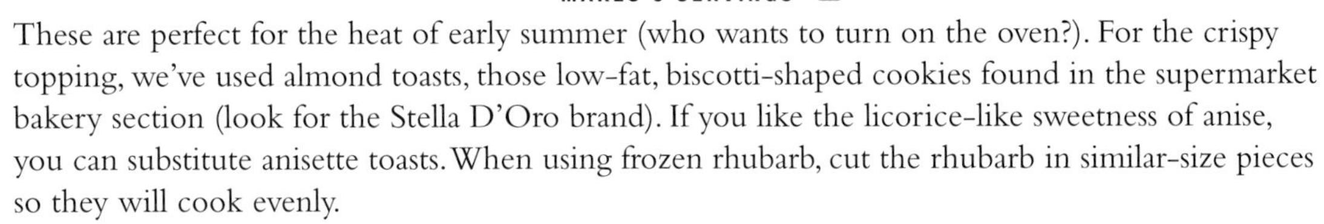
These are perfect for the heat of early summer (who wants to turn on the oven?). For the crispy topping, we've used almond toasts, those low-fat, biscotti-shaped cookies found in the supermarket bakery section (look for the Stella D'Oro brand). If you like the licorice-like sweetness of anise, you can substitute anisette toasts. When using frozen rhubarb, cut the rhubarb in similar-size pieces so they will cook evenly.

- **½ cup sugar**
- **1½ tablespoons cornstarch**
- **1½ cups sliced fresh or frozen rhubarb**
- **½ cup water**
- **1 teaspoon grated lemon zest**
- **½ teaspoon ground ginger**
- **2 cups trimmed and halved strawberries**
- **3 almond toast cookies (1½ ounces)**
- **1 tablespoon packed light brown sugar**
- **⅛ teaspoon cinnamon**
- **1 tablespoon unsalted butter, melted**

1. Stir together the sugar and cornstarch in a medium saucepan. Add the rhubarb, water, lemon zest, and ginger. Cover and bring to a simmer over medium heat. Cook, stirring occasionally, until the rhubarb is tender and the sauce has thickened, 8 minutes. Stir in the strawberries and cook 2 minutes more. Pour into a 9-inch pie plate or serving dish.
2. Chop the cookies into ¼-inch pieces; place in a medium bowl. Crumble in the brown sugar and cinnamon. Drizzle in the butter and stir to distribute evenly. Sprinkle cookie mixture over the fruit right before serving. Serve warm or at room temperature.

Per serving (⅙ of crisp): 142 Cal, 3 g Fat, 1 g Sat Fat, 6 mg Chol, 28 mg Sod, 30 g Carb, 2 g Fib, 1 g Prot, 75 mg Calc. ***POINTS: 3.***

> "People sometimes wonder why the Program used to only call for white bread. It was because at that time, packaged, presliced white bread was the only type that consistently measured one ounce per slice [and] could be portioned out accurately. Later, when other types of sliced breads (such as whole-grain, rye, or pumpernickel) became more widely available, they were incorporated into the Program."
>
> *—Felice Lippert, Cofounder, Weight Watchers International*

Bread Pudding with Winter Fruits

MAKES 8 SERVINGS

Bread pudding, everyone's favorite nursery food, enjoyed a second coming in the "cocooning" days of the new millennium. We bake ours in a water bath to insure a smooth and creamy pudding. If you like, feel free to substitute your favorite dried fruit, such as dried cranberries, cherries, apricots, or dates, for the mixed dried fruit. Teetotalers can substitute orange juice for the bourbon.

- **¾ cup mixed dried fruit, diced**
- **3 tablespoons water**
- **2 tablespoons bourbon (optional)**
- **1 ripe pear, peeled, quartered, cored, and sliced crosswise**
- **4 cups cubed day-old whole-grain bread (1-inch pieces)**
- **½ cup sugar**
- **¾ teaspoon cinnamon**
- **¼ teaspoon nutmeg**
- **3 cups low-fat (1%) milk**
- **2 large eggs**
- **1 egg white**
- **2 teaspoons vanilla extract**
- **1 teaspoon grated orange zest**
- **2 tablespoons confectioners' sugar (optional)**

1. Combine the dried fruit, water, and bourbon, if using, in a small saucepan. Bring to a simmer over medium heat. Remove from the heat, stir in the pear, and let cool.
2. Spray an 9 x 11-inch baking dish with nonstick spray. Scatter the bread in an even layer in the pan. Spoon the soaked fruit evenly on top.
3. Whisk together the sugar, cinnamon, and nutmeg in a medium bowl. Whisk in the milk, eggs, egg white, vanilla, and orange zest. Pour over the bread, pressing down the cubes to soak up the liquid. Cover with foil and let stand 30 minutes. (The pudding can be made ahead up to this point, then stored in the refrigerator overnight.)
4. Preheat the oven to 350°F. Pull the oven rack partly out. Place a large roasting pan on the rack; place the bread pudding inside it. Carefully pour enough hot water into the roasting pan to fill it halfway up the side of the baking dish. Bake, covered, 30 minutes. Uncover and continue baking until puffed and golden, 30 minutes more. Remove from the pan and let cool. Serve warm, sifting the confectioners' sugar on top, if you wish.

Per serving (⅛ pudding): 197 Cal, 3 g Fat, 1 g Sat Fat, 57 mg Chol, 161 mg Sod, 37 g Carb, 3 g Fib, 7 g Prot, 142 mg Calc. ***POINTS: 4.***

WW THEN AND NOW

French Toast

MAKES 2 SERVINGS

The sixties-era Weight Watchers French Toast recipe was simple, but not exactly authentic: plain white bread, dipped in a beaten egg, then "fried" in a dry skillet. No need to miss out on all the goodness and flavor of real French toast today. Double the recipe, if you like.

1 large egg
2 egg whites
2 tablespoons fat-free milk
¼ teaspoon vanilla extract
Pinch cinnamon
2 slices firm or day-old whole-wheat bread

1. Beat the egg, egg whites, milk, vanilla, and cinnamon until frothy in a shallow dish. Dip the bread into the egg mixture, soaking well. Repeat with the remaining bread slice.
2. Spray a large nonstick skillet with butter-flavored nonstick spray. Heat until a drop of water sizzles. Add the bread and cook until golden, turning once, until golden brown on both sides, 2–3 minutes.

Per serving (1 slice): 131 Cal, 4 g Fat, 1 g Sat Fat, 107 mg Chol, 244 mg Sod, 15 g Carb, 2 g Fib, 10 g Prot, 55 mg Calc. ***POINTS: 3.***

"I think Weight Watchers has maintained its position as the leading weight-loss organization because people know they can trust us. We have changed over the years to keep relevant to real people's lives, while reflecting the best nutritional thinking. At the same time, we've never strayed from our core values of providing a comprehensive weight-loss program delivering safe, healthy weight loss."

—Linda Huett, President and CEO, Weight Watchers International

Fruit-and-Nut Granola,
Ambrosia, and
French Toast
(clockwise from top)

Bananas Foster

MAKES 4 SERVINGS 

Although Bananas Foster was a classic long before the eighties, that decade's interest in Cajun and Creole cooking gave the dessert star billing nationwide. And no wonder: The combination of bananas flambéed in rum with vanilla ice cream is a match made in heaven. Even though this version is much lower in fat than the original, it hasn't lost any of its richness. While vanilla is the classic flavor to serve with this dish, try substituting fat-free chocolate or coffee ice cream for a yummy variation.

- **⅓ cup packed light brown sugar**
- **3 tablespoons unsalted light butter**
- **½ teaspoon cinnamon**
- **2 large ripe bananas, peeled and sliced ¼-inch thick**
- **2 tablespoons dark rum**
- **1 pint low-fat vanilla ice cream**

1. Combine the sugar, butter, and cinnamon in a large nonstick skillet over medium-low heat. Cook, stirring often, until the butter melts and the sugar dissolves. Add the banana slices and cook, tossing to coat, until the bananas begin to soften, 2–4 minutes. Increase the heat to medium and, off the heat, pour in the rum. Return the skillet to the heat and ignite the rum with a long wooden match (or, if you have a gas stove, tilt the skillet toward the flame to ignite); cook, shaking the pan, until the flame goes out, about 30 seconds. Cook 1 minute longer to thicken the sauce slightly; remove from the heat.
2. Place a ½-cup scoop of the ice cream into each of 4 wineglasses or serving dishes. Top each with ½ cup of the warm banana mixture. Serve at once.

Per serving (½ cup each ice cream and bananas): 293 Cal, 11 g Fat, 7 g Sat Fat, 34 mg Chol, 63 mg Sod, 48 g Carb, 2 g Fib, 3 g Prot, 112 mg Calc. ***POINTS: 6.***

top tip

If you'd rather omit the rum, try substituting 1 teaspoon imitation rum extract—or add 2 tablespoons pineapple juice and a few drops of vanilla extract to the bananas, and cook 1 minute before serving.

Mini Cheesecake Bites with Blueberry Topping

MAKES 12 SERVINGS

Everyone loves cheesecake, and in those days before reduced-fat cheeses were invented, Weight Watchers cooks satisfied their cravings very creatively. A 1973 cheesecake recipe called for whipping cottage cheese with eggs, nonfat dry milk, and flavorings, then lightening it with beaten eggs—not a bad solution. But today it's much easier (and tastier) to whip up these mini cheesecakes and enjoy all their creamy goodness with little compromising. Bake the cheesecakes up to two days in advance and store them in the refrigerator; they taste even better with a day of chilling. The blueberry topping can be assembled in minutes.

- **2 teaspoons honey**
- **8 gingersnaps, crushed to fine crumbs (about ½ cup)**
- **1 (8-ounce) package light cream cheese (Neufchâtel), room temperature**
- **¼ cup sugar**
- **1 large egg**
- **1 teaspoon grated lemon zest**
- **1 teaspoon vanilla extract**
- **¼ cup all-fruit blueberry jam**
- **1 cup blueberries**

1. Place the oven rack in the center of the oven; preheat the oven to 375°F. Line 24 mini-muffin cups with paper liners, then spray the liners with nonstick spray.
2. Place the honey in a medium microwavable bowl. Microwave on High for 10 seconds. Add the gingersnap crumbs to the bowl, stirring to form a crumbly mixture. Spoon a scant teaspoon of the crumbs into the bottom of each muffin cup liner.
3. With an electric mixer on high speed, beat the cream cheese, sugar, egg, lemon zest, and vanilla in a medium bowl until light and fluffy, 3 minutes. Spoon 1 level tablespoon of the mixture into each muffin cup. Bake until puffed and set in the center, 9 minutes. Cool in pans on a rack.
4. Place the jam in a medium microwavable bowl and microwave on High, just until the jam begins to bubble, 15 seconds. Gently stir in the blueberries until evenly coated with the jam. Spoon the berries over the cheesecakes (about 5–6 blueberries each). Refrigerate until ready to serve.

Per serving (2 cheesecake bites): 117 Cal, 5 g Fat, 3 g Sat Fat, 32 mg Chol, 108 mg Sod, 15 g Carb, 1 g Fib, 3 g Prot, 21 mg Calc. ***POINTS: 3.***

top tip

To crush the gingersnaps, place them in a zip-close plastic bag, squeeze out the air, and seal. Use a rolling pin to flatten the snaps to fine crumbs.

WW THEN AND NOW

"Danish" Pastry

MAKES 1 SERVING

This Weight Watchers classic, once made with cottage cheese and white bread, has long been in need of an update. Here's our newer take, with calcium-packed ricotta and more interesting raisin bread.

¼ cup low-fat ricotta
1 teaspoon packed dark brown sugar
¼ teaspoon vanilla extract
1 slice cinnamon raisin bread, lightly toasted
Pinch cinnamon

Combine the ricotta, brown sugar, and vanilla in a small bowl. Spread the ricotta mixture on the toasted bread and sprinkle with the cinnamon. Bake in the toaster oven until hot and bubbly, 3–5 minutes.

Per serving: 177 Cal, 6 g Fat, 3 g Sat Fat, 19 mg Chol, 180 mg Sod, 22 g Carb, 1 g Fib, 9 g Prot, 192 mg Calc. ***POINTS: 4.***

Lemon Bars

MAKES 16 SERVINGS

Everybody's favorite on the cookie tray, lemon bars are traditionally made with a shortbread crust and a rich lemon-curd topping. With animal cracker crumbs, plenty of fresh lemon, and a lot of ingenuity, our updated version measures up in every way to the original.

- **⅔ cup plus 2 tablespoons all-purpose flour**
- **⅓ cup animal cracker crumbs or vanilla wafer crumbs**
- **1 cup + 2 tablespoons sugar**
- **3 tablespoons unsalted butter or margarine**
- **2 large eggs**
- **2 egg whites**
- **2 teaspoons grated lemon zest**
- **½ cup fresh lemon juice (from about 4 lemons)**

1. Place the oven rack in the center of the oven; preheat the oven to 350°F. Line an 8-inch-square baking pan with heavy-duty foil, extending 2 inches beyond the sides. (This creates a "handle," so that the bars can easily be lifted out of the pan.) Spray the bottom and sides of the foil with nonstick spray.
2. To prepare the crust: Stir together ⅔ cup of the flour, the animal cracker crumbs, 2 tablespoons of the sugar, and the butter in a medium bowl until the consistency of wet sand. Pat evenly into the pan to form a crust. Bake until firm, 12 minutes.
3. Whisk together the remaining 1 cup sugar and the remaining 2 tablespoons of the flour in a medium bowl. Add the eggs, egg whites, lemon zest, and lemon juice, and whisk to thoroughly combine, about 1 minute. Pour over the hot crust, return to oven, and bake until golden and set in the center, about 30 minutes. Cool completely on a rack. Lift out the bars, holding on to the foil ends, and place on a cutting board. Cut into 16 squares.

Per serving (1 bar): 119 Cal, 3 g Fat, 2 g Sat Fat, 32 mg Chol, 2 mg Sod, 21 g Carb, 0 g Fib, 2 g Prot, 6 mg Calc. ***POINTS: 3.***

top tip

Before you squeeze the lemons, why not trim off their zest to save for another use? Remove the zest with a vegetable peeler, being careful to avoid the bitter white pith beneath, and store the strips in a small airtight freezer container for up to a month.

Boston Cream Pie

Boston Cream Pie

MAKES 8 SERVINGS

A retro favorite, Boston Cream Pie is actually a light sponge cake with a cream filling and dense chocolate icing. Our cake is quite easy to make, and amazingly low in fat.

CUSTARD

- **⅓ cup sugar**
- **3 tablespoons cornstarch**
- **¼ teaspoon salt**
- **1½ cups low-fat (1%) milk**
- **1 large egg**
- **1 tablespoon unsalted butter**
- **2 teaspoons vanilla extract**

CAKE

- **1 cup cake flour (not self-rising)**
- **1½ teaspoons baking powder**
- **¼ teaspoon salt**
- **3 large eggs, at room temperature**
- **¾ cup sugar**
- **¼ cup hot water**
- **2 tablespoons unsalted butter, melted**
- **1 teaspoon vanilla extract**

GLAZE

- **⅓ cup confectioners' sugar**
- **3 tablespoons unsweetened Dutch-process cocoa powder**
- **½ cup fat-free sweetened condensed milk**
- **½ teaspoon instant coffee powder**

1. Custard: Whisk together sugar, cornstarch, and salt in a medium saucepan. Whisk in milk and egg until blended. Cook over medium heat, stirring constantly, until just boiling, about 3 minutes. Cook 1 minute more, stirring until thickened; remove from heat. Stir in butter and vanilla. Press a piece of wax paper onto surface to keep a skin from forming on the custard; set aside to cool.
2. Cake: Place oven rack in the center of oven; preheat oven to 350°F. Spray two 9-inch cake pans with nonstick spray; line with wax paper rounds and spray with nonstick spray. Sift together the flour, baking powder, and salt onto a sheet of wax paper; set aside. With an electric mixer on high, beat eggs in a medium bowl until thickened, about 3 minutes. Gradually beat in sugar, until fluffy, 3 minutes. On low speed, beat in water, butter, and vanilla, until just blended. Beat in flour mixture, until just incorporated. Pour into the pans. Bake 25–30 minutes; cool completely on a rack. To remove cake from the pans, run a knife around the edge of the cake layers and invert onto the rack. Peel off wax paper.
3. Glaze (prepare just before assembling): Sift the confectioners' sugar and cocoa into a small saucepan. Add the condensed milk and coffee powder; stir to combine. Heat over low heat, stirring, until the mixture bubbles and thickens, about 2 minutes; cook 1 minute more. Remove from heat and set aside to cool in the pan for 10 minutes, or until thickened.
4. Cake assembly: Place 1 layer, bottom-side up, on serving plate. Vigorously stir custard until smooth. Spread on inverted cake layer in an even thickness, leaving a ½-inch border along the edge. Top with remaining cake layer, top-side up. Spread the chocolate glaze evenly on top. Use a serrated knife to cut the cake, and serve at room temperature or slightly chilled.

Per serving (⅛ of cake): 336 Cal, 8 g Fat, 5 g Sat Fat, 120 mg Chol, 318 mg Sod, 60 g Carb, 1 g Fib, 8 g Prot, 180 mg Calc. ***POINTS: 7.***

Citrus, Date, and Raisin Baklava

MAKES 16 SERVINGS

This classic Greek dessert takes a little time to make, but it's well worth the effort. And with our simple instructions for handling the phyllo dough, you'll assemble it like a pro. We've cut fat substantially by substituting golden raisins and dates for most of the nuts traditionally used and by brushing the phyllo layers with light butter. And for good measure, we've freshened up the flavorings with a hint of lemon and orange. As with any baklava, a small portion is plenty!

GLAZE

- **⅓ cup sugar**
- **2 tablespoons water**
- **3 tablespoons honey**
- **2 tablespoons fresh lemon juice**
- **1 tablespoon fresh orange juice**

BAKLAVA

- **2 cups pitted dates, chopped**
- **1 cup golden raisins**
- **½ cup + 2 tablespoons sugar**
- **1 tablespoon freshly grated lemon zest**
- **1 teaspoon freshly grated orange zest**
- **½ teaspoon ground allspice**
- **⅛ teaspoon anise seeds**
- **⅛ teaspoon nutmeg**
- **3 tablespoons fresh orange juice**
- **2 tablespoons fresh lemon juice**
- **½ cup finely chopped walnuts**
- **12 sheets phyllo dough, thawed, if frozen**
- **8 tablespoons (½ stick) light unsalted butter, melted**

1. Preheat the oven to 350°F. Spray an 8-inch-square baking dish with nonstick spray.
2 Glaze: Combine the sugar and water in a small saucepan; bring to a boil. Continue boiling, without stirring, until the sugar dissolves, 1 minute. Remove from the heat and stir in the honey, lemon juice, and orange juice; let cool and reserve.
3. Baklava filling: Combine the dates, raisins, 2 tablespoons of the sugar, the lemon and orange zests, allspice, anise seeds, and nutmeg in the work bowl of a food processor. Pulse until dates and raisins are finely minced. Add the orange and lemon juices; pulse until mixture forms a thick paste. Transfer to a bowl and stir in walnuts.
4. Place the phyllo sheets on a cutting board in a stack. Using the bottom of the prepared baking pan as a guide, cut out 2 (8-inch-square) stacks, to make 24 sheets (discard the dough trimmings). Cover the sheets with plastic wrap to keep them from drying out as you work. Place 1 sheet on the bottom of the baking dish, brush lightly with the melted butter, and sprinkle with 1 teaspoon of the sugar. Repeat with another 9 layers of phyllo, butter, and sugar. Spread with half of the date mixture, then top with 4 more layers of phyllo, butter, and sugar. Spread with the remaining half of the date mixture, then top with 10 more layers of phyllo, butter, and sugar. With a sharp knife, lightly cut the top of the baklava to indicate 16 squares, being careful not to cut all the way through.
5. Bake 30 minutes, until crisp and lightly golden. Cut the baklava into pieces along the scored lines. Drizzle the reserved glaze over the top, and cool completely before serving.

Per serving (1-inch-square piece): 249 Cal, 8 g Fat, 4 g Sat Fat, 16 mg Chol, 30 mg Sod, 45 g Carb, 2 g Fib, 2 g Prot, 20 mg Calc. ***POINTS: 5.***

Banana Cream Pie

MAKES 8 SERVINGS

Adding fat-free half-and-half to the cream filling gives this old-fashioned pie a wonderfully rich flavor and silky smooth texture. To make the crust, we've used chocolate-flavored graham crackers. Feel free to substitute plain or cinnamon grahams, if you prefer.

CRUST

- **9 chocolate-flavored graham crackers (5 x 2½-inches each)**
- **2 tablespoons honey**
- **1 tablespoon vegetable oil**
- **1 tablespoon low-fat (1%) milk**

FILLING

- **½ cup sugar**
- **¼ cup cornstarch**
- **1½ cups low-fat (1%) milk**
- **1 large egg**
- **⅛ teaspoon salt**
- **¼ cup fat-free half-and-half**
- **1 teaspoon vanilla extract**
- **3 medium bananas, well ripened**
- **½ tablespoon orange or lemon juice**

1. To prepare the crust, place the oven rack in the center of the oven and preheat the oven to 375°F. Spray a 9-inch glass pie plate with nonstick spray. Break up the graham crackers into a food processor or blender, and process until finely ground. Add the honey, oil, and milk; process until well combined and evenly crumbly. Press evenly into the bottom and sides of the pie plate. Bake for 9 minutes; cool completely on a rack.
2. To prepare the filling, whisk together the sugar and cornstarch in a medium saucepan. Whisk in the milk, egg, and salt. Bring to a boil over medium heat, whisking constantly as the mixture begins to thicken; let boil 30 seconds, whisking constantly. Remove from the heat and gradually whisk in the half-and-half and vanilla. Place a sheet of wax paper on the surface to prevent a skin from forming; set aside to cool for 15 minutes.
3. Slice two of the bananas lengthwise in half; cut crosswise into slices. Place the slices in an even layer in the bottom of the baked pie shell. Spoon in the cooled filling and spread evenly. Place a sheet of wax paper on the surface to prevent a skin from forming, and chill thoroughly, at least 3 hours or overnight.
4. To serve, slice the remaining banana and toss with the juice in a small bowl. Arrange on top of the pie and serve.

Per serving (⅛ of pie): 234 Cal, 5 g Fat, 1 g Sat Fat, 29 mg Chol, 163 mg Sod, 46 g Carb, 1 g Fib, 4 g Prot, 80 mg Calc. ***POINTS: 5.***

Key Lime Pie

MAKES 8 SERVINGS

If you're old enough to fondly remember the popular lime-flavored gelatin-based Key Lime Pie recipe that circulated in the seventies, you'll love this update. After all, it uses fresh limes—and nowadays, it's easier to find genuine key limes (from the Florida Keys) in better supermarkets. They are smaller, with golden-yellow flesh, and slightly more tart than the common Persian lime. If they're not available, use Persian limes. Just don't use bottled lime juice, key lime or otherwise; it has an unwelcome, slightly tinny flavor.

- **½ cup fresh lime juice**
- **2 teaspoons unflavored gelatin**
- **1 (14-ounce) can sweetened condensed milk**
- **2 teaspoons grated lime zest**
- **1½ cups fat-free whipped topping**
- **1 (9-inch) reduced-fat graham cracker crust**
- **1 small lime, thinly sliced**

1. Pour the juice into a small bowl and sprinkle with the gelatin. Let stand until the gelatin is softened, 5 minutes. Transfer to a small saucepan and heat over low heat, stirring, until the gelatin dissolves.
2. Stir in the condensed milk and cook, stirring occasionally, 5 minutes longer. Remove from the heat and let cool 10 minutes. Transfer to a large bowl and refrigerate 30 minutes, or until the mixture starts to set.
3. Whisk the thickened filling until creamy and smooth; stir in the lime zest. Using a rubber spatula, gently fold in the whipped topping until combined. Pour into the pie crust and refrigerate until firm, at least 3 hours or overnight. Garnish with the lime slices just before serving.

Per serving (⅛ of pie): 300 Cal, 9 g Fat, 6 g Sat Fat, 22 mg Chol, 163 mg Sod, 50 g Carb, 0 g Fib, 5 g Prot, 149 mg Calc. ***POINTS: 7.***

top tip

You'll need about 3 or 4 Persian limes, or 10 to 12 key limes, to yield ½ cup fresh juice.

Lattice-Topped Cherry-Almond Pie

MAKES 8 SERVINGS

This pretty pie is the ultimate American classic. For a well-cooked bottom crust, start the cooking in a hot oven. Cover the decorative edge with foil during the baking to prevent overbrowning.

CRUST

- **1½ cups pastry flour or all-purpose flour**
- **1 tablespoon confectioners' sugar**
- **¾ teaspoon salt**
- **3 tablespoons vegetable shortening**
- **2 tablespoons unsalted butter, cut into small chunks**
- **4½ tablespoons cold water**
- **¾ teaspoon cider vinegar**

FILLING

- **2 (15-ounce) cans pitted dark cherries, packed in juice or lite syrup**
- **½ cup packed light brown sugar**
- **1 tablespoon fresh lemon juice**
- **¼ teaspoon almond extract**
- **3 tablespoons cornstarch**

1. Crust: Pulse the flour, confectioners' sugar, and salt in a food processor. Add the shortening and butter; pulse until the mixture resembles coarse meal. Stir together the water and vinegar in small bowl. Add to flour mixture and pulse until just combined. Remove one-third of mixture (about ½ cup) onto a sheet of plastic wrap, flatten into an oval, and wrap airtight (this will be used for the lattice top). Repeat with the remaining dough (for bottom crust). Refrigerate doughs for 1 hour or up to 2 days.
2. Roll out the larger dough piece between floured sheets of wax paper to a 13-inch circle. Fit into a 9-inch pie plate. Leaving a 1-inch border, trim off any excess dough. Add trimmings to remaining dough piece, and roll it between floured sheets of wax paper to a 9½ x 7-inch oval. Cut lengthwise into ½-inch-wide strips. Place oven rack in the center of oven; preheat oven to 425°F.
3. Filling: Drain the cherries in a strainer set over a large bowl. Shake the strainer to remove any excess juices. Reserve ½ cup of cherry juice and place in a large bowl; discard the remaining juice. Stir in the brown sugar, lemon juice, and almond extract. Add the cornstarch and stir until smooth. Stir in the drained cherries, and spoon the mixture into the unbaked pie shell.
4. Arrange lattice strips on top of the pie, going in one direction, starting with the longest strips in the center and spacing them 1 inch apart. Repeat with the remaining strips, placing them at a 90-degree angle to the first set, to form a lattice top. Brush the edge of the pastry lightly with water and roll in to form an edge. Pinch the edges together to seal, and crimp decoratively. Cover the crimped edge with strips of foil to prevent overbrowning.
5. Bake 30 minutes. Slide a baking sheet under pie; reduce oven temperature to 350°F, and bake 30–40 minutes more, until crust is golden brown and the filling is bubbly. Cool on a rack for at least 3 hours. Serve pie slightly warm or at room temperature.

Per serving (⅛ pie): 272 Cal, 9 g Fat, 3 g Sat Fat, 8 mg Chol, 225 mg Sod, 48 g Carb, 2 g Fib, 3 g Prot, 27 mg Calc. ***POINTS: 6.***

Baked Alaska

MAKES 8 SERVINGS

This miraculous dish amazes diners as much today as it did in the sixties, but the real miracle is how easy it is to create when you make it in a pie plate. Just make sure the ice cream and cake are frozen solid before baking the meringue.

- **6 (½-inch-thick) slices fat-free pound cake (about 10 ounces)**
- **1 pint low-fat vanilla ice cream, softened**
- **1 pint strawberry sorbet, softened**
- **6 large egg whites, at room temperature**
- **⅛ teaspoon cream of tartar**
- **¾ cup sugar**

1. Spray a 9-inch pie plate with nonstick spray. Line the bottom of the plate with cake slices, cutting some pieces as needed to fill any holes. Cut the remaining cake slices in half lengthwise, and place them around the edge of the plate, patching any gaps that remain. Freeze 20 minutes.
2. Remove the pie plate from the freezer, and immediately spread the ice cream over the bottom layer of cake. Freeze 20 minutes, then remove from the freezer and spread the sorbet evenly over the ice cream. Freeze until solid, 2–4 hours.
3. Preheat the oven to 450°F. Place the oven rack in the middle of the oven.
4. With an electric mixer on low speed, beat the egg whites and cream of tartar in a medium bowl until soft peaks form, about 4 minutes. Increase the speed to high and gradually beat in the sugar, until stiff and glossy, about 3 minutes more.
5. Remove the pie plate from the freezer and mound the meringue over it, spreading to the edge of the plate to completely cover the sorbet. Bake until just golden brown on top, 3–4 minutes. Serve at once.

Per serving (⅛ of pie): 300 Cal, 1 g Fat, 0 g Sat Fat, 1 mg Chol, 206 mg Sod, 67 g Carb, 0 g Fib, 6 g Prot, 73 mg Calc. ***POINTS: 6.***

top tip

For a wonderfully dramatic presentation of this dessert, create it the traditional way [pictured]: Spray a 6-cup bowl with nonstick spray and line with plastic wrap, letting the wrap come up over the bowl's rim. First layer in the sorbet; freeze 20 minutes. Layer in the ice cream; freeze 20 minutes. Then slice the pound cake into wedges and make a pinwheel pattern atop the ice-cream layer, patching in any gaps. Freeze until solid, 2 to 4 hours. Continue with Steps 3 and 4, above. Remove bowl from freezer, and invert onto an ovenproof plate; remove plastic wrap. Continue with remainder of step 5.

Baked Alaska

Sweet Potato Pie

MAKES 8 SERVINGS

Back in the sixties, a Weight Watchers pie crust recipe called for bread crumbs and water—and our "sweet potato pie" was made with yellow squash, gelatin, and artificial sweetener. Today, we proudly serve the real thing—with butter, sugar, and, of course, real sweet potatoes!

CRUST

- **1 cup all-purpose flour**
- **1 tablespoon confectioners' sugar**
- **1 teaspoon salt**
- **2 tablespoons solid vegetable shortening**
- **1 tablespoon unsalted butter, cut into 6 small chunks**
- **3 tablespoons cold water**
- **½ teaspoon cider vinegar**

FILLING

- **2 large sweet potatoes (about 1½ pounds), peeled**
- **2 large eggs**
- **3 egg whites**
- **½ cup packed light brown sugar**
- **¾ cup evaporated fat-free milk**
- **1 tablespoon fresh lime juice**
- **1 teaspoon pumpkin pie spice**
- **¼ teaspoon ground nutmeg**

1. To prepare pie crust, combine the flour, sugar, and ½ teaspoon of the salt in a food processor. Add the shortening and butter; pulse until the mixture resembles coarse crumbs. Stir together the water and vinegar in a small bowl; pour mixture through the feed tube, pulsing until the mixture is just combined. Scrape dough with a spatula onto a sheet of plastic wrap, flatten into a disk, wrap airtight, and refrigerate until chilled, at least 1 hour.
2. Roll out the chilled dough between floured sheets of wax paper to a 13-inch circle. Fit into a 9-inch pie plate, crimp the edges and prick lightly with a fork. Line the inside of the crust with heavy-duty foil; fold the foil over to completely cover the edge of the crust. Bake for 12 minutes. Remove the foil, pierce any bubbles in the crust with the tip of a knife, and bake until very lightly browned, 8 minutes more.
3. To make the filling, place the potatoes in a medium saucepan with enough cold water to cover. Bring to a boil and simmer until fork-tender, 45 minutes. Drain, then add enough cold water to cover. When the potatoes are cool enough to handle, drain and mash with a potato masher in a large bowl until smooth. Measure out 1⅓ cups of the puree (save any extra for another use), and return it to the bowl.
4. Add the eggs, egg whites, and brown sugar; whisk together until smooth. Whisk in the milk, lime juice, pie spice, the remaining ½ teaspoon salt, and the nutmeg until blended. Pour the mixture into the pie crust. Bake until the center is set, 35–40 minutes (the pie should still quiver like gelatin when the pan is nudged). Cool completely on a rack and refrigerate for at least 3 hours or overnight. Serve chilled or at room temperature.

Per serving (⅛ of pie): 267 Cal, 6 g Fat, 2 g Sat Fat, 58 mg Chol, 368 mg Sod, 46 g Carb, 3 g Fib, 7 g Prot, 111 mg Calc. ***POINTS: 5.***

Fudgy Brownie Pudding Cake

MAKES 9 SERVINGS

The ultimate dessert for a chocoholic, this chewy, gooey creation hearkens back to the "impossible" cakes of the seventies (remember that cake with the fudgy tunnel in the center?). This cake magically reverses itself as it bakes—forming a wonderfully sugar-crusted brownie-like topping over a soft pudding base.

- **¾ cup all-purpose flour**
- **¾ cup sugar**
- **⅓ cup + 4 tablespoons unsweetened cocoa powder**
- **1 teaspoon instant espresso powder or instant coffee powder**
- **2 teaspoons baking powder**
- **¼ teaspoon baking soda**
- **¼ teaspoon salt**
- **½ cup low-fat (1%) milk**
- **1 tablespoon unsalted butter, melted**
- **1½ teaspoons vanilla extract**
- **⅓ cup packed light brown sugar**
- **1⅔ cup boiling water**

1. Place the oven rack in the center of the oven; preheat the oven to 350°F. Spray a 9-inch baking pan with nonstick spray.
2. Stir together the flour, sugar, ⅓ cup of the cocoa, the espresso powder, baking powder, baking soda, and salt in a large bowl. Make a well in the center, and pour in the milk, butter and vanilla. Stir together until just blended and spoon evenly into the pan, spreading level.
3. Stir together the brown sugar and the remaining 4 tablespoons cocoa in a small bowl. Sprinkle evenly over the batter. Gently pour the boiling water over the top; do not stir. Bake until the top of the pudding is set, 35 minutes. Cool in the pan on a rack for at least 30 minutes. Serve warm or at room temperature.

Per serving (⅑ of cake): 165 Cal, 2 g Fat, 1 g Sat Fat, 4 mg Chol, 220 mg Sod, 37 g Carb, 2 g Fib, 3 g Prot, 94 mg Calc. ***POINTS: 3.***

Tiramisu

MAKES 12 SERVINGS

So popular on eighties dessert menus that it became a cliché, tiramisu (which translates loosely as "lift-me-up" in Italian), nonetheless never fails to live up to its name. One of the great things about this heavenly dessert is that it can be made up to three days ahead—and it only gets better as the flavors develop.

- **½ cup boiling water**
- **5 teaspoons instant espresso powder**
- **1 cup + 1 tablespoon sugar**
- **1 (13-ounce) fat-free pound cake, sliced ½-inch thick**
- **2 (8-ounce) packages tub-style light cream cheese**
- **1 teaspoon vanilla extract**
- **1 (8-ounce) tub fat-free whipped topping**
- **6 ounces semisweet chocolate, finely chopped**

1. Combine the boiling water, espresso powder, and 1 tablespoon of the sugar in a medium heatproof bowl; stir until dissolved, and let cool slightly.
2. Spray a 9 x 13-inch glass baking dish with nonstick spray. Line the bottom of the dish with the cake slices, cutting some pieces as needed to fill any gaps. Brush with the espresso mixture to saturate the cake; set aside.
3. Combine the cream cheese, the remaining 1 cup sugar, and the vanilla in a food processor. Process just until smooth; transfer to a large bowl. Gently fold in the whipped topping and spread over the cake in the baking dish. Sprinkle the top evenly with the chopped chocolate. Wrap with plastic wrap, being careful not to let the wrap touch the surface of the tiramisu and refrigerate at least 4 hours, or up to 3 days.

Per serving (1/12 of tiramisu): 347 Cal, 12 g Fat, 7 g Sat Fat, 14 mg Chol, 336 mg Sod, 55 g Carb, 1 g Fib, 6 g Prot, 67 mg Calc. ***POINTS: 8.***

"The people who are most successful are the ones who learn to enjoy their 'trouble' foods in a safe environment—say, enjoying a scoop of ice cream in an ice cream shop, and enjoying every bite, instead of eating a whole carton of the stuff at home [in secret]. The ones who fail are those who try to cut out their trigger foods altogether. They need to learn that they deserve to enjoy food."

—Sandy Foley, Leader, Long Island, New York

Panna Cotta with Raspberry Sauce

MAKES 4 SERVINGS

After the tiramisu phenomenon of the eighties, chefs of the following decade became enamored of another Italian dessert import: panna cotta (literally, "cooked cream" in Italian). This silky, eggless custard is traditionally served cold with a fruit sauce, so it's a great do-ahead dish. Yes, that's real cream in the ingredients list; Weight Watchers has come a long way! (P.S. You can freeze the leftover cream in an airtight container for up to two months.)

- **2 tablespoons water**
- **1 teaspoon unflavored gelatin**
- **6 tablespoons heavy cream**
- **¼ cup + 1 tablespoon sugar**
- **1 cup fat-free vanilla yogurt**
- **½ teaspoon vanilla extract**
- **Scant ¼ teaspoon almond extract**
- **2 cups fresh or thawed frozen raspberries**
- **1 teaspoon grated orange zest**
- **1 teaspoon fresh orange juice**

1. Pour the water into a small bowl and sprinkle with the gelatin. Let stand until the gelatin is softened, 6 minutes.
2. Combine the cream and ¼ cup of the sugar in a medium saucepan. Cook over medium heat, stirring, until the sugar dissolves. Remove from the heat and add the gelatin mixture, stirring to dissolve. Stir in the yogurt, vanilla, and almond extract until smooth. Divide the mixture among 4 (½-cup) custard cups. Cover and chill 4 hours or overnight.
3. Meanwhile, to prepare the raspberry sauce, combine the raspberries, the remaining 1 tablespoon sugar, the orange zest, and orange juice in a blender; puree until smooth. Strain through a fine sieve, cover, and refrigerate until ready to use.
4. To unmold the custards, run a thin-bladed knife around the edge of each cup, then dip the cups in a bowl of hot water for about 15 seconds. Immediately invert the cups onto a plate. Top each with 1 tablespoon of the raspberry sauce.

Per serving (1 custard with 1 tablespoon sauce): 202 Cal, 7 g Fat, 4 g Sat Fat, 26 mg Chol, 35 mg Sod, 32 g Carb, 4 g Fib, 4 g Prot, 111 mg Calc. ***POINTS: 4.***

Chocolate Fondue

MAKES 6 SERVINGS (2½ CUPS)

Here's another reason to dust off that old fondue pot: Chocolate fondue is actually a pretty low-*POINTS* way to get a chocolate fix, since it makes a small bit of great chocolate go very far. Pairing it with fresh fruit and fat-free angel food cake makes it a guilt-free indulgence. By the way, unlike its Swiss cousin cheese fondue, chocolate fondue has an American origin. It was created in 1964 at New York's Swiss Chalet restaurant by chef Konrad Egli.

- **⅓ cup whole milk**
- **½ cup evaporated fat-free milk**
- **¾ cup unsweetened cocoa powder**
- **6 ounces semisweet chocolate, chopped**
- **1 cup sugar**
- **¼ cup water**
- **2 tablespoons light corn syrup**
- **4 ounces angel food cake, cut into 1-inch cubes (about 5 cups)**
- **12 strawberries, stemmed**

1. Whisk together the whole milk, evaporated milk, and cocoa powder in a medium saucepan until the cocoa dissolves. Add the chocolate and cook over medium-low heat, stirring constantly, until the chocolate is melted and the mixture is smooth.
2. Stir in the sugar, water, and corn syrup. Cook, stirring constantly, until the mixture is smooth, 4–6 minutes. Transfer to a fondue pot and set over moderate heat. Serve at once, with the angel food cake cubes and the strawberries for dipping.

Per serving (generous ⅓ cup fondue with ¾ cup cake and 2 strawberries): 396 Cal, 11 g Fat, 6 g Sat Fat, 3 mg Chol, 187 mg Sod, 79 g Carb, 6 g Fib, 7 g Prot, 107 mg Calc. ***POINTS: 8.***

Chocolate Fondue

Crêpes Suzette

MAKES 6 SERVINGS

In classy restaurants of the sixties and seventies, this dish came to a flaming conclusion with much fanfare when flambéed tableside by a tuxedoed waiter. Our version skips the flames but keeps all that wonderful caramelized-orange flavor.

- **½ cup all-purpose flour**
- **4 tablespoons sugar**
- **⅛ teaspoon salt**
- **¾ cup low-fat (1%) milk**
- **2 large eggs, lightly beaten**
- **1 tablespoon grated orange zest**
- **⅓ cup fresh orange juice**
- **2 oranges, peeled and cut into segments (about 1½ cups)**
- **2 tablespoons orange-flavored liqueur, such as Grand Marnier**
- **3 tablespoons unsalted light butter**

1. Combine the flour, 1 tablespoon of the sugar, and the salt in a medium bowl. Combine the milk, eggs, and orange zest in a separate bowl. Slowly whisk the milk mixture into the flour mixture until smooth. Let stand 15 minutes.
2. Spray a small nonstick skillet or crêpe pan with nonstick spray and set over medium heat. Stir the batter, then pour a scant ¼ cup of the batter into the skillet, tilting in all directions to form a thin, even layer. Cook until the top is set and the bottom is golden, 1–1½ minutes. Flip and cook until the second side is lightly browned, 15–20 seconds. Transfer to a plate and repeat with the remaining batter to make 6 crêpes. Cover loosely with plastic wrap and reserve.
3. Combine the orange juice, the orange segments and their juices, and the remaining 3 tablespoons sugar in a large skillet. Cook over medium heat, stirring occasionally, until the sugar dissolves. Working one at a time, dip 1 crêpe into the hot juice mixture. Fold the crêpe into quarters and transfer to a warmed serving platter. Repeat with the remaining crêpes. Add the liqueur to the skillet and bring to a boil; continue boiling 30 seconds. Remove from the heat and swirl in the butter until melted. Pour the hot sauce over the crêpes and serve at once.

Per serving (1 crêpe, with about ⅓ cup sauce): 178 Cal, 6 g Fat, 3 g Sat Fat, 82 mg Chol, 84 mg Sod, 26 g Carb, 1 g Fib, 5 g Prot, 67 mg Calc. ***POINTS: 4.***

top tip

If you prefer to make this sauce without the alcohol, simply substitute 1 tablespoon of lemon juice for the orange liqueur and omit boiling the sauce. When you swirl in the butter, add 1 teaspoon of grated lemon zest.

Mocha Espresso Granita

MAKES 4 SERVINGS

Granita (or in France, *granité*) is a flavored ice dessert with a slightly granular texture. Did we create this one as a homage to the coffee-crazed nineties, or to the many coffee-laced frozen desserts and shakes of past Weight Watchers cookbooks? Either way, it's great way to satisfy an ice cream craving. A little hazelnut liqueur adds a seductive, nutty flavor; if you prefer, leave it out and deduct ***1 POINT*** per serving. Try serving the granita in hollowed-out lemon shells [see below for our easy method].

- **½ cup packed light brown sugar**
- **⅓ cup Dutch-process unsweetened cocoa powder**
- **2 cups strong brewed espresso coffee, hot**
- **2 (3 x ½-inch) strips lemon zest**
- **5 tablespoons hazelnut liqueur (such as Frangelico)**

1. Stir together the sugar and cocoa in a medium saucepan. Add the coffee and lemon zest; bring to a boil, reduce the heat, and simmer 3 minutes. Remove from the heat and let cool to room temperature. Remove and discard the lemon rind. Stir in 3 tablespoons of the liqueur.
2. Pour into a 9-inch square metal pan. Freeze until the mixture is frozen around the edges but still slushy in the center, about 1½ hours. Stir with a fork, breaking up the ice crystals. Return to the freezer and freeze until just solid in the center and firmer around the edges, about 1½ hours. Place in an airtight container and freeze until firm at least 4 hours or up to 1 month.
3. To serve, scrape the granita with a fork to lighten its texture. Spoon into serving glasses, and drizzle each serving with ½ tablespoon of the remaining liqueur.

Per serving (⅔ cup): 172 Cal, 1 g Fat, 1 g Sat Fat, 0 mg Chol, 15 mg Sod, 37 g Carb, 2 g Fib, 2 g Prot, 35 mg Calc. ***POINTS: 3.***

top tip

Next time you juice lemons, save the shells for serving up treats like this. Just scoop out the pulpy centers from the juiced lemon halves, then trim a little off the rounded edges of the shells, so they can stand upright. For a decorative touch, cut a zig-zag effect on the cut edge of each lemon. Freeze in zip-close freezer bags for up to a month.

sweets and shakes

WW THEN AND NOW

Piña Colada Smoothie

MAKES 4 SERVINGS 

The creaminess of this refreshing whip comes from freezing the pineapple first. When poured, the smoothie is reminiscent of a Caribbean umbrella drink. That's your cue to kick back, relax, and sip!

- **1 cup ice cubes**
- **1 cup crushed pineapple in juice, drained**
- **1 cup frozen low-fat vanilla yogurt**
- **1 cup coconut water**
- **½ cup pineapple juice**

1. Freeze the pineapple in a freezer container or zip-close freezer bag until solid, at least 3 hours. Let stand at room temperature 10 minutes to thaw slightly.
2. Crush the ice cubes in a blender (or place them in a zip-close freezer bag, crush them with back of heavy skillet, and place in the blender). Add the frozen yogurt, the pineapple, coconut water, and pineapple juice; puree until smooth.

Per serving (1 cup): 115 Cal, 2 g Fat, 1 g Sat Fat, 2 mg Chol, 93 mg Sod, 24 g Carb, 1 g Fib, 3 g Prot, 90 mg Calc. ***POINTS: 2.***

top tip

Don't confuse nearly fat-free coconut water (the clear liquid found inside a whole coconut) with fatty coconut milk, which is made from shredded coconut and boiling water. Look for coconut water in the ethnic aisle of the supermarket—no need to buy a whole coconut and crack it yourself!

Mango-Soy Smoothie

MAKES 4 SERVINGS

The nineties soy craze meets the Weight Watchers penchant for fruity frozen shakes: It's a healthy match made in heaven. This refreshing drink is equally delicious made with peaches.

- **1 cup ice cubes**
- **1 small mango, cubed (about 1 cup)**
- **1 cup vanilla-flavored soy drink, well chilled**
- **¾ cup mango nectar**
- **1 tablespoon sugar**
- **1 tablespoon sweetened lime juice, such as Rose's Lime**

Crush the ice cubes in a blender (or place them in a zip-close freezer bag, crush them with back of heavy skillet, and place in the blender). Add the mango, soy drink, nectar, sugar, and lime juice; puree until smooth.

Per serving (1 cup): 101 Cal, 0 g Fat, 0 g Sat Fat, 0 mg Chol, 8 mg Sod, 25 g Carb, 2 g Fib, 2 g Prot, 110 mg Calc. ***POINTS: 2.***

"A week past September 11, membership was down. People felt, what value is weight loss when the world is ending? And the people who did show up at meetings were mostly in shock. But they really needed to talk things out, and we helped them cope: coping without using food to eat over their feelings—and also learning how to get comfort from food, without damaging themselves. We helped them refocus, to understand that 'yes, this terrible thing happened, but I'm still here.' I think our members were better equipped for the aftermath of that terrible time than most other New Yorkers."

—Stephanie Del Valle, Leader and Area Trainer, New York City

Double-Chocolate Malt

MAKE 3 SERVINGS 

Recipes for malteds took up a lot of room in old Weight Watchers cookbooks; they were a great way to satisfy desires for treats and snacks—and meet the required daily milk servings. But today there's no need to use imitation chocolate extract, as so many of the old faux-chocolate recipes did. Our new version delivers plenty of chocolate power with the real thing.

- **1½ cups fat-free milk**
- **1 cup low-fat chocolate ice cream**
- **2 tablespoons lite chocolate syrup**
- **2 tablespoons malt powder**

Whirl the milk and ice cream in a blender until smooth. Add the chocolate syrup and malt powder; puree until smooth and frothy.

Per serving (1 cup): 168 Cal, 4 g Fat, 2 g Sat Fat, 13 mg Chol, 123 mg Sod, 29 g Carb, 0 g Fib, 7 g Prot, 227 mg Calc. ***POINTS: 4.***

Orange Dreamsicle Shake

MAKES 4 SERVINGS 

The beloved Orange Shake of early Weight Watchers days was simple: orange juice, nonfat dry milk, vanilla extract, and sugar substitute shaken over ice. It came close to the frozen treat on a stick we all craved—but not close enough. Today's version achieves that goal, deliciously.

- **1 cup ice cubes**
- **1 cup orange sherbet**
- **1 cup sugar-free fat-free vanilla frozen yogurt**
- **1 cup fat-free milk**
- **2 tablespoons thawed frozen orange juice concentrate**

Crush the ice cubes in a blender (or place them in a zip-close freezer bag, crush them with the back of heavy skillet, and place in the blender). Add the sherbet, yogurt, milk, and orange juice concentrate; puree until smooth.

Per serving (1 cup): 135 Cal, 1 g Fat, 1 g Sat Fat, 4 mg Chol, 71 mg Sod, 28 g Carb, 0 g Fib, 4 g Prot, 144 mg Calc. ***POINTS: 3.***

Mango-Soy Smoothie, Double-Chocolate Malt, and Orange Dreamsicle Shake (clockwise from top)

Peanut Butter–Banana Shake

MAKES 4 SERVINGS

Nuts and peanut butter used to be no-nos, but now we know a little bit of nuts can be positively heart healthy. This yummy shake can't help but bring out the kid in you.

- **1 medium banana, cut into chunks**
- **1 cup ice cubes**
- **2 cups fat-free chocolate milk**
- **2 tablespoons creamy peanut butter**

1. Freeze the banana chunks in a freezer container or zip-close freezer bag until firm, at least 2 hours.
2. Crush the ice cubes in a blender (or place them in a zip-close freezer bag, crush them with back of heavy skillet, and place in the blender). Add the banana chunks, chocolate milk, and peanut butter; puree until smooth.

Per serving (1 cup): 153 Cal, 6 g Fat, 2 g Sat Fat, 4 mg Chol, 114 mg Sod, 21 g Carb, 3 g Fib, 6 g Prot, 149 mg Calc. ***POINTS: 3.***

"Group support is what makes Weight Watchers different—and better. We've all had weight problems; we all understand how a new member feels when he or she walks in. We're having more fun in life when we help others help themselves. That's what will keep Weight Watchers around for another 40 years—for another 100 years."

—Florine Mark, Franchise Owner, Detroit

DRY AND LIQUID MEASUREMENT EQUIVALENTS

If you are converting the recipes in this book to metric measurements, use the following chart as a guide.

TEASPOONS	TABLESPOONS	CUPS	FLUID OUNCES
3 teaspoons	1 tablespoon		½ fluid ounce
6 teaspoons	2 tablespoons	⅛ cup	1 fluid ounce
8 teaspoons	2 tablespoons plus 2 teaspoons	⅙ cup	
12 teaspoons	4 tablespoons	¼ cup	2 fluid ounces
15 teaspoons	5 tablespoons	⅓ cup minus 1 teaspoon	
16 teaspoons	5 tablespoons plus 1 teaspoon	⅓ cup	
18 teaspoons	6 tablespoons	¼ cup plus 2 tablespoons	3 fluid ounces
24 teaspoons	8 tablespoons	½ cup	4 fluid ounces
30 teaspoons	10 tablespoons	½ cup plus 2 tablespoons	5 fluid ounces
32 teaspoons	10 tablespoons plus 2 teaspoons	⅔ cup	
36 teaspoons	12 tablespoons	¾ cup	6 fluid ounces
42 teaspoons	14 tablespoons	1 cup minus 2 tablespoons	7 fluid ounces
45 teaspoons	15 tablespoons	1 cup minus 1 tablespoon	
48 teaspoons	16 tablespoons	1 cup	8 fluid ounces

Note: Measurement of less than ⅛ teaspoon is considered a dash or a pinch.

VOLUME	
¼ teaspoon	1 milliliter
½ teaspoon	2 milliliters
1 teaspoon	5 milliliters
1 tablespoon	15 milliliters
2 tablespoons	30 milliliters
3 tablespoons	45 milliliters
¼ cup	60 milliliters
⅓ cup	75 milliliters
½ cup	125 milliliters
⅔ cup	150 milliliters
¾ cup	175 milliliters
1 cup	225 milliliters
1 quart	946 milliliters

OVEN TEMPERATURE	
250°F	120°C
275°F	140°C
300°F	150°C
325°F	160°C
350°F	180°C
375°F	190°C
400°F	200°C
425°F	220°C
450°F	230°C
475°F	250°C
500°F	260°C
525°F	270°C

WEIGHT	
1 ounce	30 grams
¼ pound	120 grams
½ pound	240 grams
¾ pound	360 grams
1 pound	480 grams

LENGTH	
1 inch	25 millimeters
1 inch	2.5 centimeters

"40 Years of Weight Watchers" photo credits: **page 25:** Twiggy, Redgrave: Everett Collection; **page 45:** Cooper: courtesy of Cooper Aerobics Enterprises; **page 65:** Food: Rita Maas; **page 77:** Fixx: Bettmann/Corbis; **page 107:** Fonda: Douglas Kirkland/Corbis; **page 129:** Beals/*Flashdance*: Everett Collection; **page 145:** Logo: courtesy of the National Cholesterol Education Program; **page 167:** Burger: Burke/Triolo Productions/Brand X Pictures; Pyramid: John Kelly/Stone; Candles: Michael Deuson/FoodPix; **page 195:** Popcorn, burger: Burke/Triolo Productions/Brand X Pictures; **page 235:** Crowd: C Squared Studios/Photodisc. Illustrations by Rob Blackard.

WEIGHT WATCHERS GREATEST HITS INDEX

D

E

Q

R

S

WEIGHT WATCHERS GREATEST HITS INDEX

T